The Monster Within

The publisher gratefully acknowledges the generous support of the General Endowment Fund of the University of California Press Foundation.

The Monster Within

The Hidden Side of Motherhood

Barbara Almond

UNIVERSITY OF CALIFORNIA PRESS

Berkeley   Los Angeles   London

University of California Press, one of the most distinguished
university presses in the United States, enriches lives around
the world by advancing scholarship in the humanities, social
sciences, and natural sciences. Its activities are supported by
the UC Press Foundation and by philanthropic contributions
from individuals and institutions. For more information, visit
www.ucpress.edu.

University of California Press
Berkeley and Los Angeles, California

University of California Press, Ltd.
London, England

Library of Congress Cataloging-in-Publication Data

Almond, Barbara.
    The monster within : the hidden side of motherhood /
Barbara Almond.
        p.   cm.
    Includes bibliographical references and index.
    ISBN 978-0-520-26713-8 (cloth : alk. paper)
    1. Motherhood—Psychological aspects.   2. Mother
and child—Psychological aspects.   3. Love, Maternal—
Psychological aspects.   I. Title.
    HQ759.A436   2010
    306.874'3—dc22   2010020836

Manufactured in the United States of America

19   18   17   16   15   14   13   12   11   10
10   9   8   7   6   5   4   3   2   1

This book is printed on Cascades Enviro 100, a 100%
post consumer waste, recycled, de-inked fiber. FSC
recycled certified and processed chlorine free. It is
acid free, Ecologo certified, and manufactured by
BioGas energy.

This book is dedicated lovingly
to the memory of my three mothers:
my real mother, Anne Rosenthal,
my grandmother Bessie Feinsod Rosenthal,
and my dear aunt Madeline Greenberg,
all of whom loved and encouraged me
in all my endeavors to the end of their lives

CONTENTS

PREFACE

This book developed from two primary sources: my own experiences, struggles, and anxieties as a mother and my clinical work with patients in psychotherapy and psychoanalysis over the course of thirty-seven years of practice. Having gone through medical school thinking I would become a pediatrician, I became a mother first. And once I was a mother I found it too disturbing to imagine taking care of ill and sometimes dying children. I decided to pursue instead further training in adult psychiatry. Within psychiatry, my interests turned to the practice of psychotherapy and eventually to psychoanalysis. Despite the many amazing and helpful developments in psychopharmacology over the past thirty years, my deepest interest was and is in the mind, its conscious and unconscious aspects and how these connect to disturbed feelings and behaviors.

The work I do with my patients, whether psychotherapy or psychoanalysis, is based on the premise that what you don't know *can* hurt you. Our personalities are deeply connected to our experiences in early life, most of which we have forgotten. However, these experiences and relationships live on in our unconscious minds. They are brought to life in the "talking therapies," during which they are relived between patient and therapist and subsequently understood. Medications can have an important role in treatments of this sort because their regulation of mood disorders leads to the capacity for tolerating difficult thoughts and feelings and controlling destructive behaviors, thus optimizing chances for a good therapeutic outcome.

In my work I treat outpatients—people who do not need to be hospitalized but who suffer from neurotic problems and personality disorders, often a mixture of both. Neurotic disorders are characterized by symptoms (in particular, anxiety and depression) and inhibitions in work, love, and creative endeavors related to unconscious impulses, fantasies, thoughts, and memories. Much of the suffering of people with neurotic problems is internal; neurotics tend to take out their misery on themselves. Personality disorders are somewhat more severe; people who suffer from them behave in characteristic maladaptive ways that cause much interpersonal difficulty and anguish. People with such disorders also grapple with painful moods, difficulty achieving goals, and disordered relationships, but they act them out behaviorally. They do not suffer in silence.

There is an aspect of my clinical experience that it is important to keep in mind throughout this book. I see a wide range of patients in terms of the problems that bring them to therapy. However, most of them are middle or upper middle class in their upbringing and economic status. Two circumstances account for this. First, I am in private practice, where the frequency of visits and fees cannot be dictated by insurance companies. Second, education about psychotherapy, as well as acceptance of it as a way to treat problems of mind and feeling, is far more frequent among the middle class.

For most of my professional life I have treated more women than men. These women came to see me because of dissatisfaction, depression, and anxiety connected with their work and their intimate relationships. As I grew older, my patient population also aged. I saw more and more women with children—and some without children, either by choice or failure to conceive. I began to tune in more to women's fears surrounding their reproductive activities—pregnancy, childbirth, and, most of all, mothering. I believe my sensitivity to these issues increased as I got older and as my own children grew up. I no longer had to deny, out of anxiety, shame, and guilt, my own maternal ambivalence and shortcomings. Furthermore, it became increasingly clear to me that the shame and guilt that my ambivalence engendered had made it extremely hard for me, as a young mother, to come to terms with my limits. And I began to see that this was true for most mothers.

In my situation, I was deeply conflicted about how much time to devote to my mothering versus my profession. My children were born when I was in my mid-twenties, before I had completed my psychiatric training. I feared if I waited too long to return, I would lose confidence in my role as a professional. But there was a truth even harder to face. As much as I loved my children, they were demanding and exhausting, and my work, although also demanding and exhausting, was often a respite. I made an important compromise in arranging to do my residency part-time, taking five years to complete a three-year training program.

For many years after I began my private practice, I tailored it to the school schedule. Nevertheless, when I was at work my children were always on my mind. The first day of my psychiatric residency was also the first day of nursery school for my two-and-a-half-year-old son. When I left him at school, he was crying, and by the time I got into my car, I was also in tears. Unable to concentrate on my work, I called the head teacher at least three times that first morning. Finally, she tactfully suggested that I have my husband bring him to school in the future. This solved the immediate problem of my son's crying but not the chronic problem of my guilt and anxiety about my children and my mothering.

During the mid-nineties I happened to be treating several women who were conflicted about whether or not to have children. Having wanted children myself, as a much younger woman I had not thought much about this issue. I assumed *all* women wanted children, and if they were not aware of this therapy or analysis would put them in touch with this wish and, if it was not too late, lead to motherhood.

As it turned out, this assumption was wrong. The fears and conflicts some women feel about motherhood are so strong that treatment cannot tip the scales in favor of having children. I came to realize that all my female patients, past and present, had been or were (at least part of the time) dealing with guilt and shame about the quality of their mothering or their avoidance of motherhood. This was true even if they were devoted and conscientious mothers. It gradually became clear to me that fears about adequate mothering span a spectrum in time, beginning long before the prospective mother's decision about childbearing and extending throughout her life as both a mother and a daughter. These fears often manifest clinically in disguised forms such as rationalized deferments of pregnancy (often until it is too late), poorly understood abortions, or, in direct form, difficulties mothering or difficult feelings about mothering.

The first theme that engaged me because it appeared in the treatment of several women during the same period concerned the fear of bearing, or creating, *monstrous offspring.* Thinking about this fear from a psychological point of view, I began to speculate about the meaning of monsters and our fascination with them in literature and popular culture. Every Halloween I can count on young Frankensteins and Draculas appearing at my door, along with ghosts, witches, bats, black cats, pirates, and other icons of horror. True, princesses and butterflies and an assortment of other benign animals also appear, but monstrous figures far outnumber them among the young suppli- cants who ring my doorbell, hungry for sweets. Why Frankenstein, and why Dracula? And why have the grim novels from which they sprang remained best-sellers for more than a hundred years? They must speak to very basic human psychological issues. One of the rea- sons we read is to find out more about how others deal with the con- flicts that consciously and unconsciously trouble us, to understand how their stories play out, how they deal with closeness and distance, love and hate, damnation and redemption.

As I reflected on the subject of monstrous offspring, my thoughts gradually turned to a more general issue: women's difficulties dealing with the negative side of maternal ambivalence through all the phases of child-rearing—what I think of as the "dark side of motherhood," the central subject of this work. Conflict is the bedrock of human psychology and is always manifested in some form of ambivalence, the word we use for feelings of both love and hate toward the same person, goal, or desire in our lives. It is a completely normal phenom- enon. What we love can disappoint us. What we love, we can also lose. What we lose causes us pain. That mothers have mixed feelings about their children should come as no surprise to anybody, but it is amazing how much of a taboo the *negative* side of ambivalence carries in our culture, especially at this time. I believe that today's expec- tations for good mothering have become so hard to live with, the standards so draconian, that maternal ambivalence has increased and at the same time become more unacceptable to society as a whole.

I feel very strongly that women suffer unduly from the anxiety and guilt that their ambivalence engenders in them and the disapproval that it engenders in others. Ambivalence needs to be understood as a phenomenon that can be both constructive and destructive—constructive when it leads the mother to think creatively about her difficulties mothering and how they can be managed, destructive when it leads to hopelessness, intractable guilt, self-hatred, and punitive behaviors.

Motherhood itself is a highly invested phenomenon, both as a concept and as an experience. Social scientists, especially sociologists and anthropologists, have explored many aspects of gender behavior, including maternity. A number of excellent works have explored the different facets of maternity: women's wishes to work as well as care for their children, how motherhood is passed on from mother to daughter, how motherhood is a source of growth and self-development (e.g., Betty Friedan's *The Feminine Mystique,* Nancy Chodorow's *The Reproduction of Mothering,* Daphne DeMarneffe's *Maternal Desire*). All these works contain many references, explicit and implicit, to maternal ambivalence.

Mental health professionals of many stripes have also contributed their insights to our understanding of ambivalence. I am thinking of two in particular. Roszika Parker, an English psychotherapist, tackles this subject from a Kleinian psychoanalytic perspective in her 1995 book, *Mother Love / Mother Hate: The Power of Maternal Ambivalence.* She makes a bold and well-thought-out case for the inevitability and normality of ambivalence throughout the human life cycle. In particular, she views maternal ambivalence as a result of the differing needs of mother and child. Parker discusses and illustrates her contention that ambivalence creates space for thinking about one's child and coming to more individual and original ways of dealing with mother-child tensions: "The conflict between love and hate actually spurs mothers on to struggle to understand and know their baby. In other words, the suffering of ambivalence can promote thought—and the capacity to think about the baby and child is arguably the single most important aspect of mothering" (6–7). Parker sees the guilt and anxiety that stem from widespread public condemnation of the negative side of ambivalent feelings as the *real* problem for mothers rather than the ambivalence itself, which is normal. Daphne DeMarneffe, in her recent book, *Maternal Desire,* emphasizes the powerful and positively motivated desire to mother and the growth and development that mothering enables. Nevertheless, she too does not forget how useful, inevitable, and ubiquitous ambivalence is even in the most devoted and loving mothers.

My approach to the subject of maternal ambivalence is informed by these insightful writers but is my own. It is both clinical and literary, born out of my own experiences, as doctor, psychiatrist, and psychoanalyst, and my lifelong love of reading. I think the subject of mothers and children has been gestating inside me for a long time. My medical school thesis, which I cite in chapter 2, was a clinical research study of first-time mothers and social class differences in how they learned about infant care. It was a subject I chose because I was interested in pediatrics and it gave me access to observing mothers and babies. My internship in pediatrics gave me more opportunity, when I had the time, to observe mother-infant relationships. My psychiatric training was a complex mixture of different kinds of experiences, treating inpatients and outpatients and dealing with an initial, bewildering exposure to many schools of thought about how the human mind and brain work. These many schools of thought still bewilder me periodically, but what the psychoanalytically oriented ones all have in common is an emphasis on the unconscious mind and the importance of early childhood experiences throughout the life cycle. In general, the trend in psychoanalytic thinking, since Freud made his groundbreaking discoveries, has moved from an emphasis on the primacy of the Oedipal situation to the *centrality* of the early mother-child relationship as the foundation for all future development. That's where I hang my professional hat.

During my psychiatry residency I had an unusual experience that I have always remembered but was only recently able to connect to my thinking about maternal ambivalence. When I was working on the Consultation service of the Washington, D.C., Veteran's Administration Hospital, I was called to see a woman who had developed a sudden case of blindness after giving birth to her first child. Her eye exam was completely normal, except for the fact that she couldn't see. Interviewing her about her emotional reactions to the birth of the baby yielded nothing helpful. That, in itself, was interesting. I realized I was witnessing a case of hysterical blindness, something rarely encountered in the twentieth century, although common enough in Dr. Freud's nineteenth-century Vienna. It was accompanied, as were so many of those early cases of hysteria, by "la belle indifference"— an attitude of seeming not to care, certainly not to the degree that one would expect with the sudden onset of blindness.

Not quite knowing what else to do, I transferred the patient to the psychiatric unit. When I came to work the next day, the patient had regained her sight. The staff all understood that she did not want to be seen by psychiatrists, did not want her thoughts and secrets exposed, and regained her sight in order to get off the psychiatric ward! We also understood that she did not want the baby, but this she was totally unable to acknowledge. Early in his work Freud pointed out that hysterical symptoms are a condensation of an unacceptable wish and the defense against this wish. I now see this woman's blindness as a primitive response to her wish to be rid of her baby; she literally could not see it. If you can't see your baby, *you can't take care of it, but you also can't hurt it.*

The more intense my further training as a psychotherapist and later as a psychoanalyst became, the more important the mother-infant and mother-child relationship was revealed to be. I note here that I have not studied fathers, not because they aren't important, but because paternal ambivalence merits its own book. Furthermore, since I obviously have not been a father, the issue is not as personally invested for me as the issue of maternal ambivalence.

In this book I use two kinds of material as evidence of how problematic maternal ambivalence can be: clinical vignettes and case histories from my own practice and examples from the practices of some of my colleagues; and discussions of certain highly pertinent literary works, which I refer to as "case stories." Clinical material requires disguise and omission, out of considerations of privacy and confidentiality. It does not take too much of a disguise for someone to be unrecognizable to themselves or others. The essential dynamics in each clinical instance are unchanged, but certain facts, such as appearance and vocation, when changed, go a long way toward increasing anonymity. In disguised form I also have mined the experiences of some of my friends and relatives. This kind of material, clinical and familial, is very useful because it is real. Inside or outside my office, it happened to *someone.*

Works of literature, on the other hand, can illustrate quite dramatically and thoroughly the issues I wish to discuss and do not present the same constraints as clinical examples. They are part of the public domain, available to everyone, but their usefulness goes much further than that. Psychoanalysts have long drawn on literary works as examples of the unconscious mind at work. Freud wrote that "the poets discovered the unconscious" before he did. He drew on literature and the arts to illustrate psychoanalytic ideas and on psychoanalytic ideas to understand literature and the arts in depth. Apparently, he was able to put together the dynamics of the Oedipus complex after seeing Sophocles' play *Oedipus Rex*. He also wrote about dreams in fairy tales and folklore and published psychoanalytic studies of Leonardo da Vinci and Michelangelo's Moses. His papers are full of more references to literature, especially Shakespeare's plays, than I can enumerate.

Other analysts and therapists have followed in his footsteps, beginning with his early pupil, Marie Bonaparte, in her psychoanalytic study of the works of Edgar Allan Poe. A recent issue (vol. 78) of the *Psychoanalytic Quarterly*, a highly respected professional journal in the United States, is devoted entirely to articles on psychoanalysis and literature. The *International Journal of Psychoanalysis* (published in North America, South America, and Europe) regularly carries a section on interdisciplinary studies, in which literature figures prominently. Marilyn Yalom, in her book *Maternity, Mortality, and the Literature of Madness*, draws heavily on the work of women writers, such as Sylvia Plath, Virginia Woolf, and Anne Sexton, to demonstrate women's fears that motherhood will drive them crazy.

However, it is not just imitation of Freud that leads therapists and analysts to use literary material in their professional writing. Writers draw on their own unconscious in their writing, and readers bring their unconscious thoughts and anxieties to their reading. There is no *one* meaning or reading of a complex literary work, but each reader finds the meanings that resonate within her psyche.[1]

Bruno Bettelheim, in his classic study of fairy tales, *The Uses of Enchantment*, discusses why children love fairy tales and want to hear them over and over. Fairy tales deal with the basic anxieties of childhood—separation, loss of parents and siblings, good and bad parents and stepparents, envy, jealousy, and the dangers of leaving home. Fairy tales provide solutions and, usually, happy endings. True, they are often magical solutions, but hearing them over and over reassures children, making it possible for them to process their anxieties. Likewise, adult novels deal with basic anxieties and with solutions.

About twenty years ago, my husband, Richard Almond, wrote a paper on *Pride and Prejudice*, focusing on the therapeutic aspects of the relationship between the central characters, Elizabeth Bennet and Mr. Darcy. With my husband's encouragement I wrote a similar paper using a modern novel, *The Needle's Eye*, by Margaret Drabble, to illustrate another healing relationship. Our mutual interest in healing relationships portrayed in literary works resulted in a book we cowrote, *The Therapeutic Narrative: Fictional Relationships and the Process of Psychological Change* (1996). We discussed various well-known nineteenth- and twentieth-century novels in which a therapeutic relationship figured importantly, making the point that people often read and write to work out their own internal conflicts. Sometimes the conflict is worked out in relationship to another character in the novel. We also used clinical experiences in writing *The Therapeutic Narrative*.

I found this kind of writing, interweaving literature and clinical examples, very congenial. When I began to write this book, I wrote it the same way but with much more clinical emphasis. My clinical experiences are my primary source for my work, but wherever it seems pertinent I intersperse clinical and literary examples, using the latter as strengthening evidence. For instance, Mary Shelley's *Frankenstein* contains powerful references to fears of monstrous births and their outcomes. I became interested in this novel in connection with Amanda, a patient I treated who directly expressed her fear of infants as "monsters." In fact, my interest in Mary Shelley and her novel as they related to Amanda's conflicts is the springboard for this work; it led to my interest in the general phenomenon of maternal ambivalence and its effect on both mother and child.

My goal is to further our grasp of ambivalent mothering as a normal phenomenon that can be understood and managed and to help women who are dealing with their own versions of ambivalence. In the first chapter I define maternal ambivalence and elaborate a psychological spectrum of maternal behavior, from normative "good-enough mothering"—which includes normal, everyday ambivalence—to highly disturbed ambivalent mothering. The rest of my book follows the trajectory described below.

It should be understood from the outset that while mothers struggle with ubiquitous concerns about monstrosity in their children, they also look to them as objects of love and hope, the enablers of new possibilities for growth and development, for repair of the past and its disappointments. In chapter 2 I describe some of my clinical experiences with these phenomena, then use Margaret Drabble's novel *The Millstone* as further illustration. *The Millstone* captures the intense love and bonding that develop between a troubled young mother and her child, facilitating growth and development in the mother. This kind of maternal experience has a highly positive outcome; it stands in contrast to the mother who uses her child as a narcissistic extension of herself, or becomes so involved with the child and its meanings to her that she cannot draw realistic boundaries between herself and her offspring. That kind of difficulty is addressed in some of the ensuing chapters, in which I elaborate a spectrum of ambivalent behaviors and phenomena, their possible origins, manifestations, and consequences.

In chapter 3 I discuss some forms of hidden ambivalence, an especially troubling situation because of the mother's obliviousness and denial. If a mother does not have *some* conscious recognition of her problems, she will not attempt change or seek treatment. The hallmark of such a situation is that the mother feels she is raising her children perfectly while those around her feel worried and uneasy.

In chapters 4 and 5 I present and illustrate the hypothesis I have developed to explain the underlying factors that may lead to ambivalence about childbearing. I use a trilateral case example: Mary Shelley's life, her novel *Frankenstein*, and my patient Amanda. All three share a concern about monstrousness, their own or that of their potential offspring. Clinical examples from my own practice that elaborate parts of this hypothesis follow and enrich Shelley's story.

Chapter 6 is a detailed case history of Rachel, a patient who struggled with the less disturbed, more guilt-ridden side of ambivalent feelings. I suspect that most readers of this book will be able to identify with some aspect of Rachel's experience. She was a very forthcoming patient whose story illustrates some common sources of maternal ambivalence and the passing on from one generation to another, by means of unconscious identification, of maternal difficulties that the daughter *consciously* wishes to avoid.

From Rachel's story I proceed to an increasingly dark part of the maternal spectrum of disturbance. What characterizes the clinical and literary material in chapter 7 is the mother's projection of her own "badness" into her child, whom she then may blame or hate. Four literary examples, which are really about mothers who externalize their ambivalence, make up the core of this chapter. In Doris Lessing's novella, *The Fifth Child*, a mother's baby greed and ruthlessness produce a "monster" child who unconsciously represents herself. Lionel Shriver's recent novel, *We Need to Talk about Kevin*, is a raw and disturbing rendering of a mother's most horrifying fears—that she will be totally unable to love her baby and that her baby will be totally unable to love her. The last two novels are popular and sensational, mainly because they deal with universal and frightening maternal fantasies disguised in lurid horror stories. *Rosemary's Baby,* by Ira Levin, concerns a devil-child whom I view as a fantasy resulting from his mother's peripartum psychosis. Finally, *The Bad Seed,* by William March, involves early trauma, dissociation, and survivor guilt in the mother and the child as a receptacle of what the mother cannot accept in herself.

In chapters 8 and 9 I turn to the impact on *children* of maternal ambivalence. Chapter 8 deals with the management of maternal ambivalence "when the worst happens," that is, when a child is abnormal—physically, mentally, or emotionally. Mothers often experience a child's deformity as a punishment, and there is always an element of the negative side of ambivalence in their reactions. As with other forms of maternal ambivalence there are both internalizing and externalizing ways to deal with such situations. Those mothers who blame themselves attempt reparation. Those who see the deformity as something being done to *them* may reject the child. As for the child's reaction, it may blame or protect its mother. I present several cases from my own clinical experience that illustrate these various possibilities and follow them with a case story example: *Stones from the River,* by Ursula Hegi, a novel in which an afflicted child comes to terms, psychologically, with her own deformity and her relationship with her mother.

Chapter 9 poses the question of what children do in the face of maternal ambivalence. How do they manage the anxiety and damage to their self-esteem that results from the recognition that mommy doesn't always love them? Many children are able to work out this reality positively, if they are emotionally strong and flexible and/or have other sources of support within the family. Others withdraw, act out, or adopt a negative identity. I discuss two clinical situations in which the latter situation occurred and illustrate one of them with a case story from Günter Grass's novel *The Tin Drum*.

In chapter 10 I describe a spectrum of maternal overinvolvement—from stage mothers who never miss a performance and whose lives seem totally taken up with feeding themselves through what their children bring them to invasive mothering, a form of child abuse in which the mother invades the child's autonomy both physically and psychologically so that the child cannot act or think for itself. To illustrate I discuss two clinical cases and several case stories. *Dracula* is a classic example of destructive vampyric mothering, in which the Count-mother lives off his victim-children, turning them into "undead" creatures, devoid of soul, will, and choice. Two recent novels—*Anywhere but Here,* by Mona Simpson, and *Other People's Children,* by Joanna Trollope—bring these themes into contemporary life.

Child murder is the issue I address in chapter 11. A shocking phenomenon, it is usually the result of mental illness and desperation on the part of mothers who are catastrophically overwhelmed by the circumstances of their lives. I discuss the case of Andrea Yates, a nurse who drowned her five children while in the grip of a postpartum psychosis, and two dramatic case stories—Toni Morrison's masterful novel *Beloved* and the Greek tragedy *Medea*—as well as the case of a patient who took her own life, thus abandoning her small child to the care of a hated mother.

Chapters 12 and 13 form the concluding section of this work. In chapter 12 I discuss some of the vicissitudes of maternal ambivalence in later life, when children grow up, leave home, marry, have children themselves, and their parents become grandparents. Different mothers find different stages of child-rearing difficult, but maturity and the passage of time may alleviate problems engendered by ambivalence. Grandparenthood is an especially pivotal event in resolving difficult emotional situations between mothers and daughters. The resolution of these tensions is helpful to daughters in developing their *own* identities as mothers.

In chapter 13 I review and expand on the pressures mothers in our society face—in particular, the pressures of contemporary prescriptions for perfect mothering. I discuss various forms of help and treatment available to mothers—from the corrective and balancing role of other family members to the helpfulness of other mothers and mothers' groups and of professionals other than therapists, such as pediatricians, obstetricians, and lactation consultants. These sources of help are most pertinent where the problems in mothering are stage related and temporary. My main emphasis, cases in which problems are more serious and less stage related, is on psychotherapeutic treatment, short and long term. I elaborate some of the elements of intensive psychotherapy and psychoanalysis for those readers unfamiliar with these options. In this, my concluding chapter, what I want to drive home is that no matter the level of ambivalence a mother is experiencing, she is not alone. If she can be honest with herself about her feelings and if she can seek professional help, as well as support from family, friends, and other mothers, her chances of a happy motherhood are greatly enhanced.

Although this book is dedicated to the three women in my early life who were most crucial to me, it should also be dedicated to all the loving women who struggle to be good mothers in the face of their own human limitations and a highly demanding society.

ACKNOWLEDGMENTS

First and foremost I want to thank my husband, Richard Almond, for his help with this project every step of the way. He encouraged me to start writing about my clinical work about twenty years ago. He co-wrote a book with me, read the papers I wrote for scientific journals, and listened endlessly to my ideas about this present book. He made many useful suggestions about the issues I discuss here and directed me to helpful references. I cannot count the times he rescued me from computer difficulties. Most important of all, he conveyed his confidence in my ability to do this project.

My three children, David, Michael, and Steven, deserve high praise for putting up with me as a mother who worked and for teaching me to be a mother who loved. They are all wonderful, creative people, as well as good fathers and uncles. My sister, Alice Rosenthal, formerly an editor and currently a writer, has read many of these chapters in the earlier phases and commented very helpfully. My son Steve and his wife, Erin, both writers, have read some of the later material, supported me, listened to me, and, when necessary, yelled at me and pushed me to keep going.

My work on the subject of maternal ambivalence began when I was a candidate at the San Francisco Psychoanalytic Institute. Many people helped me in this endeavor, in particular, Stanley Steinberg, Phil Stein, Lisby Mayer, Marshall Bush, and Bob and Judy Wallerstein. Over the years I presented much of the material in this book to the Palo Alto Writers Group, and I want to thank all the members of that group for their support and helpful comments: Ric Almond, Laura Seitel, Bob Harris, Alan Sklar, Emily Lyon, and Mariquita West. Many other friends were also very helpful, in particular, Jennie Dishotsky, Gail Bates, Bob Hessen and Karin Bricker, Nancy Peters, Suzi Rosenstreich, Barbara Blatner, Ken Roberson, Jan Mill, and Eve Bridberg. Susanne Chassay generously permitted me to use some of the clinical material from her excellent paper, "Death in the Afternoon." I was given the opportunity to present some of these chapters in person to interested audiences, through the kindness of Maureen Ruffell, Dena Sorbo, Mark Snyder, and Sharon Levin.

An experienced editor, Cindy Hyden, read an early version of this work and got me started on a major revision, which resulted in the present book. Two people who have been enormously helpful are my excellent and hardworking agent, Gillian MacKenzie, who wouldn't give up, and my editor at UC Press, Naomi Schneider, the first editor to read my manuscript who actually understood what I was doing and why I was doing it this way. Many thanks also to my copy editor, Sheila Berg, and my production editor, Kate Warne.

For reading the final product before publication, my deep appreciation goes to Nancy Chodorow, Daphne DeMarneffe, and Stephanie Brown.

CHAPTER ONE

The Ubiquity
of Maternal Ambivalence

Ambivalence is a combination of the loving and hating feelings we experience toward those who are important to us. Maternal ambivalence is a normal phenomenon. It is ubiquitous. It is not a crime or a failing. This book is about maternal ambivalence.

.   .   .

"Admitting to Mixed Feelings about Motherhood," by Elizabeth Hayt, appeared as the lead article in the Styles section of the *Sunday New York Times* on May 12, 2002—Mother's Day. Here was one expression of the current groundswell of revolt against the idealization of motherhood in the 1980s and 1990s resulting from the enthusiasm and perfectionism of the baby boomers as they took on the "job" of parenting. Two days before reading this article I had talked with a young woman in her mid-thirties, the mother of two small children, about a parenting class she had attended. Although she had taken the class to learn more about child development, especially during toddlerhood, her most intense reaction was one of vast relief on discovering that other parents could feel exhausted, lonely, bored, and short of temper with their children. She learned she wasn't alone. As this woman is both educated and emotionally sensitive, the *degree* of her relief was impressive. I suspect that the majority of women taking that class shared her feelings.

On July 2, 2001, ten months before the publication of the *New York Times* article, the cover of *Newsweek* carried the shocking headline, "'I Killed My Children': What Made Andrea Yates Snap?" Andrea Yates was a depressed nurse, the mother of five children under the age of seven, who one morning, in the grip of severe postpartum psychosis, became desperate, lost control, and drowned all of them. The article was followed by Anna Quindlen's Last Word column, titled "Playing God on No Sleep," in which Quindlen admitted frankly that as horrified as she and others were by the murders, some part of her understood all too well how it could happen.

This book addresses the subject underlying the young mother's reaction to her parenting class and the two articles, maternal ambivalence—that mixture of loving and hating feelings that *all mothers* experience toward their children and the anxiety, shame, and guilt that the negative feelings engender in them. If you hate your parents, siblings, spouse, friends, colleagues, or people of the opposite sex, or other races, religions, and nationalities, you are considered unfortunate, unreasonable, bigoted, interpersonally difficult, even seriously disturbed. But if you hate your children, you are considered monstrous—immoral, unnatural, and evil. It is my purpose to explore and understand the spectrum of maternal ambivalent feelings, thoughts, and behaviors and where possible to see them for the normal, inevitable, and ubiquitous phenomena they are. My secondary purpose is to encourage women to seek help of various kinds, including the kind of psychological treatment in which they can be heard and understood without negative judgment or condemnation. Controversies surrounding the emotional investments and duties of motherhood have probably existed for centuries, but this past century is most pertinent to the unique dilemmas of contemporary women. Before World War II the "ideal" middle-class mother stayed home and cared for her family. Of course, many women worked out of necessity or inclination, but that was not considered ideal. World War II partially disrupted this arrangement as middle-class women put their children into day care centers and went to work. In the late 1940s, 1950s, and 1960s they returned to the "bliss" of domestic suburban life. When Betty Friedan exposed their hidden, and largely unexpressed, misery in *The Feminine Mystique,* she acknowledged women's wishes to *also* have work and a life outside of the home. Her ideas heralded the more open expression of ambivalence about motherhood that characterized the feminist movement of the late 1960s and 1970s. This ambivalence may have been more openly expressed at that time, but it was never *really* acceptable then, nor is it now.

Several contemporary writers have tackled the idea that motherhood is not automatically an all-fulfilling state. Their work has been greeted with outrage and discomfort. As cited in Hayt's *New York Times* article, these writers are acutely aware of the controversial nature of their writing. For example, Peggy Orenstein says of the mothers she interviewed for *Flux: Women on Sex, Work, Love, Kids and Life in a Half-Changed World:*

> It was almost furtive for them to admit motherhood is not
> fulfilling.... It actually makes me feel deviant and anti-mother

to say that. But I'm not. It's like being anti-American. Mother-hood silences women. The Kryptonite words for women are fat, slut, bad mother and selfish. The words make us lose our powers just like Superman loses his in the face of Kryptonite.[1]

While "fat" reflects the mania for being thin and in shape that has possessed American women for the past forty years, regardless of whether they are mothers, "slut" and "selfish" are intimately connected to "bad mother," the most Kryptonite-laden term of all. Good mothers are not sexy—that is, they are not sluts—and they put their children's interests before their own at all times—that is, they are not selfish.

The concept of maternal ambivalence and its forbidden quality has been explored by various writers but still remains highly unacceptable in our culture. This book sets out to present the spectrum of maternal ambivalence, its presence in all women, the dangers inherent in keeping it a silent phenomenon, and the means with which women can approach their own ambivalence in a healthier way. The negative, or hating, side of maternal ambivalence is the crime "that dares not speak its name" of our time. Aggression in women—the *behavioral* manifestation of their hating feelings—is generally considered problematic, that is, not feminine. But when women's aggression is aimed at their children, it becomes even more unacceptable. It is one of those societal problems that fill us with outrage and horror, even as some part of us secretly understands its normality.

Since the Enlightenment and especially during the Victorian era, childhood has come into its own.[2] This increased valuation of childhood developed hand in hand with the gradual rise in importance of the nuclear family and the recognition of the value of education in the growing middle class. Although the children of the poor continued to labor in mines and factories, especially during the industrial revolution, child labor laws and universal education eventually released them to be children.[3] With the increased importance of the family came an idealization of the mother-child bond and greatly heightened expectations of maternal care. This idealization was most marked in upper- and middle-class society, but it was not absent in working-class families. A major class difference in child rearing was the reliance of the upper classes on domestic help for child care and household work. It should be noted that it is much easier to idealize motherhood when someone else is doing the lion's share of actual child care.

The idealization of motherhood has continued into the present and grown in intensity. Two additional problems increase the strains that contemporary mothers face. First, as families move great distances from each other in search of better jobs and housing, the extended family living in one place has become less common. Fifty years ago, grandparents, aunts and uncles, and older siblings often helped raise children. The breakup of the extended family now places the burden of child care squarely on the parents, usually the mother. Second, the breakdown of the nuclear family—the current divorce rate is about 50 percent and the number of children born to single mothers 25 percent—more often than not leaves both mother and child quite on their own to deal with their complicated mutual psychological needs and interactions.

Paradoxically, as the conditions of mothering become more difficult, more is expected from mothers, and mothers, in turn, expect more from themselves. Fierce and demanding pressures surround contemporary mothering. Perfectionistic standards of child care in every area—feeding, sleep, play, emotional and intellectual development—prevail. Breast-feeding, the healthy and natural way to feed infants, has become more a fanatical pursuit than a preference; babies must, at all costs, sleep on their backs even if they sleep better on their tummies, so they won't die of sudden infant death syndrome (SIDS); toys must be carefully vetted for their educational value rather than their appeal; and so on.[4] Add to this conflicts between work and home and the absence of family support systems, and you have a situation that leads inevitably to increasing frustration and resentment as mothers are expected, and expect themselves, to be perfect.

Here's a recent example of what I'm describing. "Cosmopolitan Moms," an article by Stacy Lu published in the Fashion and Style section of the *New York Times*, describes a group of eight Philadelphia mothers who meet every Friday afternoon with their children for a play group. But this is a very unorthodox play group, for on this one afternoon each week, while the children play and drink fruit juice, the mothers treat themselves to a glass or two of wine or beer. The article highlights that these women are merely seeking a release from the pressures of motherhood. They are not out to get drunk, nor are they acting irresponsibly. Instead, they are seeking, as the article put it, "a way to hold on to a part of their lives that existed before they had children and to bond over a shared disdain for the almost sadistically stressful world of modern parenting."

Maternal ambivalence must be increased in this "world of modern parenting" where women feel they should be able to do it all. One could argue that the deferment of childbearing, so common among educated and professional people and so rationalized by the availability of assisted reproduction in the form of in vitro fertilization and other techniques, is in no small part an expression of this ambivalence. The declining birthrate in first world countries may be another manifestation of ambivalence about parenting. Advanced reproductive technology doesn't always work, but it allows the delay of a decision that is more difficult for many women than they can easily admit. For not only is it unwomanly not to love your children *unconditionally*, but it is considered unnatural not to want children in the first place.

Interestingly from the paternal point of view, these issues seem to play out a bit differently. The father's concerns have more to do with providing the means for the biological and social survival of the family. Although men struggle with wishes to have or not have children, and with issues of good fathering, they do not hold themselves so thoroughly responsible for the emotional care of their offspring. While those concerns can be deep and terribly troubling, striking at the heart of what it means to be a man and manly, the emotional well-being of the family is generally laid at the mother's doorstep. The emotional well-being of the children especially is seen as the mother's territory, for the father plays a very important role in protecting the needs of the adults in the family.

Although it is not my purpose to discuss the biological validity of our assumptions about women and children, current sociobiologists and primatologists, such as Sarah Blaffer Hrdy, maintain that loving motherhood is not automatically programmed into the female of our species but is an extremely complex equation of genetic, evolutionary, emotional, and social factors aided by powerful hormonal influences.[5] My interest lies in exploring some of the emotional dimensions and qualities in the spectrum of maternal ambivalence in an effort to describe, understand, and "normalize" it—that is, to recognize that however problematic this ambivalence may be, it is part of the human condition. And this recognition is crucially important. Too many women suffer as they attempt to be perfect mothers, an effort driven in part to cover over their ambivalence. Modern "maternally correct" mothers are literally driving themselves and their offspring crazy in their quest for maternal perfection, which can only be proven by the perfection of their offspring. And it doesn't work! It's hard on the mothers themselves, their children, and their spouses, and it needs to be seen for the impossible goal that it truly is.

WHAT IS AMBIVALENCE?

Before setting out to uncover the dimensions of maternal ambivalence, it is important to understand what the term itself means. Part of this understanding involves clarifying the difference between hatred and aggression. "Ambivalence" refers to a *conflicted mental state*, in which one has both loving and hating feelings for the same person. It characterizes *all* human relationships, not just that of mother and child. Being able to tolerate both kinds of feelings, at different times, without having one feeling destroy the other, is a sign of good mental health. Having to deny or suppress either love or hate leads to depleted and rigid relationships in which the other person is not experienced in his or her full emotional reality. For instance, in Jane Austen's novel *Pride and Prejudice*, Elizabeth hates Mr. Darcy because he has snubbed her and belittled her family. Her negative feelings protect her from knowing that she is deeply attracted to him and that he is an honest and complex person who loves her. Until she comes to know him better, she can't love him, but to know him, she must first give up her single-minded dislike of him.

Hate and love are *feelings*, states we experience inside ourselves. Aggression and loving nurturance are *behaviors*, actions we carry out toward others. Aggression comes into play whenever our own needs are not met, expressing itself in the form of hateful feelings, angry fantasies, or actions. However, hate, which is inevitable whenever people have intense conflicting and unsatisfied needs, may also foster a sense of separateness. That is, as long as hate exists alongside love, it may facilitate individual development. For example, a younger sibling may resent his older brother's superior strength, knowledge, and power; at the same time he deeply admires and wishes to emulate him. Yet he cannot *be* his brother. He must find his own individuality, his own talents and abilities, and he is aided in doing this by his admiration for the older brother and his knowledge that the brother, too, has had to struggle to grow up.

The English analyst Roszika Parker, who has written brilliantly about maternal ambivalence, sees it as a potentially creative process in which the mother has to actively *think* about the differences between herself and her child and come to solutions that allow for more attuned mothering. Parker feels that the anxiety and guilt that ambivalence generates in today's society keeps us from seeing its creative aspects. This anxiety and guilt has roots not only in cultural imperatives and expectations but also in the deep-rooted fear that hate will overrun and destroy love.

Maternal ambivalence starts rather mildly, with occasional bouts of impatience, anger, even hate in otherwise loving mothers. There can be an enormous range of ambivalent behaviors that are fundamentally harmless, meaning that they are ultimately mitigated by love. A mother may lose her temper when, behind her back, her toddler tries to pour a glass of juice by himself and spills it all over her newly mopped kitchen floor. Yet she is also impressed by his independence and wish to "do it himself," and she quickly picks him up and hugs him. Another mother has reminded her adolescent daughter repeatedly that she is supposed to do the dinner dishes. Tempers flare, insults fly, and the daughter suddenly performs a flawless imitation of the mother's voice and gestures. Both mother and daughter break out into helpless laughter. When this mitigation does *not* occur, maternal ambivalence can extend to the depths of the dark side—expressed in behaviors ranging from psychological and physical abuse to child murder. Maternal ambivalence comes in all shapes and sizes. This book identifies some important phenomena along the spectrum of ambivalence.

Using both clinical vignettes and literary works as illustrations, I hope to shed some light on these concerns about the dark side of maternity. The guilt and shame associated with my patients' feelings of aggression toward their children make it difficult for me to use the clinical material that contributed to my interest in this subject to the full extent I could. Maternal aggression is extraordinarily difficult to deal with honestly in psychotherapy, as are most hateful feelings or loaded issues, like sex and money. Out of respect for former patients, who have confided these difficult feelings and fantasies, my own clinical vignettes (and those of colleagues) are kept, for the most part, brief and disguised. Out of respect for my now-grown children, I also disguise some of my own experiences. The content is not disguised, only the dramatis personae. I hope that my use of these real-life examples will help those readers troubled by what they feel are disorders of maternal feeling to be emboldened to seek help and treatment or, if already doing so, to view these worries as less shameful and more universal, certainly as legitimate human and therapeutic concerns.

In my clinical work with women, the fear that one might produce a monstrous offspring, or that one already has done so, through faulty—even monstrous—mothering occurs with great frequency, albeit often unconsciously. Some women seek treatment specifically because of their fears of becoming mothers, but they are in the minority. More often, fear of an incapacity to mother or of inadequate mothering will appear in the treatments of women that were focused, originally, on other types of conflicts, such as work and relationship problems. In thirty-seven years of clinical practice, I cannot think of a single mother I have treated whose concerns about mothering—"bad" mothering, really—were not an important element in psychological life. Of course, the intensity of concern has been greatest in mothers with newborn and very young children, when they suffer the strains of interrupted sleep and inexperience. Although the fear of being a bad mother tends to taper off as children become older (with a blip of increased intensity when the child reaches adolescence), it never disappears completely. Many of these women are as good at mothering as one could hope for, others less so, but all *fear* they are bad mothers.

Women face a painful dilemma in coming to terms with their aggressive feelings toward their children, whether or not they have expressed them. In my experiences with patients, I have found that this aggression is both psychologically inevitable and socially unacceptable to a *very* marked degree. While defective and harmful parenting, with its painful emotional consequences, is the concern of any enlightened society, the guilt produced by the pressure on women to be all-loving and all-giving toward their offspring takes a powerful toll on both mothers and their children. This guilt only makes the aggression worse, as women fail in their attempts to fulfill impossible standards of mothering. They feel angry and disappointed with themselves and, in turn, angry and disappointed with their children. Anger and disappointment make them feel even guiltier, so they try harder and harder. It is a repetitive and exhausting cycle.

Certain works of literature illustrate quite dramatically the complexities involved in maternal ambivalence and, being part of the public domain, they don't present the same privacy constraints as clinical material. Throughout this book, literary case stories as well as clinical case vignettes will help to underscore the issues at hand.

For instance, maternal ambivalence often begins with the fear of having children in the first place. Mary Shelley's novel *Frankenstein* is a stunning illustrative case story that connects with the fantasies of those women whose reproductive anxieties appear as a fear of giving birth to a monster. While clinical material is "real" and therefore very valuable, some literary works convey painful feelings and situations so vividly and imaginatively that they say to the reader what many patients cannot.

THE SPECTRUM OF MATERNAL AMBIVALENCE

Maternal ambivalence reveals itself across a broad spectrum. This book describes this spectrum along an axis of increasing severity, taking into account the possible roots of ambivalence, how it manifests, and what some of the consequences are, that is, where it began, how it looks, and what happens over time. The point of this book is *not* to depict motherhood as a negative experience. There is a clear and powerful "bright side of maternity"—which I term *motherlove*. As a starting point, I examine this phenomenon. For while ambivalence is ubiquitous, so is motherlove. Motherhood is primarily an experience of fulfillment, growth, and, in some cases, healing and redemption. I feel it is very important to remember this base point of motherhood as we look at some of the disturbing situations that follow.

I go on to explore how different forms of maternal ambivalence manifest chronologically—from preconception through pregnancy to after the child is born. The "before the beginning" phase concerns fears about *having* children and some of the psychological issues that lie behind these fears. Once motherhood is achieved, maternal ambivalence can be explored by looking at women who function at different levels of ego strength and object-relatedness. These are technical terms, but they are important ways to describe the mother's psychological abilities. "Ego strength" refers to the mother's ability to function realistically and adaptively, in relationship both to her own needs and to the needs of her children. It assumes her ability to recognize her child's changing needs as development proceeds but equally to protect her own need to not be swallowed up by the demands of motherhood. For instance, children should not be forced to become toilet-trained before they are ready, but often they are ready long before they are willing. A mother who is fed up with dirty diapers and who has the courage of her convictions may be willing to move things along firmly and encourage potty use. Another mother may have a more laissez-faire attitude and be comfortable with it. She does not push potty use, even if others advise her to do so. Both mothers have good ego strength in the sense of balancing their needs and the needs of their children.

"Object-relatedness" describes the capacity to relate to the child as a whole other person, not as a clone or an extension of the mother. A mother with mature object-relatedness has the ability to allow for both dependence and independence, similarities to and differences from herself, in her children. She has the capacity for emotional flex-ibility and control in dealing with them. It does not mean she feels constant and unfailing love but rather that she can judge when a child needs security and when it needs freedom and separateness. Setting limits sensitively involves the ability to understand that the child is not a replica of the mother but that he or she, nevertheless, needs to be socialized within the sociocultural milieu in which he or she is being raised. Since this often leads to intergenerational conflict, it arouses frustration and anger, the negative side of ambivalence. There is no way to really avoid this, because total indulgence infantilizes and weakens children, but the way in which the mother handles her ambivalence is a measure of her capacity to recognize her child as an "other," worthy of respect regardless of how much in need of discipline. Recognizing the child's individuality is a crucial part of sensitive mothering. It allows the mother to manage the child's need for discipline and parental control, as well as the child's need for freedom to develop in his or her own way.

A shy and sensitive acquaintance of mine gave birth to a wonderful little boy whose temperament was active and exuberant at all times. Sometimes this got him into trouble with other children and with their mothers. It was difficult for my friend to have a child so unlike herself, but she worked at understanding his capabilities and limits. This is what Parker means when she talks about the "creative function" of ambivalence. My friend had to think about and imagine what her child really needed. She could not assume she knew him because he was just like her. It goes without saying that mothers with good ego strength take into account their own needs for satisfaction as well as the needs of their children. It is the failure to recognize that most ambivalence springs from conflicts between the child's and the mother's needs, both legitimate, that explains much of the social and cultural condemnation of "imperfect" mothers. Recognizing their own mixed feelings, mothers themselves add self-condemnation to this brew.

ESTABLISHING A MORE REALISTIC BASELINE: THE GOOD-ENOUGH MOTHER

When talking about problems or failures in mothering, we must begin with the question, What *is* a good mother? Since the standard for good mothering in contemporary society has become so demanding of maternal perfection and selfless devotion, it is time, for the well-being of both mother and child, to consider a new and more realistic standard. The British psychoanalyst Donald Winnicott, who began his career as a pediatrician, coined the phrase "good-enough mother." He was describing the "ordinary devoted mother" who was able to establish a loving relationship with her baby through identification with its needs from the very beginning, a state he also called "primary maternal preoccupation." The good-enough mother is, in Winnicott's words, "the person who, in the early days and weeks, was temporarily identified with her infant, and for the time being was interested in nothing else but the care of her own infant."[6] Winnicott elaborates on the critical nature of the early days: "The important thing, in my view, is that the mother through identification of herself with her infant knows what the infant feels like and so is able to provide *almost exactly* what the infant needs in the way of holding and in the provision of an environment generally."[7] By "holding," Winnicott is referring to all the soothing and calming activities the mother provides in addition to actual feeding—activities like cuddling, speaking, singing, and rocking that are a crucial part of early infant care. In Winnicott's words there is "no such thing as an infant without a mother." What he means is that all growth, development, and survival depend on the mother, or mothering person. But Winnicott does *not* mean that the mother reads all the baby's cues perfectly. Far from it. "Almost exactly" is not exactly. A mother who perfectly and *omnisciently* anticipates her child's every need does not allow the child the experience of frustration. Optimal frustration—not too much and not too little—leads to the capacity in the child for thinking, for internal development, and for recognizing the existence and needs of other people.

When Winnicott emphasizes the role of the good-enough mother in providing a safe and holding environment for her child, much as a therapist does for his or her patient, he does *not* mean an environment that is always loving or perfectly gratifying. In his well-known psychoanalytic article "Hate in the Countertransference," Winnicott lists eighteen reasons why a mother (presumably an "ordinary devoted mother") may temporarily hate her baby. Here, in his words, are a few of them: "The baby is a danger to her body in pregnancy and at birth. He is ruthless, treats her as scum, an unpaid servant, a slave. He is suspicious, refuses her good food, and makes her doubt herself, but eats well with his aunt. After an awful morning with him she goes out, and he smiles at a stranger, who says: 'isn't he sweet!'" (201). Hating your child at these times is perfectly normal and, furthermore, *necessary* for the child to eventually learn that he or she is a different and separate person from the mother.

The American writer Anne Lamott underscores the inevitability of temporary hate in her journal of her son's first year of life. A loving mother, worn out after an evening of baby colic, she muses, "I wonder if it is normal for a mother to adore her baby so desperately and at the same time to think about choking him or throwing him down the stairs."[8] She continues:

> He's so fine all day, so alert and beautiful and good and then
> the colic kicks in. I'm okay for the first hour, more or less, not
> happy about things but basically okay, and then I start to lose it
> as the colic continues. I end up incredibly frustrated and sad and
> angry. . . . I have gone so far as to ask him if he wants me to go get
> the stick with the nails which is what my friend Kerry says to her
> dogs when they are being especially bad. I have never hurt him
> and don't believe I will, but I have had to leave the room he was in,
> go somewhere else, and just breathe for a while, or cry. . . . I hope
> that somehow I am and will be a wonderful mother for Sam. Per-
> haps I should stop asking him about the stick with the nails. (59)

In her humorous and self-deprecating way Lamott expresses the honest emotions of a worn-out new mother who loves her baby and desperately needs her sleep!

Paradoxically, these months of early infancy, while the most difficult physically, are so often the most successful emotionally as the mother falls in love with her new baby and turns her single-minded concern to its survival and welfare. We will explore in more detail the concept of motherlove later in this book. Like the heroine we will meet in the case story drawn from Margaret Drabble's novel *The Millstone*, many women will discover that they are good-enough mothers and that their motherhood is, *in itself,* a therapeutic experience for them.

Many women are concerned about not being good-enough mothers at certain stages in their children's lives. The truth is that the demands of mothering shift with the child's development, and here is where emotional flexibility becomes crucial. Some mothers are wonderful with small babies but edgy and impatient with toddlers; others are strained to the limit with the demands of infancy but comfortable with their children once more autonomy has been achieved, or marvelously relaxed and creative with their school-aged children and disastrous with adolescents. The identifications mothers make with the needs of their babies go on beyond infancy—throughout the life of mother and child, in fact. Such identifications are the source of good interpersonal attunement and management but also of much trouble and grief. Since the identifications occur largely unconsciously, the mother just seems to know what is needed. However, when the mother, through these unconscious knowings, relives a time in her own life that was traumatic, it may lead to unconscious and disturbing repetitions. For example, a socially adept and friendly mother who was shy and awkward as a child may find herself very impatient with her six-year-old daughter's difficulty making friends and adjusting to school. Having recovered from such painful difficulties herself, she doesn't want to remember them, and her impatience makes the situation worse. Paradoxically, she is of less help to her daughter than is her husband, who was never shy and awkward.

Later I discuss Rachel, a patient of mine who had a mild version of a phenomenon that I think of, somewhat ironically, as the psychosis of early child rearing. Although this kind of disturbance is *not* usually a psychosis, it is always related to the mother's own disturbing early experiences, generally ones that have been repressed or forgotten. Because of this forgetting, such experiences are not processed and are therefore more likely to be repeated in a disturbing way between mother and child. *The Bad Seed*, a case story, tells how a mother's severe early trauma, dissociated from her consciousness, is repeated with her child, in an attempt at mastery. Paradoxically, it is often the mother's unconscious, empathic attunement to the child's struggles that stirs up her own unresolved issues, which can then lead to disruptions in good mothering.

MATERNAL AMBIVALENCE: INTERNALIZING VERSUS EXTERNALIZING SOLUTIONS

Throughout this book I am seeking not only to expose the nature of maternal ambivalence but also to explain the means that women use to cope with this phenomenon. The fantasy of giving birth to a monster—*something going wrong*—is the first fear that haunts women as they wrestle with their ambivalence, but an even more pervasive fear is that the child will begin normally and develop into one. The idea that the mother will make the child monstrous because she cannot love him enough or mother him properly is, in my experience, handled psychologically in two different ways. Either the mother blames herself or she blames others, especially the child. That is, her solution is either internalizing, guilty, and masochistic—*"It's my fault"*—or externalizing, paranoid, and blaming—*"It's someone else's fault."* As I discuss in greater detail in later chapters, when I speak of an internalizing solution, I am describing a situation in which the mother tends to feel guilty about her ambivalently motivated behaviors, to take the blame, usually by trying harder and harder to be a good mother, to punish herself for her failures, real or imagined.

The externalizing solution involves a mother who sees her child as an embodiment of hated or problematical parts of herself or important others, especially parents, siblings, and spouses. This mother tends to blame the child and becomes angrier. In my view, this second solution is more likely to occur if the mother's relationship with her own mother has been disturbed or if there have been traumatic disruptions in the early mother-child relationship or other kinds of traumatic experiences—which are *all* experienced by infants and young children as maternal failures of protection.

The mother who blames herself attempts to repair her failures. She is more likely to seek psychotherapy, and once in treatment she is more accessible to looking at her own inner thoughts, feelings, fears, and fantasies. She is less afraid of what she will find out since she has already condemned herself. To complicate matters, her need to make up to the child for her own failings may lead to overindulgence and a failure to recognize that the child's demands are often related to inborn temperament and character development. It was not Lamott's "fault" that her baby was colicky in his early months, but she couldn't help experiencing it as her own failure. Because of her basic devotion to her baby's needs, she sought help from La Leche (which fortunately it was able to give) and thus solved her problem. She did not get paralyzed by her own guilt or by painful ruminations about either her own or her baby's badness.

The mother who blames others tends to experience shame and rage rather than guilt. She sees in her child unacceptable qualities of her own inner life, and she does ruminate about the baby's badness. She needs to extrude from within herself impulses and feelings she cannot face or accept, and once she sees these parts in her child, she does not need to make reparations. It is, rather, the child who owes *her* something. These mothers have difficulties experiencing their children as separate and autonomous people. They are less likely to seek treatment, for to change the relationship they have with their children is too much of a threat to their shaky equilibrium.

In Doris Lessing's disturbing novella *The Fifth Child*, we see a case story of a mother whose child represents her darkest side, her greed and ruthlessness. This mother is eventually able to understand the problem as coming from within herself, the child being a projection of what she once could not accept about her own needs and behaviors.

Some mothers see their children as bad and spoiled; others *make* their children so through unempathic mothering. Dr. Frankenstein's monster is an example of a "baby" made monstrous by abandonment and parental incapacity to love.

Sometimes a parent's hungers are so compelling that the child's most basic needs and autonomous strivings are ignored, neglected, or subsumed. In these instances the child is not allowed to have a mind of its own, and mothering can then be considered "vampyric," a form of possession in which the mother needs to colonize the child's body and soul for her own survival.

In a separate yet related category are situations in which unbearable life circumstances lead to severe breakdowns in mothering, including child murder. Here is where the Andrea Yates story becomes relevant, *if* we include disordered states of emotional functioning, including postpartum psychosis, as unbearable circumstances. Toni Morrison's magnificent novel *Beloved* is a very complex case story that belongs in this category, for it describes with passion and sensitivity the desperate attempt of a devoted but temporarily deranged mother to prevent her children from being taken into slavery, by murdering them.

Although readers will discover that there is a wide spectrum of disturbance in mother-child relationships, this book strongly takes the position that there can also be movement in the direction of healthier functioning. Even in the most dysfunctional situations, there may be islands of strong mothering. At different times of life and under different stresses, areas of strength and weakness may come to the fore. If unconscious identifications and memories of a negative quality can wreck relationships, those of a positive quality can also rescue them. In all but the most extreme cases, substantial motherlove survives at the core of the relationship. As an analyst, I believe strongly that therapeutic work and intervention can ameliorate many disturbances of feeling and behavior. Exposing unconscious forces to the light of day allows for choice and control rather than a blind drivenness to action. So why would this not also be true even when the dark, or hidden, side of maternity holds sway?

In the chapters that follow I discuss examples of mother-child conflicts that, in some unfortunate cases, could not be ameliorated but also many instances of successful intervention. A central premise of my book is this: if women can come to understand their maternal ambivalence as a *normal part* of their emotional lives, they will seek help to deal with it more effectively, thus vastly increasing their chances of the happy and fruitful motherhood for which they so deeply long.

CHAPTER TWO

Motherlove

The Power of Maternal Desire

A character in Joanna Trollope's novel *Other People's Children* tries to warn his daughter about the perils of becoming a stepmother:

> It's as if stepmothers have come to represent all the things we fear, most terribly, about motherhood going wrong. We need mothers so badly, so deeply, that the idea of an unnatural mother is, literally, monstrous. So we make the stepmother the target for all these fears—she can carry the can for bad motherhood. You see, if you regard your stepmother as wicked, then you need never feel guilty or angry about your real mother whom you so desperately need to see as good. (309)

He is right. We expect everything from mothers, and we excuse little. We come out of their bodies totally helpless and dependent, and human consciousness, in coming to grips with this reality, attributes to them enormous power for good and evil, for our survival and destruction. We expect mothers to be able to do magic, and, furthermore, we deeply wish it. Cinderella's "fairy godmother" is the missing good mother come back to rescue her. Interestingly, Cinderella hates her wicked stepmother, who is *there,* and idealizes her missing good mother, who only makes fantasied and intermittent (albeit important) appearances. Our need for mothers leads to an idealization in which they are expected to be all-loving, all-giving, and self-sacrificing, an idealization that makes little room for normal emotional reactions, such as ambivalence. It is a need that lasts way beyond childhood.

In *The Fantasy of the Perfect Mother,* Nancy Chodorow and Susan Contratto elaborate a shift in the feminist position on motherhood. From an open acknowledgment, in the 1970s, of the *inevitability* of women's aggression toward children and the need for women to liberate themselves from unfulfilled bondage within their families, feminists and nonfeminists alike have tended to hold mothers responsible for all emotional and developmental problems of their offspring. Chodorow and Contratto wisely point out that such an attitude ignores the influence of infantile wishes and fantasies, persisting in the present unconscious, on our perceptions of both past and present. Somewhere deep inside we expect our mothers to care *for* us and *about* us now as they did when we were children. We still want mothers to "make it all right" as we wished them to do in infancy, when at least some of the time they really could. Since, unconsciously, we prefer to ignore the necessity to relinquish wishes for parental magic, a relinquishment that is part of normal adulthood, we often blame our mothers (and fathers, of course) for our shortcomings and disappointments.

When Donald Winnicott writes of the good-enough mother as the necessary foundation for future emotional health, he eloquently describes ordinary maternal absorption in the welfare and care of infants and children. When he also elaborates the many reasons a mother may (temporarily) hate her baby, he is acknowledging that good-enough mothers *are* ambivalent and that it is perfectly normal. To be hated, sometimes, is a necessary part of the child's grow-

ing awareness of separation and reality. That is, the child becomes
more aware of his own mind and wishes when his mother does not
automatically meet his every need. He comes to realize he and his
mother are not one and the same person. Roszika Parker elaborates
further when she points out that ambivalence *itself* is not the problem
but rather the guilt and anxiety that ambivalence provokes. I completely agree with her assessment. The poet Adrienne Rich writes
that our fear about ambivalence is that "hate will overwhelm love and
lead to isolation and abandonment." She tells us, "My children cause
me the most exquisite suffering of which I have any experience. It
is the suffering of ambivalence: the murderous alternation between
bitter resentment and raw-edged nerves and blissful gratification."[1]
It is important to note that this gratification stems, not from total
maternal sacrifice but from mutual pleasures between mother and
child in which the mother's needs are also gratified.

Motherlove, the bright side of maternity, is fueled by intense biological strivings inextricably bound to powerful psychological wishes.
As an analyst, I make the assumption that bodily needs are *always*
translated into psychological wishes for nurturance and relief; even if
the wishes are unconscious, they are always connected to an underlying need. Take, for example, the phenomenon of falling in love with
one's baby, especially one's first baby, as an example of the intertwin-
ing of biological necessity and psychological response. It is one of
those experiences that always surprises with its intensity. (Adolescent
falling in love, with all its power and turmoil, is comparable but more
evanescent and rarely as altruistic.) This loving attachment feels
almost involuntary. For women who have been ambivalent about their
pregnancy, it is especially surprising. It must account, in large part,
for the number of women planning to give up babies for adoption who
change their minds at the last moment. Because they did not want,

or could not keep, their babies, they did not plan to love them, but the power of the love they suddenly feel can turn the best-laid plans upside down.

A psychologically sophisticated patient, returning after a maternity leave, described a dramatic instance of the "falling in love" phenomenon. She had been excited and pleased with the birth of her first child and comfortable with early nursing and infant care. On her third day in the hospital, her obstetrician appeared to circumcise the baby, as previously arranged. My patient, who is Jewish, was surprised at her own response. She felt protective and alarmed on the baby's behalf. She couldn't refuse circumcision, but she also felt she couldn't bear to hand him over, even to a doctor she felt was experienced and compassionate. When the procedure was finished, the baby was brought back, asleep. While my patient was showering next to the nursery, her son woke and started crying. She suddenly broke into a fit of weeping. "It was so unexpected," she explained to me. "It just came over me. It wasn't just that I felt bad that the circumcision might be painful to him, although that did concern me. It was as if he and I were one person. His tears were my tears. Not even dry, I ran back into the nursery to pick him up and soothe him."

This kind of incident is not unusual. It illustrates the mother's identification with her baby and her empathic response. Like my patient, at the moment of her baby's cry, a mother unconsciously senses what the baby feels and needs and takes care of it. Mothers unconsciously relive all the stages in their children's development, adjusting their expectations based on empathic identifications. This is how they "instinctively" know what to do. At the same time, these identifications can be very troubling during phases in the infant's or child's life that were difficult and poorly satisfied in the mother's own childhood. My patient Rachel, discussed in chapter 6, developed a serious depression at the time of her grandmother's death when her own first child was three years old. Unconscious memories and anxieties connected to a separation from her own mother when *she* was three years old were evoked. When that kind of disturbance arises, the mother's response may not be empathic, any more than that of her own mother. Rachel expected more resilience and maturity from her three-year-old, Ethan, than he could manage, as her own mother had done with her. Confidence in her mothering suffered a temporary but very troubling setback. Motherhood can lead to powerful developmental growth, even transformation, in many women, or to regressive breakdown, partial or total, in some unfortunate others. For most women the experience lies somewhere in between.

Many years ago I had the opportunity to observe the passionate bonding between mother and child in the earliest days of life. As a medical student at Yale University, I did a research thesis on social class differences in sources of information on infant care. In the course of this study, I interviewed twenty first-time mothers in their first few postpartum days. Most of them were blissful and delighted, happy to be through their childbirth and convinced that their babies were beautiful and special. But two were not.

One of the unhappy women was a graduate student who had given birth to twins, a boy and a girl. She knew in advance that she would be having twins. When I interviewed her, three days postpartum, she was talking about the girl as "my baby" and the boy as "my husband's baby." Overwhelmed and frightened at the prospect of caring for two children, she didn't want to nurse the boy. She was, however, quite distressed at these feelings, and some emergency supportive psychotherapy was very helpful. When I saw her a few days later she had decided she didn't have to nurse both babies entirely—she could supplement each with a bottle—and she was already noticeably calmer and more attached to the little boy. Her husband's willingness to participate actively in infant care was also helpful to her in regaining her balance. This was a situation worth noting: a potentially harmful degree of ambivalence was arrested by a combination of crisis intervention therapy and spousal support. I believe the brief therapy was helpful because her feelings were treated with respect and understanding rather than the condemnation she expected. The ensuing relief of her anxiety and guilt allowed her to solve her dilemma, with practical measures that were previously unacceptable to her—sharing the nursing between the two babies and using supplementary bottles. I did not get a chance to follow up her situation, but it would not surprise me if she became gradually able to nurse both babies fully. Even if she did not, her confidence in her motherhood was not derailed at this crucial, early time.

The second situation seemed much more ominous. The mother, an eighteen-year-old married woman, was so upset and anxious I could barely interview her. What her sources of information on infant care were seemed irrelevant. She wanted nothing to do with the baby; he frightened her. She talked of the difficult birth and implied he would be hard to take care of. (He was peacefully asleep during the entire interview.) I found myself feeling very alarmed. It was clear that this woman's mother and large extended family would, in effect, care for the child. This study did not involve later follow-up but in retrospect I realize I was witnessing the development of a monster baby in the mind of the mother. And unlike the mother of twins, this woman had no interest in psychotherapeutic intervention. She wanted out of a situation she found intolerable. I should add that there didn't seem to be any relationship between reported difficulty of birth and enthusiasm for the infant in the other nineteen women. This patient was disturbed and unprepared for motherhood in *any* form.

Motherhood reconfigures family relationships, giving women a different status, usually a more special one. An experienced male colleague mentioned to me that it had been his repeated experience with patients who had recently given birth that they desired to have their mothers available, in some capacity, even if previous tensions existed between them. This wish for closeness to one's own mother has been the experience of many of my patients, although not all. Becoming a mother changes things in a family, sometimes allowing separations and "declarations of independence" to occur, at other times strengthening affectionate bonds and repairing previous ruptures and in unfortunate instances creating envy and hostility.[2]

Most mothers are delighted to have their daughters follow them into motherhood, but not all. Caroline, a patient who for both medical and psychological reasons was only able to have one child, confessed to a feeling she "knew" was irrational—that her mother would find something wrong with her baby daughter and somehow spoil her pride and pleasure in the newborn. In this instance anxiety and envious spoiling were projected into her mother *and* correctly perceived as already existing in her mother. Motherhood is an intensely powerful event in the lives of women, and spouses, parents, and siblings are the supporting and sometimes undermining cast in this complicated drama.

Motherhood, in itself a major opportunity for further development, provides new ground to rework old issues as well. For example, having an infant creates possibilities for gratification of the mother's sensual needs, through skin contact, soothing, and cuddling the baby. Sometimes this leads to a decreased sexual interest in her husband, sometimes to enhanced sexuality in the marriage. (For both physiological and psychological reasons, some previously frigid women become sexually responsive after giving birth.)[3] Caring for an infant provides an opportunity for gratification of needs that were poorly met in the mother's own infancy, but this gratification can be problematic. If the mother's relationship with *her* mother has not led to solidly internalized experiences of good mother-infant interactions, she may envy what the baby is getting from her. Or she may feel rage at a baby who cannot be easily soothed, because it deprives her of the experience of being *able* to soothe. This, in turn, arouses fears that she cannot mother any more effectively than her own mother could. In the background of the relationship between mother and child is always the mother's own experience during infancy and childhood.

Daphne DeMarneffe, in *Maternal Desire,* speaks of what she feels is a relatively disregarded aspect of mothering, the *desire* to mother. She feels that this desire is overlooked, especially in middle-class and educated women, out of a "motivated sense that preserving one's selfhood depends on shutting out an interest in children." What concerns DeMarneffe "is understanding mothers' desire to care for their children as a feature of their self-development and self-expression, rather than its negation" (25). Motherhood is a major opportunity for both personal growth and the emotional fulfillment of unmet needs. Many young mothers "grow up" through taking care of their babies. Others experience closeness, security, nurturing, and playfulness in deep and meaningful ways, sometimes for the first time in their lives. The literary case story that follows illustrates motherhood as a potentially healing, therapeutic, even redemptive experience.

REDEMPTIVE MOTHERING: *THE MILLSTONE*

In her first session with me, Dorothy told me that she had one child and that "if it weren't for her, I wouldn't be here." She did not mean that mothering her daughter was the problem that brought her into treatment. Rather, it was that the relationship with her child had given her confidence for the first time in her life that she could form a positive emotional connection, where the gratification of dependent longings didn't spell inevitable disappointment and humiliation. She had come from a stable family but one that was emotionally inhibited and withholding. At the time she came into therapy with me, she longed for closeness with friends and a more intimate relationship with her husband, but the risks involved were too frightening. As her trust in me gradually developed, she learned to experience these feelings in the transference relationship with me.[4] This allowed her to become closer to people in her life other than her daughter—her husband, family, and friends.

This patient reminded me in many ways of Rosamund Stacey, the heroine of Margaret Drabble's novel *The Millstone,* in which the redemptive and curative aspects of motherhood are the subtext in a story of an emotionally distant young woman who complicates her life through a seemingly self-destructive and masochistic choice—to become an unwed mother.

Though Rosamund is a beautiful, young, upper-middle-class woman and a successful scholar, her emotional relationships are shallow and duplicitous. She goes about with two different men, each of whom thinks she is sleeping with the other. Craving their admiration and attention, she does nothing to set the record straight. Of her disordered relationships with men, Rosamund says, "The idea of love ended in me almost the day it began" (7). Being terrified of sex and intimacy, she has given up hoping for love. As readers, we don't learn much about her early years, except that she is the youngest of three children and she feels her parents are not very interested in her. They live, Rosamund believes, by ascetic, left-wing principles that emphasize self-punishing sacrifice and independence. "I believed dependence to be a fatal sin," she says (9). It is not the act of sex that Rosamund fears so much as the underlying vulnerability and need it may involve. She sees being female as a weakened, inferior state. When she accidentally becomes pregnant, she feels it serves her right "for having been born a woman in the first place" (16). This is a statement that speaks to her masochistic view of femininity, her feeling that women are inferior and doomed to suffer, an attitude that does *not* speak well for the quality of her internalized relationship with her own mother.

Rosamund also sees her pregnancy as a judgment for her first intercourse. She had chosen George, a casual acquaintance who is certainly bisexual (and whom she thinks is gay), and allowed him to seduce her. There is not much danger of intimacy developing in this relationship. Although Rosamund yearns after George intermittently, she cannot ask him for anything or expose herself as having any needs. She never tells him of his paternity. In all her relationships she has to maintain an "illusion of self-sufficiency," which the psychoanalyst Arnold Modell has described as a defense against feelings, in particular, loving feelings. Because loving feelings bring vulnerability to loss in their wake, such an illusion supports a person's need to deny all dependency on other people.[5]

Rosamund feels that her "attempts at anything other than my work have always been abortive" (7), reflecting her lack of belief in the possibility of a safe and enduring relationship with another person. Underneath her narcissistic exterior, she is depressed and masochistic; this is the most fundamental stratum of her personality. The masochism, among other things, represents an identification with her parents' self-deprivations. It leads her to deny her need for loving relationships, leaving her depleted and depressed. For Rosamund, pregnancy represents an emotional compromise. Unconsciously, she longs for, but cannot allow, a relationship that she hopes will relieve her depressive isolation. Consciously, since having a baby as a single mother will involve much hardship, suffering, and self-punishment, she *can* allow herself to have it.

When she realizes she is pregnant, she makes a halfhearted and botched attempt at self-abortion. "I felt threatened. I felt my independence threatened. I did not see how I was going to get by on my own" (39). At this point Rosamund is unaware of her deep wish for a baby. Seeing herself as having to get by on her own denies that having a baby means having a relationship. She sees the other women at the maternity clinic as mired in misery, but I think this view is a projection of her own depressed state. Rosamund thinks, "I was trapped in a human limit for the first time in my life and I was going to have to learn how to live inside it" (58). In the clinic setting she feels herself an outcast because of her unmarried status and class, but it is in fact her emotional withdrawal that isolates her. Rosamund does not need to go to a clinic and has the means to obtain an abortion. In her state of denial, however, she can only see the pregnancy as a punishment she deserves.

Gradually, as the pregnancy progresses (and perhaps once she feels the fetus move inside her, making its presence more real), she begins to wonder if perhaps she has hidden reasons for wanting a baby. She wonders if she seeks a different scheme of things: "totally different from the scheme which I inhabited, totally removed from academic enthusiasms, social consciousness, etiolated undefined emotional connections, and the exercise of free will" (67), which is to say, a scheme less cerebral and emotionally impoverished, more connected to her body and her feelings.

Although she has fears about her capacity to mother, when her older sister suggests she give the baby up for adoption she realizes how determined she is to keep it. At this point she does not yet feel love but rather "an extraordinary confidence in myself, in a conviction, quite irrational, that no adoptive parents could ever be as excellent as I myself would be" (72). Although this confidence sounds unrealistic and like a reflection of narcissistic attitudes, it really represents Rosamund's early bonding with her fetus. This baby is part of her; if she can care for herself, she can care for it. Other changes occur. Rosamund feels energized. Her creativity and ability to work increases—many women note this during pregnancy—but she is also aware of being less masochistically submissive. On a bus two older women, unaware of Rosamund's pregnancy, comment to each other on her inconsiderateness in taking the only remaining seat. Normally, Rosamund would have immediately relinquished her place; now she allows herself to admit she needs to sit more than they do.

Rosamund is getting ready to accept the baby into her life. When, after a relatively easy labor, she sees her for the first time, she says, "What I felt it is pointless to try to describe. Love, I suppose one might call it, and *the first* of my life" (102; emphasis mine). She is proud of her baby's beauty and the ease with which she takes to nursing. When it comes time to hand "Octavia" back to the nurses, she does so without reluctance "for the delight of holding her was too much for me" (103).

I remember speaking to a friend who had just had her first baby. In all seriousness, she said, "And the best part of this is they are going to let me take him home from the hospital with me!" She, like Rosamund, could hardly believe this wonderful baby was really hers.

For several months, sleepless nights notwithstanding, Rosamund is surprised and delighted by her reactions, especially when she experiences the baby's smiling preference for her. But when Octavia is a few months old, Rosamund decides to stop nursing. Despite her awareness that the baby likes nursing very much, she can't stand the mess of leaking breasts, or so she tells herself. When she gives the baby her first bottle and sees the milk descending, ounce by ounce, she feels as if this has been the baby's first *real* meal. This is the first hint we are given of maternal ambivalence. Rosamund is not comfortable with her female body. She doesn't feel natural about having her breasts full and dripping, and paradoxically, despite her ease and adequacy in nursing, she fears she doesn't have enough to give the baby. She has no confidence in her female, nurturing self. We don't know if Rosamund was nursed, but we do know her mother didn't encourage dependency. The closeness and mutuality of nursing, especially as the baby becomes more conscious and responsive, may be too threatening to women like Rosamund, reminding her of dependent longings she does not wish to acknowledge. It is a decision not really in the baby's best interest, but her generally loving attitude and care for Octavia seem to mitigate it.

In this very insightful and emotionally realistic novel, there are two dramatic developments in Rosamund's maternal growth—developments that exemplify the phenomenon of maternal ambivalence in a mother who cherishes her baby. The first is Rosamund's positive response to the baby, the surprise and delight of being able to love someone and of being loved in return. The second is a disturbing series of events that threaten Rosamund with feelings of painful ambivalence, much more basic and troubling than those she had about nursing. When the baby is about eight months old, she is discovered to have a congenital heart defect that requires immediate surgery. Rosamund feels both dread for the baby and the fear of losing her, but she is also aware of her own resentment because of the vulnerability to which she, loving Octavia, is exposed.

But now for the first time I felt dread on another's behalf, and I
found it insupportable.... As I emerged from each fit of grief, I
felt bitter resentment against Octavia and against the fate that
had thus exposed me; up to this point, I had been thoroughly
defended and protected against such onslaughts, but now I
knew myself to be vulnerable, tender, naked, an easy target
for the malice of chance. (120)

Rosamund feels burdened by her love for the baby, which she still
sees as a weakness. More burdensome than this is her knowledge
that the baby can't survive emotionally without her. She finds herself
thinking about George, the baby's father. She wants someone else to
love the baby, so that Octavia won't have to depend solely on her. She
is experiencing what most mothers, if they are honest, admit to feeling: a child is with you for life, for better or for worse, and that is both
reassuring and a burden. The title of the book expresses this irony.
Octavia is indeed a millstone around her mother's neck, yet her birth
has been the most important emotional *milestone* in Rosamund's life.

During the baby's operation Rosamund is in a daze, but once it is
successfully completed, she begins to worry about how Octavia will
respond to the separation, how she will feel when she wakes up alone.
She understands that because infants can't communicate their terror, it does not mean they do not experience it—"that the innocent
suffer" (128). For most of her life, Rosamund has been able to remain
remarkably obtuse to the workings of her own psyche. Now, with
her growing sensitivity to her baby's needs, she knows more about
herself. *She* cannot bear the separation either.

Hospital rules at that time did not allow mothers to be with their
infants, but Rosamund (who *never* makes a fuss) absolutely insists
that she be allowed to stay with her baby. She becomes hysterical

in her demand to see Octavia. At the same time, she is aware of the "clearness of my consciousness and the ferocity of my emotion, and myself enduring them, myself neither one nor the other, but enduring them, and not breaking in two" (134). This kind of assertiveness and tolerance of intense feeling is absolutely new to Rosamund, a turning point. She can tolerate intense feeling, which she has in her empathy with Octavia, and she can tolerate it without shattering because she knows what the baby needs, and that comes first. Here is a perfect example of how motherhood, as a new developmental opportunity, may lead to increases in ego strength, as demonstrated by Rosamund's greater emotional range and capacity to take action.

When Rosamund finally sees her baby, she fears Octavia will have forgotten her or will become more upset, but Octavia stops crying immediately and is suffused with smiles. "She had forgiven me for our day of separation, I could see, and such generosity I found amazing for I am not generous. Fair, but not generous" (135). Good mothering is a two-way street for learning, a chance for the mother as well as the baby to grow; it is what DeMarneffe is talking about when she sees maternal desire as an opportunity for further development of the mother's self.

Rosamund can now accept that love doesn't depend on merit or beauty. "I knew something now of the quality of life and anything in the way of happiness that I should hereafter receive would be based on fact and not on hope" (142). This is another example of how Rosamund's relationship to reality, both inner and outer, is strengthened.

As the novel ends, Rosamund has to ask a favor of neighbors she had previously ignored and scorned—that they listen for the baby while she goes out to fill a prescription for antibiotics. She is touched at their kindness and concern and realizes that they can express it because she has asked them to help her and that she can now ask for help because of Octavia. Masochistic self-denial is no longer an option, nor is isolation. Finally, Rosamund's work, which has always been important to her, flourishes in a different way. It has a less schizoid, "scholarship for the sake of scholarship" feeling to it. It is her way of supporting her child and making a contribution to society, of which she and her daughter are now a part.

The capacity to love, to be involved in a relationship of mutual dependency, to deal with inner and outer reality with more flexibility and greater emotional strength—in other words to continue to develop herself as she shepherds her child's development—these are the rewards of motherlove, the bright side of maternity. It is not an unambivalent state but rather in its good and rewarding moments a nourishing and joyful one and in its darker moments an opportunity for thought, compromise, and growth.

CHAPTER THREE

The Subtle Ambivalence
of the Too-Good Mother

My patient Dorothy and Rosamund, the heroine of a fictional case story, both entered maternity in states of emotional depletion and inhibition. Through the experience of motherhood both grew and developed into more fulfilled and responsive people. They became the good-enough mothers Winnicott describes—not *without* ambivalence, but with enough real love and sensitivity to respond in flexible and realistic ways to their children. I take Winnicott's description of the good-enough mother seriously, since no mother is without needs, and these needs don't always mesh with those of her children. It is this conflict of needs that leads to maternal ambivalence.

For some mothers "good enough" is not enough; they struggle to be perfect mothers. Since that can't really be done, I think of them, ironically, as "too-good" mothers. Part of the unconscious self-expectation of the too-good mother is that she has *no* ambivalence. Since this is impossible, her ambivalence takes very subtle forms, often masquerading as a deep concern to do the best she can for her child, to do motherhood the absolutely right way. In a culture such as ours that has such limited tolerance for the negative side of maternal ambivalence, there are bound to be more women struggling to be perfect than there have previously been, especially in middle- and upper-class families. The harm they can do to themselves and their children is hidden and pervasive.

Let me give a few illustrations. Several summers ago, while on vacation with my family—including my twenty-month-old grand-daughter—I observed a mother whose interactions with *her* twenty-month-old daughter left me feeling chilled and disquieted. We were staying at a family inn in New England, where one of the "vacation extras" offered to guests was a play group for younger children. The group was supervised by friendly, competent counselors, and it freed parents to pursue their own pleasures and activities for several hours a day. The inn was generally child friendly, and there was much opportunity to observe and interact with other parents and grand-parents at meals, after meals, in a large family room full of toys set up for young children, and during drop-off and pick-up at the play group.

My granddaughter took to the play group as the proverbial duck to water. Her parents are attentive, relaxed people who treasured the time off and were able to let go of their daughter easily. Some of the other children (and parents) had a harder time letting go at first, but all got used to the play group activities and schedule.

In the midst of this pleasant arrangement, one of the mothers, Claire, and her daughter, Susie, stood out. At first this family seemed like the others with children. Although Susie was shy and didn't talk as well as other children her age, she got used to being left. But some-thing was troubling me. I realized it was the way Claire talked to her daughter—loudly and constantly, making a running commentary on the child's every move. On the surface these comments seemed perfectly normal and meant to be helpful. "Susie, try some of this cereal. You *love* Cheerios." "Susie, you don't really want that cookie. Have some of these nice grapes." "Susie, we share our toys. Let the other children have a turn." The problem was that Susie didn't seem to love Cheerios, did love cookies, and was told to share her toys even if she had just started playing with a toy by herself. She had her mother's constant attention, but there was a way in which Claire's maternal empathy was defective. What child of twenty months *really* understands the concept of sharing? And even if they understand, they don't really want to do it. Yet Claire was so busy hovering, watching, and intervening that the child's fragile autonomy and true wishes were overlooked.

It was puzzling. Claire seemed to be a devoted mother, so what was going on here? I didn't have the privileges of the consulting room since Claire was not a patient of mine. But I knew a few things. Susie was a wanted child, her first. Claire had a successful career that she now pursued part-time. Her husband did a fair amount of child care. It *seemed* to be a reasonable arrangement. Yet, I wondered, was Susie *really* wanted? If, unconsciously, Susie wasn't really wanted, did Claire have to compensate by doing everything perfectly, so she wouldn't have to face her negative feelings? Or was Claire guilty about time away from her child, feeling she had to give extra? Did she feel that "good" mothers shouldn't work? The guilt about working would also be worse if, unconsciously, the child was not fully wanted.

Claire had an inordinate need for control, but this is true of many anxious, first-time mothers. But she also had a loud voice accompanied by an uncomfortable laugh. She would glance around rapidly as she spoke. Her body language suggested that she wanted everyone to know that she was a very conscientious mother and that she *didn't make mistakes*. I felt that this need reflected her doubts about her maternal feelings and abilities. That loud grating voice gave her away.

Susie, who seemed bright and normally developed for her age, was shy, easily prone to tears, and not yet talking. Was this because her mother didn't give her a chance to talk? Not all twenty-month-old children talk a lot, although girls often develop language before boys of comparable ages. Susie didn't seem to be able to get a word in edgewise, so perhaps she had stopped trying.

Since I did not get to know Claire, I can only hypothesize about what was going on inside her. My best guess is that this child (maybe any child) was too needy and unpredictable for a woman so perfectionistic. Perhaps she had expected a different kind of child, one less anxious, more precocious. Perhaps she had wanted a boy. What I do feel certain about is that she could not admit to herself or others *any* degree of ambivalence. And yet, intuitively, most people interacting with Claire would pick up her discomfort with motherhood and her cluelessness about her effect on her daughter. ("Overweening" was the expression my son used to describe her.) In this real-life situation the negative side of ambivalence was not so much subtle as denied. Claire's need to deny the kinds of feelings that most mothers can admit, at least to themselves, points to a deep-seated insecurity about her capacity to mother. Women who become too-good mothers may have many different personality types and personal histories, although, in general, the need to be too good extends to other areas of their lives. However, most of them hide their discomfort better than Claire did.

The story of Tanya, the daughter of an acquaintance of mine, is one that is typical of too-good mothers of a certain type. These mothers are *convinced* that doing "the right thing" will protect their children from all sorts of future emotional, behavioral, and learning difficulties. This belief in the right thing can be a rationalization for a kind of fanaticism that is often deeply rooted in their early experiences. In Tanya's case these experiences involved having been raised in a family of religious fundamentalists. In her family if one *believed* something, this alone made it right. I am comparing their way of looking at the world with a more empirical and scientific point of view—that is, if something is *proven* right, it is *then* believable.

As an adult Tanya was close to her family but distanced herself from their religious fundamentalism and political conservatism. As so often happens, this discarded fanaticism reappeared in a different form. Tanya became an atheist, politically left-wing, and a deep believer in alternative medicine and child-rearing practices. These convictions and practices were right because she believed in them.

Her three children were home birthed. This was not a problem with the second and third children, but Tanya's first delivery was a nightmare. The second stage of labor was protracted and extremely painful, ending in an emergency trip to the hospital. There, reluctantly, she accepted an epidural and delivered the child within the next hour. Tanya viewed this birth as a failure on her part. Although she loved her son dearly, her childbirth wasn't "natural." Her later success at home delivery, with the easier labors she had with her two (smaller) daughters, alleviated her guilt about her son's birth. But why should she have felt guilty in the first place?

Tanya nursed all her children, in an equally fanatical way. It was only her exhaustion from long, sleepless nights and her need to get out and see friends that induced her to permit her husband to give the babies an occasional bottle—of pumped breast milk. Her children weaned themselves once they started on solid foods. If they hadn't, it is not clear when, or if, Tanya would have weaned them. She did not believe in vaccination or other forms of modern medicine, except in dire situations. Her children were not given painkillers or antibiotics. Their food was 100 percent organic and mostly vegetarian; sugar was carefully proscribed. Tanya's husband went along with his wife's convictions when it came to child rearing, but he was more relaxed about the entire project. As a result he seldom intervened.

Tanya's sense of rightness went beyond the physical care of her children. The family did not have a television set, and until they were older the children were allowed very limited time on the computer. Tanya believed that "screen time" interferes with brain development. Toys were made of wood, never plastic, and had to be educational as well as fun. The family lived in a city with good public schools. Tanya did not push her children about their school performance, which was fortunate because her son had a lot of trouble with his verbal skills for several years. He especially minded the absence of computer time, and he later turned out to be a natural at computer work. Both her daughters did well at school and were generally more compliant with the rules of the home.

One could ask where the hidden ambivalence was in Tanya's maternal behavior. Most mothers worry about doing the right thing and tend to follow the class-related popular cultural practices of their time. Tanya was certainly an involved and loving mother. But she pushed her beliefs too far. She was subtly inflexible. A story she told me illustrates this inflexibility. Because her first child weaned himself once he began to eat solids, she was worried her nursing was inadequate. It was especially important to her that she nurse her second child "adequately." This little girl was a frequent and lusty feeder, and it was hard for Tanya to keep up with her, especially now that she had two children. One afternoon, when Tanya was just exhausted, her mother urged her to try giving the baby some rice cereal. Reluctantly, Tanya agreed. The baby, then seven months old, ate it avidly. Tanya began giving her solids regularly, but again felt she was a failure as a mother. No food, she felt, is the equivalent of mother's milk.

An April 2009 article in the *Atlantic*, by Hanna Rosin, is titled "The Case against Breast Feeding." Rosin has three children and has nursed them all. Yet she makes a case in her article against the current idealization of nursing and breast milk as the *only* reasonable way to feed a baby. Rosin has nothing against breast feeding but feels that it has increasingly become a fetish and that the claims for breast milk as an inoculation against childhood infectious disease have not proven out in recent studies, nor have its salutary effects on brain development, weight gain, and so on. An earlier article in the Science section of the *New York Times*, published on May 13, 2008, reported a number of studies that debunk the idea that vaccination makes children more likely to develop autism. Tanya's reaction to this information is that both articles are wrong.

Tanya *did* exhibit a particular kind of ambivalent behavior that was striking because it was so different from her usual concern about her children's welfare. She would make dates with friends, or plan short vacations, without adequately preparing the children for her absence. She would let them know she would be gone, but often she did not give them enough time to take her absences in, and she was not entirely reliable about when she returned. She was not aware of how eager she was to get away. Since her children were all deeply dependent on her, it was very destabilizing. As the children grew older they had trouble with separation both from their parents and from each other. I believe Tanya's erratic behavior with regard to separations revealed her unconscious ambivalence as well as her unconscious worry about harming her children. The harm was projected into the "wrong" foods, the "wrong" practices, and the "wrong" toys, all of which she avoided, but it surfaced in her mistakes surrounding separation. Of these mistakes fueled by ambivalence, she was unaware.

Tanya exemplifies the too-good mother who tries to do everything right, making life more difficult for herself and her children. An example of this variety of perfectionistic mothering is portrayed hilariously in an episode of a recent movie directed by Sam Mendes, *Away We Go*. The mother (and father) in this episode carries attachment parenting to ludicrous extremes: the mother nurses her two children (six months old and four years old) frequently and sometimes simultaneously. The children sleep in the "family bed" and witness their parents' sex lives—it's "important for their development." The mother never uses a stroller but carries her children everywhere. Strollers keep the child too far away from her body. "Correct parenting" has become a fanatical folie à deux in this family.

There is another, more insidious form of too-good mothering that has been making the headlines in recent years. It involves women who feel they must have an inexhaustible supply of motherlove, who feel their needs don't count in comparison to those of their children. It is a kind of mothering that easily breaks down. For instance, it is currently the rage, or perhaps the fashion, among movie stars to have many children. Angelina Jolie is a striking example. I have a strong hunch that nannies play a very major role in raising these children. Even if my hunch is wrong, there seems to be a strong competitive and narcissistic undercurrent in this recent mommy race among the stars. This "narcissistic" undercurrent is a hidden wish to be very important to many people, not just fans. After all, who is more important to a child than its mother? In chapter 7 I explore further some of the issues underlying "baby greed" in a case story from Doris Lessing's *The Fifth Child*.

A more unfortunate example of too many babies is the case of

Andrea Yates, who I discuss in detail later in this book. She combined a feeling that she had to love and care for *everyone* in her family with her and her husband's strong religious convictions about not using birth control. Five children in seven years led to a psychotic break-down, in the grips of which Andrea murdered them all.

Along these same lines, the recent report of a young mother who gave birth to octuplets has engaged my curiosity. Nadya Suleman, a thirty-three-year-old single woman, already had six children when she gave birth to octuplets. Six embryos were implanted, resulting in eight births when two sets of twins developed. Suleman has attracted a great deal of media attention and public outrage. Why did she do it? How *can* she do it? She was interviewed on February 9, 2009, by Ann Curry on the *Today Show.* "All I wanted was children. I wanted to be a mom. That's all I ever wanted in my life," she told Curry. She talked about holding each premature baby (still in the hospi-tal) for forty-five minutes a day: "I'm loving them unconditionally, holding them, giving up my life for them." When asked how she will manage, she talked about living with her mother and going back to school to become a counselor so she can support them. She appears calm and unruffled. There is, in her voice, something very childish and unworldly—as if she has acquired a family of dolls to play with. There can never be too many of them. She will devote her life to loving them.

When asked by Gail Saltz, a psychiatrist invited to the interview, why she thinks she did this, Suleman replied, "It is my life's mis-sion." She feels it makes up for something missing in her childhood. Saltz's wry comment is that when something is missing in your child-hood, you consult a therapist; you don't have fourteen children. I am inclined to agree with her. Suleman is out of touch with the realities of what her life will be. Others will have to fill in. The children may grow up with the unconscious knowledge that they were deprived but with a strong *conscious* pressure to appreciate and love a mother who gave up so much for them.

Not long after this story broke into the media, I was standing in a line at the supermarket, looking at the headlines in the *National Enquirer* and other "yellow" purveyors of fantasy and lurid half-truths. I saw a story about Suleman locking the door on her children and leaving them to cry. The story was obviously concocted since the children were still in the hospital, but I felt that in its twisted way the tabloid had gotten it right. It had targeted the repudiated hate and rage that unconsciously lie behind actions this extreme. Time will probably tell us more, but I would venture a guess that this mother has an underlying depression, even a psychosis that may later break out clinically.

Especially interesting to me is the widespread negative public response to Nadya Suleman's behavior. It is not really the multiple birth issue; there have been other sets of octuplets born and living. The response is created by her deliberately bringing these births about when she already had six children. People are outraged. There is talk of taking the children away, or laws being enacted to prevent promiscuous childbearing. I doubt any of this will come to pass, but it is a reflection of the public's awareness of the difficulties and stresses of parenthood, motherhood in particular.

Good-enough mothers know better than to minimize the needs and demands of children or the stresses on themselves. They are frightened of what this woman has done, not because they want to do it themselves, but because they know it *can't* be done. They would feel overwhelmed—appropriately. What is wrong with this woman's thinking and sense of reality? Others are angry at the drain on diminishing public funds that such an impulsive act may carry in its wake. But even if Suleman were wealthy and able to take financial care of the children herself, the human limitations are what frighten people who are capable of dealing with reality and know what raising children involves. Rather than a loving, giving Madonna she is likely to turn out to be

> an old woman who lived in a shoe.
> She had so many children, she didn't know what to do,
> She gave them some broth, without any bread
> And whipped them all soundly and sent them to bed.[1]

In large families, older children often take care of the younger ones, ameliorating some of the problems that may occur. But when there are eight children the same age and six others young and close together, how can that happen? Thinking about the children in such a situation, I was reminded of Cindy, a young woman I treated briefly for feelings of anxiety and guilt about her attraction to another woman. She was the thirteenth of fourteen children in a family of observant Catholics. These children were spaced about two years apart, and the mother stopped having babies only because of the advent of menopause. Cindy described the members of her family rather variably. Some were happy and well adjusted, others troubled and discontented. None were in serious trouble. She saw her parents as hardworking and concerned. She, and every one of her sibs, knew that there were too many of them and that this had had consequences. None of them spoke of wishing to have large families. I had the impression that Cindy's attraction to another woman had a lot to do with what she didn't get from her mother but also what she *did* get from a favorite older sister.

Unfortunately, the therapy was very short term as Cindy was

leaving the area, so I was not able to explore that possibility with her. I do remember that she was amazed and stirred up by the experience of having me listen to her, of having me to herself. I listened to Cindy as I would to any patient seeking my help, but for her it was especially loaded with meaning and with a fear that I would soon turn my attention to someone else.

I remember an incident that took place during one of our sessions. A fire alarm went off in the building in which I worked. She and I had to leave the office and wait for the Fire Department to evaluate the situation. Instead of just waiting around tensely, I suggested we take a walk and she could continue talking to me during that time. It was very moving to her that I wouldn't just send her away, to come back for the next session, but was willing to find a way for her to use the time.

In addition to my patient Cindy, I have two friends who were the youngest children in large families, six and seven children, respectively. Both describe their mothers as old and tired by the time they came along. In both cases the eldest daughter took over their care from early on, so much so that they both felt their older sisters *were* their mothers. As adults, these two friends have been secure and affectionate people, suggesting that children can have important attachment figures other than their mothers and fathers. The key seems to be the affection and reliability of the older sibling. In families like that of Nadya Suleman intense sibling rivalry and resentment is very likely to be the order of the day.

I have delineated several varieties of too-good mothering, all characterized by the hidden quality of the ambivalence to the mothers themselves. As I will continue to emphasize, all mothers deal with some ambivalence. It may be internalized or externalized, hidden or obvious to others, or combinations of the above. What sets *this* kind of ambivalence apart is the mother's denial of the possibility that she is struggling with mixed feelings. The first task of a therapist is to bring these feelings into the open. This may be a major undertaking, but the relief that may ensue can have a very positive effect on a mother and her whole family.

CHAPTER FOUR

"Before the Beginning"

Women's Fears of Monstrous Births

My interest in maternal ambivalence began when I was treating a patient who feared any baby she had would be a "monster." Thinking about other women with similar worries, I realized that maternal aggression is frequently handled by being experienced as residing in a demanding and insatiable child, often described as a monster. Why does this word come up again and again? I think it is because children's needs and demands do exhaust parents and do provoke intense anxiety in them. Around these anxieties—which are about the *extremity* of children's needs and feelings—images of monstrosity proliferate.

Images of monsters disturb us because of two crucial psychological characteristics we attribute to them. We see them as the repository of our unwanted aggressive and sexual thoughts, feelings, and behaviors, and thus they represent what we fear is evil and destructive in ourselves. At the same time they are like caricatures—exaggerated, larger than life. By seeing them this way—larger than life—we can deny their connection to our *own* impulses and feelings. Although we often worry about grotesque *physical* attributes and differences, our real fear of monsters has to do with their emotional excesses—their out-of-control, driven behaviors that make us feel they have no concern for or connection to other human beings. Think for a moment of an extreme example—the creatures in Ridley Scott's movie *Alien*. They ruthlessly procreate using live human hosts whom they then discard. These creatures have no relationship to the humans who die giving birth to them. Insects and machines come to mind. However, most monsters, real or imagined, *do* seek an emotional connection to those who have used them as repositories of their own evil qualities. They seek connection to those who are actually, or symbolically, mothers. Dr. Frankenstein's creature follows his father/mother to the ends of the earth in an attempt to stay with him. Count Dracula is as deeply dependent on those he vampirizes as they are on him.

Fear of our own inner monstrosity is part of the human condition, taking on heightened importance when we become parents, especially mothers. The intellectual historian Marie-Helene Huet, in her 1993 work, *Monstrous Imagination,* elaborates how until the beginning of the nineteenth century the most persistent theory about the origins of monstrous progeny (birth defects) held that a "disordered female imagination" was responsible. In other words, the mother was blamed. Huet writes, "The monstrous child bore witness to the violent desires that moved the mother at the time of conception or during pregnancy" (1). Although the idea that the mother is *literally* responsible for such aberrations has disappeared, as the sciences of genetics, embryology, and reproductive physiology have developed, I maintain that worries about the maternal power to influence, for worse as well as for better, are more powerful than ever in a society that privileges its children as thoroughly as ours does and that expects so much of mothers.

Many fantasies surround the experiences of pregnancy, child-birth, and motherhood, but of these the horrifying idea of giving birth to a monster seems to be ubiquitous. This idea is usually experienced as a fear of physical birth defects, but the fear that you could give birth to a psychological monster, although often latent, may be even more disturbing. It takes the form of fearing that you will have a child you cannot love or will create a monster child *because* you cannot love it.

Variants of this fear may permeate all phases of the female reproductive process: women fear they will not be able to get pregnant because their insides are abnormal, or monstrous; they fear that pregnancy will sicken, deform, or drain them, that their fetus is a parasite; they fear being damaged or dying in childbirth; and they fear that once the child is born, they won't be able to mother it properly. Sometimes women fear that they won't be able to love a child because it is different from the fantasized child of pregnancy, in sex, appearance, or temperament. Think about it—you readers who have had children or those of you who are contemplating doing so—don't some of these fears sound familiar?

I became interested in these "monster" worries while I was treating Amanda, a woman who struggled with conflicts about whether or not to have a child. She had frightening fantasies of being damaged by pregnancy and childbirth. She feared that the child would be a "creature" (her word). Her most powerful fear was that she would be unable to mother, specifically, unable to soothe or comfort the child. Since treating Amanda, I have heard variants of all these fears in many of my female patients with and without children. In wondering why such fantasies are so common and what their deeper meanings might be, I became interested in an iconic literary representation of these themes—Mary Shelley's *Frankenstein,* a novel whose enduring fascination attests to the universality of the psychological concerns it addresses. I thought further about Mary Shelley herself and the idea I had once heard that her fears of childbirth had "given birth" to this novel, the most famous conception of a monster in the Western literary canon.

Although the psychoanalytic literature has much to say about the general meanings and concerns of women surrounding pregnancy, childbirth, and mothering, the *specific* concern about monstrous births, using *clinical* material to illustrate, is rather thin. It is not a pleasant subject to consider, for either patient or therapist. But it is a subject that needs to be addressed. Therefore, I decided to consider Mary Shelley, with her literary "progeny," *Frankenstein,* and my patient Amanda to see what themes recurred—that is, what are the psychological factors that contribute to these fears. Not surprisingly, many other patients came to mind as these ideas developed, and I talk about some of them in the next chapter.

MY HYPOTHESIS ON MONSTROUS BIRTHS

I am proposing that mothers' fears of birthing a monster reflect four different kinds of psychological concerns, all found in both my real patient Amanda and in Mary Shelley's life story and novel. First, and perhaps most important, the child imagined as monstrous is a reflection of the monster *within* the mother, that is, the fear that maternal aggression is in some form passed on to or put into the child, using the mechanism of projection. *Projection* is a technical term used by therapists that describes a way of dealing with disturbing thoughts, feelings, and behaviors by seeing them as existing in others: "I am hateful, and therefore my child will be a hateful monster, possibly even my executioner. I will be unable to love it, or it me, and this will make it even more monstrous." In different versions of this fear, the child represents evil, destructive parts of the mother's self, parts of hated siblings now reborn, or parts of hated parents. These are usually parents from whom the mother is incompletely separated or with whom she is pathologically identified.

Second, the monster is an impossible child because it is, in the *unconscious mind of the mother,* a child born of Oedipal incestuous wishes or fantasies and, as such, must be denied, rejected, and seen as monstrous. When I talk about the Oedipal period, or Oedipal fantasies, this is what I mean. Before the age of three, children's relationships are dyadic, that is, one-to-one. They are primarily connected with their mother or mother-substitute caretaker, and their bodily satisfactions have much to do with being fed, warmed, and comforted and learning to control their bodies (sitting, crawling, walking, and running) and their sphincters—becoming toilet-trained.

While the father is important in this "pre-Oedipal period," he moves more to center stage when the child is about three. At this age children become concerned, in their fantasy lives, with the power and intactness of their bodies, in particular, their sexual organs, and with pleasing and attracting the parent of the opposite sex—daddy's special little girl, mommy's big boy. During this phase both boys and girls struggle with conflicts between love and hostility directed toward the parent of the *same* sex. Frilly clothes, makeup, and jewelry are coveted by little girls; large motorized vehicles and feats of muscular strength and mastery, being like father, dominate the fantasy life of their male counterparts. In both sexes the question of babies and where they come from is implicit in their concerns and is a subject of much speculation and interest. Fantasies, largely unconscious, of *having* father's baby are a feature of the Oedipal period in the development of young girls, as is the fantasy of *giving* mother a baby in the psychology of young boys at this stage. As this fantasied baby is forbidden by the incest taboo, it is viewed, unconsciously, as a "monster" and is closely related to the concept of the bastard, the shunned outcome of an illicit or illicitly perceived sexual union. Both monsters and bastards are children who should not have been born.

Third, a mother's fears of producing a monster child may relate to shame and anxiety about the *meanings* of being female, about the insides of her body and what that body may produce. How a grown woman feels about her body and its reproductive capacities is a reflection of many factors—cultural and socioeconomic factors, to be sure, but more particularly psychological ones. Does she feel her female body was loved and admired by her parents? Does she love her mother and wish to be like her? Does she hate her mother and wish at all costs not to emulate her? Does she feel her femaleness is valued by her parents, or does she feel one or both of them would have preferred a boy? Have there been traumatic experiences—overstimulation, molestation, violence—in her life? Does she live in a culture and family where women are valued, where children, the product of women's procreative powers, are valued, too, or in a culture where women are controlled and demeaned and valued mainly for their (male) children? By the way, it is my belief that whatever the *conscious* cultural valuation of women and their reproductive abilities may be, on an *unconscious* level women—*mothers*—are always deeply needed and feared. But this does not necessarily translate into "treated" well; sometimes, precisely because they are needed and feared, they are treated quite poorly. And mistreatment, defensive or otherwise, does not contribute to positive self-valuation but rather leads to fear, shame, passivity, and self-loathing. All this may deeply color a woman's feelings about childbearing.

Fourth and finally, there is an especially crucial factor, that of the mother's relationship with her *own* mother. There are two aspects of this relationship that are very important for understanding anxieties about mothering—a woman's *identifications* with her mother and *early disturbances or disruptions in the mother-child bond*. All children identify with their parents, and this process has both conscious and unconscious elements. Children take on their parents' ways of seeing the world, their values, ideas, even their ways of moving, speaking, and expressing themselves. This is the conscious part of identification. Unconsciously, children pick up their parents' anxieties, feelings, and conflicts; it is this unconscious level of identification that leads many women to emulate their own mothers when *they* become mothers. This can, and does, happen even when a daughter does not really like her mother, because she is unaware, that is, unconscious, of what she is doing. Nancy Chodorow puts the issue of identification with one's mother's mothering very succinctly in *The Reproduction of Mothering*: "Women mother daughters who, when they become women, mother" (209).

Early disturbances or disruptions in the mother-child bond are very important, but they are hard to recapture, even in therapy, because they often have been forgotten.[1] Rather, they may be played out in subtle ways between therapist and patient and thus recaptured. Failure to meet the child's basic needs for feeding and safety may be caused by separations between mother and child, maternal depression or other psychological disorders, maternal incompetence, or physical illness in either mother or infant. These factors interfere with the formation of good images of maternal care and infant lovability, inside the infant, and either disrupt secure attachments or foster insecure attachments between mother and child. These disruptions are as likely to lead to a child's perception of *itself* as monstrous as they are to lead to disturbances in the mother in her care of the child. When disruptions are early, they may not be remembered consciously, but they leave their imprint; children, being both ego-centric (experiencing the world as revolving around them) and need-ing to protect and preserve their mothers, are likely to blame them-selves. This is a very common phenomenon that I next illustrate.

MARY SHELLEY

Mary Shelley is a dramatic example of a woman who, for all the above reasons, could have experienced herself as monstrous, and it is with her and her "hideous progeny," Dr. Frankenstein's monster, that I want to begin. They can be discussed together because there is evi-dence (both in the novel and in the author's letters and journals) that Shelley's deepest worries "gave birth" to this novel. Mary Shelley *is* Frankenstein's creature; he is the *monster within her.*

Mary Shelley was the only child of William Godwin and Mary Wollstonecraft, two famous literary figures of the late eighteenth century, both radicals and freethinkers. Neither parent believed in marriage as a social institution but married during Wollstonecraft's pregnancy to spare their child the stigma of bastardization. Mary Wollstonecraft died of puerperal fever eleven days after giving birth to her daughter. The circumstances of this death echo through *Frankenstein,* both literally and metaphorically. The midwife in atten-dance was unable to deliver the placenta. A doctor was called in. He removed the placenta manually, piece by piece, under the usual septic conditions that prevailed at that time, infecting and ultimately killing his patient. Dr. Frankenstein, too, "dabbled among the unhal-lowed damps of the grave," haunted charnel houses and slaughter-houses, and "disturbed, with profane fingers, the tremendous secrets of the human frame" (49–50). This author wreaks a painful revenge on doctors who bungle their work.

Mary Shelley, left motherless at eleven days of age, may have been burdened with two unconscious fantasies that I believe must haunt children whose mothers die in childbirth: the fantasy that she was her mother's murderer and the fantasy that her mother had abandoned her, perhaps because of *her*, Mary's, monstrous qualities. The converse of this second fantasy is that her mother's abandonment *made* her monstrous. Based on clinical observations of children who have lost mothers at a young age, we might expect such fantasies to be permeated with feelings of guilt, depression, anger, and the wish for revenge, and these indeed are the major affects expressed in Shelley's novel.

Mary was a bright, imaginative child who was highly identified with both her literary parents. Until adolescence, she was an intellectual companion to her father. Because of her stepmother's jealousy of "my excessive and romantic attachment to my father," she writes, she was sent away to Scotland from the age of twelve to fourteen to live with family friends.[2] This temporary but devastating separation from her father was followed by an outright rejection by him when, at the age of seventeen, she eloped with Percy Shelley, a married man. Although Godwin himself did not believe in marriage, he could not forgive his daughter for following his own precepts. He would neither speak to her nor write to her, and he did not acknowledge the birth of her children.

The hypothesis I am proposing is that for Mary Shelley the absence of a mother is connected with ideas of her own murderousness and unlovability, and the rejection by her father is connected with ideas of her own unacceptable sexual and incestuous impulses and that these murderous and incestuous impulses were "monstrous" to her.

On February 22, 1815, Mary gave birth, prematurely, to her first child, a girl, who died thirteen days later. This was a cruel repetition of fate for a young woman who had lost her own mother at the age of eleven days. Mary was grieved and preoccupied with the baby's death and felt very alone dealing with it. Her father would not acknowledge the birth, and she felt, with some justification, that Shelley did not love it, because it was a girl. In her journal she describes repetitive dreams of bringing the baby back to life: "Dream that my little baby came to life again; that it had only been cold, and that we rubbed it before the fire and it lived."[3] Dr. Frankenstein, too, wishes to bring the dead back to life.

In the 1831 preface to *Frankenstein,* fifteen years after the novel's conception, Mary Shelley attempts to answer a question often asked of her: "How I, then a young girl, came to think of, and to dilate upon, so very hideous an idea?"

> It is not singular that, as the daughter of two persons of dis-
> tinguished literary celebrity, I should very early in life have
> thought of writing. As a child I scribbled; and my favorite pastime,
> during the hours given me for recreation, was to "write stories."
> Still I had a dearer pleasure than this, which was the formation
> of castles in the air[,] ... the indulging in waking dreams ... at
> once more fantastic and agreeable than my writings. . . . [M]y
> dreams were all my own. . . . I did not make myself the heroine
> of my tales. . . . I was not confined to my own identity, and I could
> people the hours with creations far more interesting to me at that
> age than my own sensations. (222)

In this later explanation of her creation, Shelley seeks a reality-based reason for an unconsciously motivated behavior. She denies the personal nature of her monster fantasy (this is *not* a story about me), but the deeper reasons that drove her to write *Frankenstein* are revealed in the text.

Before turning to that text, I wish to speculate a bit more about what Mary Shelley was coping with psychologically and how these issues took form in her novel. The loss of her mother is her deepest psychological issue, certainly her earliest. Did my mother leave because I was monstrous: Did I kill her? Are some progeny so monstrous that even their makers reject them? And what, then, happens to the monster itself, left motherless? What kinds of mothers abandon their children; are they themselves monstrous? A related theme is the wish to bring the dead back to life, *her mother, her first baby,* recently lost. It is through these thematic strains that Shelley's concern about maternal aggression is expressed.

However, a father creates the monster in this book. A feminist critic, Anne Mellor, contends that *"Frankenstein* is a book about what happens when a man tries to have a baby without a woman,"* that is, what happens when the maternal presence is missing.[4] This father is horrified by what he has created; he cannot *really* give it life, he cannot mother it, and he tries to destroy it. Without empathy for his creation or for its needs, he treats it like a guilty secret. Another feminist critic, Katherine Hill-Miller, sees the novel as a disguised story of father-daughter incest and makes a persuasive case, based on close reading of the text, for the presence of such a guilty secret.[5]

I agree that incestuous themes are strongly present in the novel. The explicit incestuous concern is that of Dr. Victor Frankenstein and his passion for his mother, but the hidden issue is Mary Shelley's concerns about her own and her father's incestuous impulses and the meanings of any babies she bore. Percy Shelley was unconsciously connected with both her parents, more obviously her father. The figure of Victor Frankenstein is felt by many critics to represent an amalgam of Percy Shelley and William Godwin. I would extend this comparison and say that the doctor is a condensed figure of *all* the most important people in Mary's life, including herself. He is, like her father and Percy Shelley, a man whose ambitions and intellectual ideals are ruthlessly pursued to the neglect and detriment of those who love and depend on him.[6] He is, like her mother, a parent who abandons a child at birth. He is, like Mary Shelley herself, a parent whose children don't survive, perhaps because they are monstrous, the product of incestuous wishes.

FRANKENSTEIN

I would like to turn now to a brief discussion of *Frankenstein*, the novel in which Mary Shelley, in her disguised presence as Dr. Frankenstein's creature, expresses her deepest concerns. Recently, feminist and psychoanalytic literary critics have enriched our understanding of this novel with their recognition of the centrality of concerns about female sexuality and procreation. I am in substantial agreement with readings of this text that highlight themes of female sexual concerns and incestuous anxieties, but I feel that the primary "trauma" the author attempts to master through her writing is *maternal absence;* this is the theme that colors the novel, hovering constantly in the background and creating a sense throughout of horrible bleakness.

Frankenstein begins and ends in the frozen wastes of the Arctic Circle, the white, cold breast of the dead mother. In her journal Mary Shelley writes that as a child she heard Coleridge read his poem *The Rime of the Ancient Mariner.* It made a great impression on her; all her life she felt like the Mariner, "alone on a wide, wide sea." Dr. Frankenstein animates his monster on a cold, dreary night. He meets him later on the icy slopes of Mont Blanc, where the monster tells his story and pleads with Frankenstein to create a mate for him. The "mother earth" of this novel is a frozen, lifeless landscape.

Victor Frankenstein is the eldest son of loving and enlightened parents. He has two brothers and an orphaned cousin, Elizabeth, who is like a sister to him and to whom he will eventually become engaged. Shortly before he leaves home to study medicine in Ingolstadt, his mother dies, having contracted scarlet fever from Elizabeth.[7] Elizabeth, then, loses her own mother in infancy and "kills" her adopted mother. She is later killed, on her wedding night, by Frankenstein's monster. She symbolizes Mary Shelley's concerns about her own monstrousness, as mother killer and bearer of incestuous desires.

Frankenstein is distraught at his mother's death. He wishes to "banish disease from the human frame and render man invulnerable to any but a violent death" (49). He pursues his studies fanatically in an effort to discover the secrets of the generation of life. When he is able to do so, he fantasizes, "If I could bestow animation upon lifeless matter, I might in process of time . . . renew life where death had apparently devoted the body to corruption" (49). In his wish to resurrect the dead, he builds an enormous creature out of parts of dead bodies and brings it to life (of a sort), then turns from it in fear and loathing.

Dr. Frankenstein's creation of his monster reads like a grotesque pregnancy and childbirth. "Winter, spring and summer passed away during my labours," he tells us (51). He becomes frantic, feverish, and obsessed as the time of birth draws near: "With an anxiety that almost amounted to agony, I collected the instruments of life around me that I might infuse a spark of being into the lifeless thing that lay at my feet. . . . I saw the dull yellow eye of the creature open; it breathed hard, and a convulsive motion agitated its limbs" (52).

But Frankenstein is not filled with relief and pleasure at the "successful" birth. Rather, he is horrified at the catastrophe he has wrought.

> I had worked hard for nearly two years for the sole purpose of infusing life into an inanimate body. I had desired it with an ardour that far exceeded moderation; but now that I had finished, the beauty of the dream vanished, and breathless horror and disgust filled my heart. Unable to endure the aspect of the being I had created, I rushed out of the room. (52)

Frankenstein is frightened and repelled by the physical monstrousness of his creation, but a deeper source of his horror is revealed in the dream he has that night.

> I thought I saw Elizabeth, in the bloom of health, walking in the streets of Ingolstadt. Delighted and surprised, I embraced her; but as I imprinted the first kiss on her lips, they became livid with the hue of death; her features appeared to change, and I thought that I held the corpse of my dead mother in my arms; a shroud enveloped her form, and I saw the grave-worms crawling in the folds of the flannel. (53)

The dream reveals Frankenstein's secret wish: to bring to life and embrace his dead mother. His baby is an incest baby, an impossible and hideous progeny. As previously noted, the incest theme in *Frankenstein* condenses two incestuous situations and substitutes one for the other: in the book it is a son who wishes for his mother, not a daughter who wishes for her father. Mary Shelley's hideous progeny is the embodiment of *her* unconscious wishes and fears, not that of her male protagonist. But there is more to Dr. Frankenstein's horror of his "baby" than his incestuous anxiety. He cannot *really* create a live baby with whose needs he can identify because he (again, representing Mary Shelley) has had no steady, early maternal presence to internalize. He cannot be the "ordinary devoted mother" of whom Winnicott wrote, bringing an infant to life by identifying with and satisfying its needs, because he cannot draw on his own unconsciously relived experience.

Mary Shelley has yet another unconscious issue to deal with in this novel. Her monster is not only a baby whose creator cannot give it real life. There is another question about his monstrousness. Was he born that way, or made so by abandonment? The author's purpose appears to be an effort to *prove* the latter and thereby absolve *herself* from having been her mother's murderer. The second volume of the novel concerns the monster's failed efforts to find a loving family and his turn to vengeful aggression when he faces the final abandonment by Dr. Frankenstein, who will neither care for him nor create a mate for him. Interestingly, once Frankenstein dies, the monster does not find true revenge but rather is hopelessly grieved. He will build a funeral pyre and immolate himself on it. There is no reason to go on living once his rejecting "mother" is gone and all hope of connection, even a tormented and destructive connection, is over.

AMANDA'S STORY: A CLINICAL EXAMPLE

The concerns that may have plagued Mary Shelley appear in the fantasies and associations of several of my female patients, but Amanda's story seems especially relevant. A thirty-five-year-old married architect, Amanda was concerned about both the aggressive and incestuous meanings of childbirth and mothering. She entered four times weekly psychoanalysis to deal with relentless inner pressures in all parts of her life and to decide whether or not to have a child.

Amanda feared, admired, and emulated her scientist father and her older brother. She loved her mother but felt she was unable to be close to her. Several factors seemed important in this mother-daughter estrangement. In her first year of life Amanda spent six months in a harness to correct her congenital hip dysplasia. This meant she had to lie on her back, in her crib, with her legs rotated outward so that her hip joints would develop normally. During this time her mother had severe arthritis in her hands, which made it difficult "to hold and diaper her baby girl." Normal cuddling and soothing were disrupted. This disruption of mother-infant intimacy was partially offset by the mother's concern and presence. She may not have been able to pick the baby up, but she used her voice to soothe and comfort her. Amanda loved her mother, but something was still missing. She perceived her mother as passive and as having inferior status in the family. Amanda felt that both her parents preferred her brother, and she devalued women in general. She was not homosexual, but she repudiated many aspects of femininity. "It wasn't that I wanted to be a boy. I wanted *not to be a girl*," she told me. To Amanda, girls were crippled.

All aspects of the female reproductive cycle were a problem to her. The onset of menses was an unwelcome event that she discussed with no one, and she tried her best to hide all signs of it. Pregnancy she saw as grotesque and embarrassing, an indisputable proof of her femaleness. She wished pregnancy could end "like an appendectomy. You have something taken out, and that's the end of it. Nobody has to know. But a child is with you forever." She imagined childbirth as an endless pain-ridden process with which she would get no help. The baby would be stuck inside. They would have to cut her open to get it out. She was not referring to a cesarean; it was as if there was no vagina for the baby to pass through. "I imagine I have this painful infant inside, and I can't stand it. They'd have to cut my body open, down the middle, like a fish, and have this thing taken out."

All these worries had a frightening, claustrophobic coloring.

Amanda suffered from nocturnal panic attacks, accompanied by a violent gastrointestinal discharge. These attacks were brought on, the patient thought, by demands at work or from her family, demands that she felt she would be unable to meet. But these attacks had other meanings, one of which seemed to be that of symbolic childbirth. Amanda recalled reading the childbirth scene in *Gone with the Wind* with horror and fascination: "When I think about those images, I have a queasy feeling, a reaction that goes all through my intestines, a sort of anxiety thing." The patient and I both came to see that the panic attacks also related to her early, unremembered experiences of lying helpless and immobilized in her crib and desperately needing bodily soothing.

Amanda explored how frightened she was of the fetus itself. She described fetuses and babies as "creatures," like something out of the movies *Alien* and *Eraserhead*. "It's a frightening monster—like a vicious animal—not that it has teeth or claws, but it takes on that flavor." In *Alien* the creature splits the body of its mother/father apart. In *Eraserhead* an ambiguous creature is born; "We don't even know if it *is* a baby," the mother says.

Moreover, Amanda feared that once the baby was born, she would be unable to mother it. It would be endlessly demanding and inconsolable, and she would be all alone. She had insufficient internalized images of the experience of being soothed, especially in infancy. (She did not fear older children, those who were no longer babies.) Both in her fantasies of childbirth and in her fantasies during her panic attacks, she felt nobody would help her.

For Amanda, infants were not only demanding and aggressive monsters but incest babies, too. The disruptions in her early relationship with her mother intensified her passionate Oedipal attachment to her father. She longed more than anything to please him, even though this required, in her eyes, that she perform perfectly, never ask for help, and never show dependency. Amanda railed angrily at her father's rigid demands and standards but was deeply identified with him. She admitted sadly, "I don't want to be like him, yet I feel it's wrong not to be." She married a man much like her father. During analysis she came to recognize her husband's limitations, his rigidity and defects in empathy, but this recognition was very threatening to her. As she put it, "It makes me unhappy, but—it's hard to explain—there is no one else quite like him in the world." I felt that the person most like him in the world was her father, but this was a similarity she could barely acknowledge. Although evidence of passionate and guilt-ridden Oedipal feelings appeared in dreams and "accidents"—for instance, she injured her back when she was due to stay with her father and take care of him when her mother was briefly hospitalized—such feelings were consistently repressed and denied by the patient. Amanda did not want to see that for *her* any baby was father's baby.

In the analytic situation I was experienced, at times, like her father, critical and impatient, expecting her to have all problems understood (regardless of their unconscious components) and solved without help and seeing her as weak and spineless when she couldn't perform. As mother I was perceived as inviting her into a feminine world, a world she longed for yet saw as shameful. While she felt understood and accepted by me, especially in connection with her warded-off dependent longings, she questioned and repudiated most of my interventions, as if I did not have much of value to offer her. As the relationship with me developed, I also became the demanding baby that controlled and structured her life, insisting, for instance, that she come to four sessions a week when her life was already so heavily scheduled and overburdened. I experienced her as a woman avoidant of need and closeness, yet as someone who longed intensely for a relationship with me that would fulfill those needs and allow her to *accept and repair* her femininity.

Analysis was ultimately helpful to Amanda. Although she did not have a baby, her creativity and her relationships with other women, including her mother, blossomed, and her internal pressures to perform, at the expense of her own needs, were considerably modified.

AMANDA AND MARY SHELLEY

I began this chapter by proposing that the fear of monstrous births might have four different but interwoven psychological components. I have discussed the incest theme at some length in my analysis of Mary Shelley's life and its relationship to her novel. Important as that theme is in the novel and in the unconscious fantasies of many pregnant women, I feel that the expectant mother's concerns about her own aggression are an even more potent source of the fear of giving birth to a monstrous baby. The aggression she fears her child will "inherit" may represent hated and destructive parts of herself transmitted genetically and psychologically, the belief in the former often serving as a defense against fears of the latter. But the child may also represent hated siblings, parents, and spouses. Joan Raphael-Leff, a British psychoanalyst who has written much about the internal world of pregnant women, presents the case of a pregnant woman who wanted a boy because her fetus, if female, would represent her envious and resentful mother or her resented female siblings.[8] Raphael-Leff also feels that fears of one's own murderous feelings toward the baby, and fears of the baby as a parasitic and murderous force within, surface regularly in the dreams and fantasies of pregnant women. We have seen that Mary Shelley, a motherless child, was deeply concerned about the murderousness of babies and the meanings of being an abandoned daughter. I maintain that even if fears of monstrous babies *are* ubiquitous in the fantasy life of pregnant women, they must be more prevalent and troubling in women whose relationships with their mothers are disrupted or seriously troubled. Models of healthy and fulfilled motherhood are missing or incomplete, and identifications are formed with mothers who are conflicted or unloving. Where the mother-daughter early bond has been disrupted, there may be a failure to securely internalize a loving mother-infant relationship. Psychological factors in the daughter, too, may make healthier identifications problematic.

This was the case with my patient. Amanda's mother was concerned and well meaning, but Amanda spent much of her early life repudiating her. The trouble between this mother and daughter began with an early traumatic disruption, the patient's *real* birth defect, leading to disturbances in physical and emotional care. It was compounded later by the patient's resentment of her mother's perceived preference for her brother and by her mother's anxiety and passivity about claiming her rightful status in the family, making positive feminine identifications more difficult. Interestingly, Mary Shelley, although suffering a total maternal absence, seemed able to have and love her babies. I would speculate that resiliency based on inborn temperamental factors and good substitute mothering *early in life* (including from her father) were some of the factors that allowed Shelley to mother adequately. Only her novel reveals how deep-seated and horrifying her unconscious concerns about mothering were; her creature has no mother.

Amanda's problems highlight another factor that may operate in women who are fearful about their ability to mother. Both she and Mary Shelley had fathers who devalued women and who viewed and treated their daughters as if they were sons. I will quote from a letter written by William Godwin to his daughter in 1819, right after the death of her son, William, at the age of three. Mary had lost another baby, Clara, a year earlier, at thirteen months. In the letter Godwin chastises his daughter for the intensity of her grief.

> You must . . . allow me the privilege of a father in expostulat-
> ing with you upon this depression. I cannot but consider it as
> lowering your character in a memorable degree, and putting
> you quite among the commonality and mob of your sex, when
> I had thought I saw in you symptoms entitling you to be ranked
> among those noble spirits that do honor to our nature.[9]

Noble spirits are men, people who don't have babies. This repudiation of the female is also a theme in Shelley's novel. Frankenstein seals his fate when he refuses to create a mate for his monster out of his fear that she will "create a race of devils." Of course, Frankenstein's refusal to create a woman may also be viewed as envious, a defense against the reproductive abilities he attempts unsuccessfully to duplicate, as perhaps is true of much male envy of the female.[10]

A parallel to Godwin's devastating letter to his daughter occurred with my patient. For a long time in her analysis Amanda disavowed my observation that she felt herself devalued as a female and damaged (as she viewed her mother to be). Then one day she told me that she had been talking to her parents the previous night, and they had described finding a dead animal in their swimming pool, decapitated and eviscerated. Amanda, an animal lover, identified the animal as an opossum. Her father suddenly replied, "It was probably a girl 'possum. Probably in the 'possum culture they get rid of girls, chop their heads off, rip out their guts, and throw them away." Amanda was shocked. "It was so bizarre—it came out of left field.

But I really heard it that time. Sometimes I think I imagined all that stuff, but I didn't ... about women being second-class citizens. So where did I fit in?" Where, indeed? I think that both Amanda and Mary Shelley unconsciously felt their female bodies were damaged and shameful. Amanda knew that her own mother had had hyperemesis gravidarum (a rare but serious disorder of pregnancy involving nausea and vomiting throughout the entire nine months) with both her pregnancies. Amanda herself had had a birth defect. Perhaps she feared what her own insides would produce, whether they could produce a normal baby. Mary Shelley had a mother whose body could not survive childbirth. What did that mean to her about women's bodies? Even more important, I feel, is that both Shelley and Amanda, as young women, experienced their beloved fathers as threatened and disgusted by their femininity. Their conclusion could have been, there is something wrong with me, with my female condition, and therefore with anything that is proof of that condition. The "something wrong" could be connected to having the wrong desires and wishes, in particular, the unconscious wish to have the father's baby.

Amanda's conflict over her femininity led, in reality, to a refusal to have children and, intrapsychically, to a denial of her female anatomy as demonstrated in her fear that the baby would have no way to get out, as if she were a man. By denying her female anatomy she felt she would please her father and successfully compete with her brother while warding off any possibility of unconsciously having an Oedipal (incestuous) baby. After all, men, even imaginary men, don't have babies. Amanda, Mary Shelley, and her monster *all* turned out to share the complex of concerns I elaborated in my hypothesis at the beginning of this chapter. Examples of other patients who struggled with some of these issues follow in the next chapter.

CHAPTER FIVE

Women's Reproductive Fears

More Clinical Examples

My patient Amanda first alerted me to women's fears of pregnancy, childbirth, and mothering. My interest in her story sparked my investigation into Mary Shelley's story, illustrated in her classic horror novel, *Frankenstein.* Now I would like to offer more clinical material to illustrate that it is not unusual to fear childbearing. The situations of other patients support different parts of my hypothesis about women's reproductive fears. Although not all of them feared monster children, all did struggle with issues involving family relationships and various aspects of femininity. Their stories broaden our view of the problem.

Sarah and Phyllis were women who generally dealt with painful situations projectively, and concerns about their children were no exception. They feared they had or would produce monsters. Sarah feared her baby might hate her, and this fear reflected intense worries that she would hate the baby. Phyllis feared her child would be a replica of her own mother, to whom she was ambivalently attached. Deirdre worried about her body and its capacity to bring forth a healthy child, as well as her capacity to mother it lovingly. All this came out in her dreams during her pregnancy. Rebecca's situation illustrates the effect of tensions involving femininity and incestuous longings on fertility and sexual response. Sandra and Sybil both dealt with early disruptions in their relationships with their mothers and also with conflicts over femininity and incestuous attachments. Finally, there is Priscilla, who did not have children, despite strong conscious longings to do so, because of a deep unconscious fear that her child would be a monstrous replica of her three demanding younger siblings.

FEARING THEIR CHILDREN ARE MONSTERS: SARAH AND PHYLLIS

Sarah was six months pregnant, with a boy, when she sought therapy with a colleague of mine. She had a history of depression and self-destructive behavior starting in adolescence and was worried about the possibility of a postpartum depression or psychosis because she had to stop taking antidepressant medication during her pregnancy. She reported a history of defiant and aggressive behavior in childhood, behavior her parents were unwilling or unable to control.

Recently Sarah had been struggling with the return of an obsessional ritual (hand washing) and with anxiety about what her unborn son would be like. She described a "game" that she played with the baby: "I sort of poke him and wait to see if he'll poke me back. Sometimes he'll kick me, but when my husband comes along and puts his hand on my belly, the baby quiets right down." Sarah wondered if her son would be a bully: "How do I know what he's going to be like? Maybe he'll be angry and hurt people. He might be a scared little kid, or maybe he won't want to be around people. He might not care about anybody else and want to push people around. What will we do then?"

My colleague commented to Sarah that she seemed to believe the baby would be born "full blown" and that she and her husband would have no influence over him, just as her parents had had no influence over *her*. Sarah replied that she didn't want to talk about this, she had dealt with it before, and she wanted some practical advice about how to handle the situation. Her refusal to explore the connection between her own history of uncontrollable behavior and her fears about the baby were felt by the therapist to be setting the stage for the projection of her hostility (expressed in her poking games and defended against with obsessional hand washing) into her infant.[1]

While it was distressing for the therapist to see a "monster" being created in the mind of its mother, she was aware of the danger and able to focus on it with the patient, who was, after all, in therapy to prevent a postpartum "disaster." Furthermore, Sarah saw her husband as someone who could rescue her and neutralize the effect of her aggression on the baby. Depending on her husband to help her control her hostility was an indication of her positive feelings and concerns about the baby. As we saw in chapter 2, in the case of the woman who was afraid she couldn't manage her newborn twins, the supportive role of the father is often pivotal to avoiding a disaster.

Phyllis was deeply worried about monstrousness in her only son, three-year-old Josh, in the form of eccentric behaviors that, she feared, would lead to his being seen as a misfit. Phyllis's unwed mother had felt tied down by having a child. She expressed both her ambivalence and her immature, demanding personality in her behavior toward her daughter, alternately smothering her with inappropriate attention and demands and wounding her with cruel criticisms. Having had trouble leaving her mother, Phyllis married late. Although she, too, was ambivalent about having a child, with her husband's support and encouragement she was able to do so. She feared closeness of all kinds, but she was especially fearful that a child would be a demanding replica of her mother, endlessly needy and self-centered. She was relieved that the child was a boy, but she worried about him and struggled with *any* behavior on his part that marked him as different from other children. On very little evidence, she perceived Josh as strongly self-willed and stubborn and feared he would end up a lonely outsider, like her. In identification with her mother, Phyllis, too, was needy and demanding, so that her fears about the boy were clearly unconscious projections of something it was hard to admit in herself. Her focus on his becoming a misfit really represented her fear that he would never grow up and be able to leave her—repeating her experience with her mother. Both of these women feared their babies would end up with qualities and behaviors that they did not wish to acknowledge in themselves, the hallmark of maternal ambivalence expressed by externalizing.

FEARS OF AN INCEST BABY: REBECCA

In contrast to Sarah and Phyllis, Rebecca really wanted children but, as I learned in her therapy, feared their connection with her unconscious erotic longings for her father. Rebecca started therapy in her mid-twenties with troubled feelings about her family and her femininity. A bright woman, successful in her career, she dressed in frumpy clothes and seemed oddly unconcerned about her appearance. She *was* concerned about her inability to achieve orgasm with her devoted and passionate boyfriend. Eventually she revealed to me her uncertainty about marriage and motherhood. The eldest of three children, she was overly involved with her parents. She deeply admired her father and was ashamed and contemptuous of her mother, whom she viewed as weak and inadequate.

Both these attitudes were quickly revealed in her therapy, in relationship to me. At the time I began seeing Rebecca, I shared an office building with several other therapists, including my husband. After our first appointment Rebecca left my office and instead of exiting the way we had come in, walked into my husband's office. Claiming in the next session that his door was unmarked and that she had a poor sense of direction, on leaving she promptly walked into his office again. When I began to explore this "mistake" with her, she minimized it, but she managed to find the correct exit route from then on. As time went on, her unconscious wish to "be with her father" (i.e., in my husband's office) became more accessible, as did her thinly veiled contempt and anxiety about me, my strength and competence. Men were valuable, women weak and shaky. Much of the contempt she felt for her mother was a function of her jealousy at being replaced by two siblings, one of them a highly prized boy. Angry and disappointed, she turned to her father, as she did literally in leaving my office after the first two visits. Her interest in my husband (and my marriage) extended to some boundary violations in the form of researching his records at the university where he taught and she worked, thus discovering that we had children. (I saw Rebecca before the development of the Internet. These days, doubtless, she would have googled me, and it would have been much harder for her to see this as a violation of privacy.)

After several years of therapy Rebecca and her boyfriend married. Both wanted children, and now in their early thirties, they began to try to become pregnant. Rebecca had had a previous pregnancy with this boyfriend a few years before beginning therapy. Although the pregnancy was terminated by an abortion, she knew she could conceive. Nevertheless, she became very worried that she was infertile and would never be able to have children. After a year of trying and worrying, Rebecca finally became pregnant and was later able to conceive easily twice more. I attributed her temporary "infertility," as well as her lack of orgastic response in lovemaking with her husband, to unconscious guilt over incestuous wishes and, no doubt, to guilt over her previous abortion. To Rebecca, as to Mary Shelley and Amanda, all babies were, unconsciously, "father's babies," as they had been in childhood, and all husbands were *also* fathers.

Curiously, Rebecca was able to achieve orgasm during masturbation. There were two essential components to her masturbatory practices. She would never touch her genitals, achieving orgasm by rubbing and squeezing her thighs together, and she fantasized about sexy male movie stars, the kind of movie stars who appeal to adolescent girls rather than grown women. Through this behavior she expressed her shame about being female and having female, *not male,* sex organs. In this respect, she was like Amanda. Rebecca didn't want to touch herself and feel what was not there. Her excitement over teenage male idols (John Travolta in *Saturday Night Fever,* for instance) reflected the excited adolescent inside herself—still daddy's girl, contemptuous of the weak, incompetent mother who was a repudiated part of herself, and having to hide sexual longings behind frumpy clothes and a lack of feminine adornment of any kind.

Rebecca's concerns about having children did not stem from worries that they would be monstrous but rather from what they meant in terms of her unconscious fantasies. Sex and babies meant both having what her mother had and displacing her mother by being daddy's favorite. This, in turn, meant losing mother's love. Beneath her contempt was a deep attachment to her mother but an attachment that was disrupted (as it so often is) by the birth of two younger siblings. She showed me, in action, in the first few sessions, what her worries were. She walked into my husband's office, leaving me behind, but she also worked hard in therapy, forming a strong attachment to me. The fruit of this work was a good marriage, children whom she mothered well, and an internal shift in her attachments. After we had worked together for four years, she happened to see my husband in the hallway. She remarked on how much he had changed—no longer dashing and handsome (John Travolta?) but rather a pleasant-looking, middle-aged Jewish man!

DEIRDRE'S PREGNANCY DREAMS

Deirdre, the patient of a colleague, became pregnant during the time she was in therapy. Her thoughts and dreams illustrate several aspects of my hypothesis about monstrous births: the fear that she will make the baby monstrous, the fear that her body cannot birth a normal baby, and the fear of hidden incestuous meanings in becoming a mother.

Deirdre grew up in a family where she felt inferior. Her father was a successful and autocratic businessman whose love she craved, and her mother was a devalued housewife. She had one sibling, a younger brother. Deirdre did not achieve as much as her brother and cousins academically, and she married a man of modest aspirations and means, for which she was criticized. She grew up filled with envy and resentment toward successful men and contempt for women, including herself. She did not like her body and struggled with bulimia. Her sexual satisfaction was obtained to the accompaniment of fantasies of being tied up and beaten.

Deirdre's first and easily attained pregnancy ended in a miscarriage, and she became convinced she would *never* be able to conceive again or would habitually miscarry. Nevertheless, she became pregnant easily the second time, and the pregnancy did not miscarry. But concerns and dreams about not being able to mother successfully began to occur. In one dream she was going from empty room to empty room. These rooms represent wombs that can't hold a baby. Next she dreamed of going from one messy room to another, trying desperately to clean them up. Her husband had made these messes. The patient said, "I'm turning into my mother, cleaning up all these rooms. My husband is becoming fat. I don't want us to be fucked up for the baby!" Turning into her mother had negative meanings to her, including being fat, which also connects to being pregnant. Her therapist said that Deirdre fears she won't be a good mother. Deirdre said, "If I expect the worst, it won't upset me so much if the baby hates me."

The next week Deirdre had an anxiety dream about her cat being mutilated. In the dream she tries to help him and takes him to the vet. She associated this with how much she loves her cat and how worried she is about the baby being all right. The vet represents her therapist. Deirdre feared the baby would be anencephalic—born without a brain. She talked of her worry that the baby was not moving enough, which means it isn't growing. In this series of dreams Deirdre expressed her fear that her aggression (hatred) would be put into the baby and that the baby would hate her, that the baby would be a monster—born without a brain—and her body inadequate to grow a healthy baby.

At the same time she was thrilled when she did feel the baby move and angry at her husband when she thought of him having more time with the baby than she will. He would have more time with the baby because *she* is arranging it that way. She earned more money than he did, so she felt she should continue to work and he should stay home. But she hated and envied him for this. Here is her ambivalence—loving the active, moving baby and fearing the angry, hating baby, wanting to stay home with her baby but turning him over to her husband. Love and hate war in her mind and come out in her dreams.

Deirdre's sexual fantasies also changed during her pregnancy. From anonymous images of bondage, in which she is the victim of a faceless perpetrator, she imagined a man who verbally punishes her, makes her get undressed, spanks her, and tells her she is not listening to him. Perhaps this is her therapist. She had powerful orgasms as she imagined this scene. Interestingly, she didn't have many thoughts about *this* fantasy. She didn't want to recognize these thoughts as they connected to her childhood and her early passionate feelings about her father and now to her male therapist. This was too threatening. Fears about the incestuous meanings of a baby tend to stay unconscious in treatment, while the other fears I have described in my hypothesis are usually easier to talk about.

Many pregnant women do not remember their dreams, but that doesn't mean that they don't have them. Deirdre did remember her dreams while in therapy, and this, with her therapist's help, allowed her to understand her ambivalence before her baby was born. This understanding, in turn, decreased Deirdre's anxiety about her future mothering and increased her comfort and confidence with her baby when she was born. Women who find themselves having conscious ambivalent feelings and dreams relating to motherhood have a great deal to gain from therapy during their pregnancies.

Deirdre was also helped by therapy during her first few months of mothering. Her delivery went well, and when her daughter was two weeks old she began to bring her to sessions. She continued to worry about being a bad mother despite her obvious fondness for and attention to the baby. Some difficulty nursing in the first few weeks led her to tell her therapist that she "feels like a failure, like everything else I do." She admitted that she felt angry at the baby earlier in the week (because of the nursing difficulties) and then had "some baby blues." At Deirdre's next session she told her therapist a repetitive fantasy she had been having. After the baby feeds, when she lets go of the nipple, she smiles at Deirdre. When this happens Deirdre worries that the baby is a monster who is tricking her into thinking she, the baby, needs maternal care. She fears the baby will become a "demon-monster like in *Rosemary's Baby*." She worries she is feeding her daughter too much. Deirdre is worried about how much *she* eats and fears she has put her greed into the baby. Deirdre's comfort with talking about her maternal ambivalence with her therapist enabled her to overcome her early difficulties and to enjoy her motherhood more and more as time went on. When she finished her therapy, she was pregnant with her second child.

EARLY DISRUPTIONS AND SEPARATIONS: SANDRA AND SYBIL

Although both Rebecca and Deirdre suffered from incestuous conflicts and feelings of inferiority and shame about their femininity, there was no evidence of a disruption in their early relationships with their own mothers, other than the birth of younger siblings and the favoritism shown, in both cases, to brothers. I do not claim that the birth of siblings is not traumatic and disruptive, when it so often and so clearly is, but rather that the disruption is normal. Since sibling relationships, while complex, can provide substantial gratifications— validation and emotional support—they are usually not a net loss. For instance, Rebecca was quite jealous of her brother but had a close alliance with her sister in a shared view of the family, an alliance that supported them both in the need to become autonomous from their loving but very overprotective parents.

The next two women I describe did suffer early disruptions in their attachments to their mothers. Sandra, the second of two children born within two years to young and insecure parents, suffered a severe early disruption due to a traumatic birth. A drop in the fetal heart rate during delivery led to an emergency cesarean that endangered the lives of both mother and baby and left the mother ill and weakened. Because of this illness early bonding was severely compromised, with Sandra's father and other helpers taking care of the baby for several weeks. This acute disruption was only the beginning of an alienated relationship between Sandra and her mother. It turned out that the mother had a chronic and debilitating disease that necessitated at least one lengthy hospitalization during Sandra's early years and kept her weak, intermittently bedridden, and dependent on medications.

As is not unusual in such cases, Sandra unconsciously held herself and her own infantile needs responsible for her mother's illness. The situation was made worse by the mother's youth and immaturity. She was not emotionally ready to take care of two small children and may have taken partial refuge in her real illness. Even more powerfully than Rebecca, Sandra identified with her father and turned to him for support and approval. She tried to please him by being what she supposed he would want and admire in a daughter, overriding her real aptitudes and deeper interests. Like Amanda, she did not want to be a man, but she also felt that being a woman, in particular, a mother, was bad news.

Sandra was very uncomfortable with her feminine body, focusing mainly on her weight. Being thin was important, but not having big thighs, hips, breasts, buttocks, or abdomen was even more crucial—nothing curvaceous, nothing that jiggled. Yet dressing well and looking attractive *was* important to her. She was heterosexual and quite responsive sexually. The real danger, for Sandra, was closeness and dependency. To need someone was to destroy them or to have them disappoint you. To have a more masculine body and persona, to be totally self-sufficient, was safe. Neither she nor anyone else could be hurt.

Although she was often drawn to children, Sandra did not want any of her own. She had had an abortion during her thirties and suffered considerable unconscious guilt in consequence. Babies, she felt, weaken and sicken mothers with their endless, clamoring neediness. Even though she agreed to go into analysis to understand her conflicts, she did not want to need *me,* in any way. She sought out alternate ways to achieve self-understanding, ways that did not involve ongoing dependence on another person, ways that would allow her to be in control—slim, strong, and autonomous. A woman's body, one that could bear children, was a vulnerable body, a shameful body, and women's minds were not all that reliable either. She could only imagine using me as a disembodied psychological consultant, not as a live person, in relation to whom she could experience, and thus understand and possibly modify, her ways of seeing and being in the world. This was how she consciously felt at the beginning of our work, but gradually she was able to feel reassured by my ability to endure her needs, feelings, and anxieties without becoming ill or damaged.

Sandra was able to admit she missed having a child only when it was too late, but by then she had also made impressive strides in her life. She had met and fallen in love with a man she was later to marry, had made career changes more suitable to her personality and interests, and was able to value, deeply and realistically, the work we had done together. Had she been younger, perhaps she and her husband would have had children.

Sybil's story, in contrast, involves early separations from a very *loving* mother. She and her mother had formed a strong, reliable attachment during her infancy, but during her first five years of life she had to be hospitalized three times for the gradual correction of a congenital malformation. The first of these separations was at eight months, an especially vulnerable time for babies, marking the onset of separation, or stranger, anxiety. The next operation was at eighteen months (another period of sensitivity to separation in children) and the third at five years.[2] Although her mother stayed close by, during and after the hospitalizations, Sybil was further sensitized to issues of separation by the eighteen-month hospitalization and to issues of bodily intactness and injury by the operation at five years. Some of the latter sensitivity was intensified by the sadistic behaviors of a jealous older brother who tormented her physically.

Although Sybil was an attractive, intelligent, and successful young woman, her relationships with men felt very fraught with danger to her. Any behavior on their part that could be interpreted as rejection or insult led her to flee angrily. The danger was not only one of narcissistic injury. Being a woman and having a woman's body was, in itself, a situation of great vulnerability. Feelings about her bodily self and its weaknesses were strongly intensified by the early surgical experiences. Furthermore, her parents, her mother in particular, were very protective of their daughter, unable to give her permission to take risks in the world, out of the safe nest of the triangle the mother, Sybil's father, and Sybil formed. Although Sybil felt she would very much like to have children, she was not sure she could tolerate the difficulties of a relationship. No man would be as nice to her as her father was, and, like Rebecca, to be close to a man (who had unconscious connections to father) was to risk losing her mother. My work with Sybil ended before I could find out how her story evolved. I felt that her conscious wish was to have a family but that unconscious fears of bodily damage, in both sex and childbirth, as well as her sensitivity to injury from men, may have made that unlikely.

FEARS OF MONSTROUS SIBLINGS: PRISCILLA

Priscilla's dilemma led to a delay of childbearing until it was too late. She belongs in this discussion of the fear of monstrous offspring even though she did not struggle with most of the issues that plagued Mary Shelley and Amanda, that is, early disruption in the mother-child bond, deep incestuous concerns, and shame about her body. However, she *did* harbor a projective fantasy about monstrous babies.

A striking redhead, radiating confidence and energy, Priscilla consulted me for depressive feelings in connection with an abortion she had had two years earlier. The eldest of four children, from a well-to-do midwestern family, she told me she had always wanted a family. Yet, somehow, in the context of two consecutive, stable relationships, she had elected to abort a pregnancy, one in her thirties and the more recent one in her mid-forties. Her first boyfriend wanted her to marry him and have the baby. Despite the strength of her conscious wishes to be a mother, she had the abortion. The boyfriend then left and married someone else. The next man she became involved with had never wanted children, and she knew this. But she accidentally became pregnant, and although he said he would stay with her whatever she decided, she terminated the pregnancy. She and the boyfriend later married, but she remained depressed and troubled about her decision.

The whole situation was puzzling. Consciously, she craved children but behaved in a way that indicated the opposite. After much therapeutic work, the following factors were clarified. Priscilla suffered, as did Amanda, from claustrophobia. In her case this occurred mainly in airplanes, accompanied by the fantasy that she was trapped, and since she would be unable to get out until the plane landed, she feared that she would become overwhelmingly and catastrophically panicked. With regard to pregnancy, she had the fear that she would suddenly feel trapped, with a similar feeling of impending doom, and would want the baby out of her. She could never consciously connect this feeling with a wish to kill the baby, but if she couldn't tolerate it invading her body, how else could she get rid of it? Her focus was always on how unbearable the panic would be, never on *why* she would be so panicked.

Priscilla was not uncomfortable with her femininity, nor was she ashamed, in any way, of her body. She had a very close and secure relationship with both her parents, especially with her mother, and the only disruptions in their relationship were the three siblings born by the time she was six years old. Priscilla was the most grown-up and successful of all the children; she helped her mother with the others; they seemed to be an ideal family. But the mother, a sweet and maternal person, made life entirely too easy for her younger children, and none of them ever really grew up. (This kind of overprotection is another variant of hidden ambivalence.) Priscilla's problem, of which she was absolutely unconscious when she began therapy, was that the baby she needed to tear from her womb (and did in having two abortions) really represented her secretly hated siblings. She didn't want to share her mother's womb or attention with them, and this was the root of her claustrophobia (a sense of being unbearably crowded and trapped). On one occasion she admitted that she had sometimes worried that she might have a monster baby. But she didn't connect this with the feeling that monster babies were *already* part of her life. She had projected her experience of them as demanding and exhausting monsters into her own fantasied infant, the baby she was frightened to have.

. . .

Amanda, Sandra, and Priscilla waited until it was too late to have a baby before they sought therapy. Helpful as these therapies were in other ways, I conclude that their fears of having a child were so profound that they *unconsciously* waited until conception was unlikely or impossible. On the other hand, Rebecca, Deirdre, and Sarah were in therapy when they considered, and chose in favor of, motherhood and thus were able to negotiate their doubts and fears before their biological clocks ran out.

CHAPTER SIX

Rachel's Story

*Internalized Ambivalence
and the Dangers of Hidden Guilt*

Rachel was a woman who handled her ambivalence by blaming herself. From the outside she looked like one of those women who had it all—a good job in a respected profession, marriage to a fellow professional, a thin and attractive body, an active social life, and two bright, healthy children. She did all the things devoted mothers are supposed to do—reading to her children every night; planning play dates, birthday parties, excursions to the park and zoo; and arranging her work schedule to allow for visits to the pediatrician and meetings with her children's nursery school teachers.

But what none of her friends knew—because she only talked about it to her therapist—was that Rachel was in real trouble. She felt depressed and panicky and found her children increasingly exhausting and sometimes infuriating. Feeling that she was the only one of her friends who didn't feel unconditional love for her children, she handled her ambivalence by assuming the blame. She felt she was on the edge of breaking down.

Rachel's specific case is that of a well-meaning, relatively healthy mother whose history reveals problems in her early relationship with her mother. Her story illustrates several common situations that may intensify ambivalence—conflicts between work and mothering, the effect of rigid social expectations of "correct" child rearing on a mother's capacity to be confident and flexible with her child, and the power of early identifications with one's own mother to shape mothering behavior, to name a few.

Rachel represents the majority of women—those who try hard, mean well, and attempt to protect their children from the effects of their mixed feelings. My purpose in telling her story is to illustrate that part of the spectrum of maternal ambivalence that represents a guilty, self-blaming solution to the problem, with attempts on the mother's part at reparation. It is this less disturbed, more neurotic picture that I have seen most often in psychotherapeutic and psychoanalytic treatments. Women like Rachel are more likely to seek treatment because they tend to be less self-deluding and because they take the blame for problems with their children. Their primary concern is that their ambivalence will harm their offspring.

In contrast, for women who have been unable to have children because of psychological disturbances or who experience and treat their children as monsters, the fear is that their children will harm *them*—deprive them, drain them, or drive them crazy. Very early disturbances between the mother and her mother are usually at the core of such difficulties, and, interestingly, these disturbances appear in treatment in the fantasied relationship between the therapist and the patient. This more serious form of ambivalence is characterized by the projection of "badness" into the child by the mother or the taking on by the child of a monstrous or negative identity. In the latter situation, it is often the case that the children themselves are the patients.

Although it is true that most women use *both* internalizing and externalizing solutions, one solution usually dominates. It is helpful to discuss them separately since there is a general gradient in the direction of more serious disturbance as we move into projective mechanisms. Therefore my discussion in this chapter focuses on Rachel and her experiences with internalizing maternal ambivalence. In chapter 7 I take up the subject of externalizing ambivalence.

RACHEL

As an academic physician in her early fifties, Rachel sought psychoanalysis for work-related conflicts having to do with the extent to which she could allow herself to attain her professional ambitions. Although her children were now grown and self-supporting, she was unable to let herself "go as far as I think I could." For a long time, the previous thirty years in fact, she had attributed much of her inhibition in pursuing personal goals to painful conflicts between her role as a wife and mother and her career. Now, her children grown, she had to face her inhibitions about success in terms of internal issues relating to early identifications and attachments; these issues made up most of the work of the analysis with me. Rachel had had previous treatment, both psychotherapy and psychoanalysis. During these treatments her conflicts about her mothering were more central. The material of this case description comes from the more recent psychoanalytic work (rendered in italics) as well as the patient's self-knowledge derived from her previous treatment.

It is difficult to separate these two issues—the conflict between work and mothering roles per se and internal conflicts about success and ambition. Many women view work and the pursuit of a career as important parts of their identity and their sense of themselves as worthwhile people. Early identifications and attachments, to parents, siblings, and family members they wish to emulate and please, contribute heavily to these work and career identities. The satisfaction women derive from work can just as easily make them better mothers, more secure in themselves, and less dependent on their children for their own worth as it can derail mothering by creating exhausting conflicts, resentments, and guilt. For Rachel, success was itself a source of conflict, and this increased her ambivalence about working while raising children.

Rachel was the first child of Jewish parents in their early thirties who had postponed having children until they were economically solvent. Her birth, at the end of the Great Depression, took place to much parental, grandparental, and familial fanfare. Rachel's mother, Hannah, a schoolteacher, took a maternity leave that lasted until Rachel was eight months old. Delighted to finally have a baby, Hannah was loving, responsive, and attentive. However, she did not nurse and followed the precepts of 1930s behaviorism in her child rearing—precepts that included by-the-clock feedings and allowing babies to cry, sometimes for hours, to "strengthen their lungs and teach them to be on a schedule." Hannah later told Rachel that she often "wanted to push the hands of the clock ahead" so that she could comfort her and feed her. Rachel's paternal grandmother, Rivke, who considered such infant-rearing practices cruel and ridiculous, would come to her rescue whenever she could.

"Correct" child-rearing practices, which seem to shift generationally, can exert a tyranny of their own. Mothers want to do it right, which often involves behaviors that go against their maternal intuitions. At one time "spare the rod and spoil the child" was the guiding maxim of child discipline. These days a spanking may result in a call to Child Protective Services. Nursing, the natural way to feed babies, was out of style in the 1930s among middle- and upper-class women. Women who

would have nursed, and could have enjoyed the closeness and sense of nurturance that nursing can provide, may have deprived themselves and their babies of this experience out of a sense that nursing was low class and that they would not be doing the right thing. By the 1960s many women nursed, but using formula was still widely acceptable. Nursing is now the most highly approved way to feed babies, and any middle- or upper-class mother who doesn't nurse may be considered politically incorrect if not unnatural and lazy. Yet the discomfort that may ensue from doing something that doesn't feel natural, or that causes anxiety, can be transmitted as tension to the infant and small child. A tired mother, whose milk supply is temporarily low but who feels a bottle will harm or deprive her baby, may resent the baby for crying frequently and, by insisting on nursing, may really deprive him of a good feeding. Ambivalence takes many forms, sometimes masquerading as "correct" mothering.

Hannah was the third child of six, born to poor but ambitious immigrants from Eastern Europe. She was nursed by her mother, but this nursing was probably interrupted too early by the mother's next pregnancy, which resulted in a sibling when Hannah was fourteen months old. Although all six siblings in this family were born within a few years of each other, Hannah was the child most quickly displaced by a younger one. Hannah's mother, Malkah, died of complications secondary to a gall bladder operation while pregnant with a seventh child, when Hannah was thirteen years old. Malkah had been the "stronger" of Hannah's parents, the one who closely supervised and encouraged the education and development of her children, especially Hannah, her brightest child.

The loss of Malkah reverberated throughout the family in many disturbing ways. All the children felt unconsciously responsible for her death, and they attempted to deal with their guilt by criticizing and blaming their siblings. The combination of guilt provocation, envy, and competition between the siblings in this family was a serious emotional burden to Hannah throughout her life. Her unconscious hatred of her mother for replacing her with younger siblings and then deserting her so early in life, as well as her fear and hatred of these younger siblings, led Hannah to develop a defensive reaction in which she believed she loved children dearly. Not all of this love was defensive by any means, but the denial of her ambivalence toward babies led to some very counterintuitive behavior on Hannah's part; not bending the rules to comfort and protect Rachel was only one example.

Here is an illustration of the roots of ambivalence. Hannah suffered a maternal loss in her early adolescence and had no mother to help her deal with her developing femininity and sexuality. She was not comfortable with her own body (perhaps her real reason for not nursing), nor was she ever really relaxed and easy with Rachel's female development. Moreover, since all her brothers and sisters felt they had worked their mother to death and had to deal with their guilt by resenting and blaming each other, Hannah's dislike of siblings was unconsciously very familiar—so familiar in fact that she felt paralyzed in dealing with Rachel's later sibling hatred. A mother's early experiences are relived in her relationship with her children, especially if she remains unconscious of the meaning and impact of these experiences.

Rachel's father, Jacob, was the oldest of five children and much adored by his young and unhappily married mother, Rivke. When he was three, his younger brother, then eighteen months old, died of pneumonia. Rachel's sister once asked her father about the strawberry-colored birthmark on his forehead and was told it was the "mark of Cain." He felt, as many children do, that his wish to be rid of his younger brother had killed him. Jacob's entire life was involved with taking care of people, his parents, his siblings, his wife's siblings, and his two daughters, all of whom were seen as more fragile than they in fact were, and as having to be protected from his unconscious aggression. Unlike Hannah, Jacob was very distressed by Rachel's reaction to her younger sibling, Ruth, but unconsciously he was too guilty about the death of his own younger brother to deal with it effectively. Rachel's sibling rivalry reminded him of his own, which in his mind had had disastrous consequences.

When Rachel was eight months old, Hannah's father died. At the same time, Hannah went back to her teaching job. She would have preferred to stay home with Rachel but feared losing her position if she did not resume work. Both Hannah's grief and her absence at work represented a disruption in an otherwise loving mother-child bond.

A second disruption occurred when Rachel was just three years old. Her mother was at the end of her second pregnancy, and it was a hot summer. She sent Rachel to the country with Grandma Rivke for a period of about six weeks. During this time Rachel saw her father, who would come up for weekends. She has some memories from this period, a vague sense of how the summer colony looked and a memory of waking up one morning to find her mother in bed with her. Hannah had come up to the country, after her second daughter, Ruth, was born, to bring Rachel home. Rachel remembers being surprised and relieved and speculates that she may have thought she would never see her mother again. What Rachel could *not* remember was the new baby. She recalls the crib, the changing table with apothecary jars containing lotion, powder, and Q-tips in her parent's bedroom, but no infant. Her first memory of her sister was of eight-month-old Ruth sitting in her high chair being fed breakfast as she, Rachel, was being picked up to go to all-day nursery school.

These two early disruptions are an important part of the roots of Rachel's ambivalence. After her father's death, Hannah's grief was intense. She was reminded of her early maternal loss, especially because her father, a gentle man, had filled in as much as he could with his children; losing him was like losing a second mother. Hannah's return to work was probably less damaging. She was home midafternoons, evenings, and weekends, and she was very attentive to Rachel.

Rachel always felt the second disruption—at three years—more damaging, but it was of course the one she remembered. This second disruption was quite disturbing to both mother and child. Rachel "got her mother back" from her job when Hannah was three months pregnant with her second child, so she had five blissful months of undivided maternal attention before being sent away. Both Rachel and Hannah loved this time together, but Rachel clearly felt she had had too much and was being punished, even though her beloved grandmother was taking care of her. Six weeks apart from a mother is a lifetime to a three-year-old. It left Rachel with a lifelong anxiety that any relationship or situation, no matter how secure, could collapse instantly, that disaster was never far away. It is also of interest that Rachel had a secure and loving attachment to her mother, but this did not prevent the separation from affecting their relationship quite seriously, which was very distressing to Hannah and undermined her maternal confidence.

Ruth was a big baby who may have had infantile colic. At any rate, she had no tolerance for scheduled feeding. "We threw out the book with her," Hannah later told Rachel. When Ruth was a year old and the family was on a summer vacation, she developed streptococcal pneumonia and had to be hospitalized for about ten days. At that time parents were not allowed to stay with children in the hospital. Visits were brief, and Ruth returned upset and clinging to two parents who had been deeply frightened that they would lose her and whose need to overprotect her was much reinforced by this trauma.

Rachel does not remember much about this illness. (Later in life she taught at the hospital where Ruth had been sent and looked up her medical chart, thus verifying that the hospitalization was indeed for ten days, for the treatment of strep pneumonia, before the advent of penicillin.) However, she handled her rage at her mother for what she perceived as favoritism to Ruth by becoming closer to her father. She became his favorite, the apple of his eye, and she turned her back on her mother and sister for quite a long time. She also began to develop an identity as "the big girl," which was to become an integral part of her character for the rest of her life. Rachel remembered a photograph of herself, at the age of five, sitting in her sister's stroller, with an ashamed but determined look on her face. The need to maintain both an intense external and internal relationship with her father contributed to her "big girl" identity. Her father encouraged this; he seemed to want her to succeed, but underneath this protective defense he could brook no competition from his wife, siblings, or children. This was an important part of Rachel's professional inhibition.

Ruth's illness was traumatic to the entire family. Rachel did not recognize her own guilt about almost losing a sister that she already deeply resented. Family reports of Rachel's change from a happy, easygoing child to a bratty "wild Indian" confirm her anxiety and rage at Ruth's intrusion into the family. Hannah and Jacob, who may have been disappointed that Ruth was not a boy and were certainly worn out by her early colic and generally explosive nature, reacted by becoming very protective of baby Ruth, too protective in Rachel's jealous eyes.

Although Rachel's sibling rivalry was intense, her alienation from her mother was not total. She was identified with her mother in a number of ways—in her longing for babies and in her commitment to a career and to combining work and mothering. Rachel's first child was born two years after she married, when she was in her mid-twenties. In her first pregnancy she did not want a girl and was delighted when her son, Ethan, was born.

Rachel came to understand her strong desire for a boy as a hope of avoiding a repetition of her own early experiences with Hannah and as an unconscious Oedipal wish to give Jacob the son he had never had. Defensively contemptuous of both Ruth and Hannah, she secretly felt men were superior. Here we can see some of the factors I discussed in chapter 4: the fear of not being able to love a girl and then projecting those hateful feelings into the baby who might, in turn, not love her; incestuous fantasies reflecting her attachment to Jacob; a secret devaluation of femininity; and the results of an early mother-child disruption. In Rachel's case this did not lead to ambivalence about having a baby but rather about having a girl baby. Sadly, she later came to regret that she had never had a daughter. More assured of her ability to form an attachment to a baby, she came to feel that she would have enjoyed a daughter and mothered her very well.

Rachel and Ethan did well together, although she was later aware of her tendency to rush him out of infancy. She took great pride in his developmental landmarks, and in an unconscious identification with her mother, she did not nurse him long enough. Although initially very determined to nurse, she was poorly instructed and worried, as many women are, that she did not have enough milk, although the baby gained well and seemed satisfied. In the grip of her identification with Hannah, Rachel became discouraged after a couple of months and switched to formula.

Rachel became pregnant again when Ethan was sixteen months old—a planned pregnancy, which she now hoped would yield a daughter. Instead, she had another boy, Sammy, shortly after Ethan's second birthday. Although Sammy was full term and healthy, he was a difficult and colicky baby, later a clingy and demanding toddler, prone to tantrums and needing a lot of attention from his mother. Rachel felt overwhelmed. She handled the situation with obsessional planning and control and denied the extent of the strain. Hannah helped as much as she could, and again, nursing was minimal. Rachel later realized that she had expected her first child to grow up too quickly, as she had. She was very guilty about turning from him to Sammy, yet in some ways it was more comfortable for her to attend to a baby. It was also biologically driven.

Until Ethan was two and a half years and Sammy was eight months, Rachel was largely at home with her children, so that the situation was manageable. At that time several changes occurred. For reasons connected with her husband's professional needs, the family moved out of the area, where help from Hannah and other supportive friends and relatives had been easily available. Rachel herself returned to residency training on a part-time basis and obtained live-in help. Things between Rachel and her husband, Robert, became increasingly strained as both struggled to manage two young children, two careers, and their relationship.

Trying to do it all—work, raise children "properly," relate intimately to your husband, maintain hobbies, a social life, and an exercise schedule, all without the help of an extended family—is a common profile of maternal expectations these days. Ambivalence can only be worsened by the exhaustion and inevitable failure that such goals engender. At the time Rachel returned to training, feminist perspectives on motherhood strongly supported mothers returning to work and tended to denigrate mothers who remained at home. However, Rachel's too early return to work was not really based on middle-class cultural mores. Given her identification with

two working parents, she was very invested in her career and unconsciously shaky
about her mothering, especially after there were two children.

About ten months after the move Grandma Rivke died. Rachel
became depressed and began to experience panic attacks. The unconscious determinants for the onset of these attacks were gradually
clarified in treatment. Shortly before her grandmother's death, Rachel
had sought therapy to help her manage the strains of being a mother
and a medical resident. She developed a strong positive relationship
with her older female therapist, a relationship that intensified after her
grandmother died. She felt that the therapist was her lifeline, as her
grandmother had been when she was three years old.

Two months after Grandma Rivke's death Rachel's parents came
for a visit. One afternoon the adults took the two children swimming at a local pool. The weather was very hot, the children cranky,
and the atmosphere strained. As they were walking back to the car,
Hannah was struggling to carry several heavy beach chairs. When
Rachel asked her to hurry up, her frustrated mother gave her a look
of "hatred." Rachel was hurt but also realized she had been impatient. However, that night, during dinner with her parents and some
friends of theirs, Rachel began to feel panicked, couldn't eat, and
finally asked her husband to take her home. What she later realized,
in analysis with me, was that her mother toiling in the hot sun to
carry the chairs evoked unconscious memories of Hannah's second
pregnancy during that hot summer when Rachel was three. She had
unconsciously condensed the look of hatred from her mother with
her childhood conviction that she was sent away for being demanding and too much for her pregnant mother to handle. Only now there
was no grandmother to take care of her. Furthermore, strains in her
marriage made Rachel fear she could lose Robert, who in her uncon-

scious mind she condensed with her father. Jacob had been there for her part of the time she was separated from Hannah. This was a second way in which the early maternal disruption was stirred up by her grandmother's death.

Although at that time Rachel had a therapist who intuitively understood that her neediness was increased in an unconscious identification with her children's needs and developmental stages, a therapist who helped her manage her guilty self-chastisement, this was not enough to stave off a period of intense, almost debilitating anxiety. It is an example of the "psychosis" of early child rearing to which I referred in chapter 1. In Rachel's case this took the form of a depression with severe anxiety. The panic attacks were fueled not only by Rachel's unmet needs but also by her fear of her own rage. She feared she would lose control and either hurt her children or possibly kill herself. These were true obsessive thoughts, painfully unwelcome and tormenting. In fact, her children were often a source of comfort to her during this difficult time. Still, she was aware that Sammy, who was very attached to her, was vulnerable and depressed. (Later in life he was diagnosed as having a mood disorder, but who can know that when a child is eighteen months old, and what would they do if they did know?) Both children felt short-changed, and in fact *were*, despite good household help and genuine efforts on the part of both parents to meet the children's needs.

For Rachel, these repetitions of her own early history were devastating and contributed to her maternal ambivalence. Her identification with Ethan, an oldest child, replaced as she had been by a colicky younger sibling of the same sex, increased her need to have him be a big boy and evoked rage at Sammy, the baby. Her identification with Hannah led her to repeat some of Hannah's "mistakes" in child rearing (giving up nursing especially) and to return to work too quickly and perfectionisti-

cally. Furthermore, and this was perhaps most important, Hannah, as a maternal model, was a shaky figure. Hannah's replacement early in life by a younger sibling and the loss of her mother in adolescence left her insecure about her own maternal instincts and choices, despite her external persona as someone who loved babies. With Rivke now dead, Rachel, unable to depend on Hannah, felt unmothered, regressed, and very frightened.

With the help of her therapist, the worst of Rachel's shakiness began to abate after about nine months.[1] A move to another city, with better weather and the proximity of Robert's parents, made life considerably easier, but some of the psychological scars of this difficult period remained, in the children's insecurities and powerful sibling jealousies.

This is an example of the consequences of maternal ambivalence in the next generation. Rachel's sons identified with her, as she had with Hannah. In all three generations anxiety and sibling problems were severe. Identifications were passed on from grandmother to mother to children, as is so often the case.

Because of her own intense sibling rivalry, about which Rachel felt both defensive and guilty, she remained relatively blind to how much of a problem this rivalry was for her children. Furthermore, the fear of her own aggression, which had fueled her panic states, led her to remain somewhat withdrawn from her children's emotional needs. Rachel loved them and attended to them, but some part of her became too easily upset when they did. She walled herself off so that she often ignored the signs of trouble or its extent. These behaviors, denial of sibling problems and emotional withdrawal, were aspects of her identification with Hannah. With extensive analytic treatment she and Robert gradually repaired their marital alienation and her mothering improved as her children got older. But she remained guilty and con-flicted about the years of their childhood.

DISCUSSION OF RACHEL

I am presenting this case history to illustrate several points. It is not an unusual story. Many parts of it could not be helped. Control of the vagaries of biology—the sex of children and their temperaments—are not really options for prospective parents. Conscious and unconscious identifications are passed on from mothers to daughters, manifested in this case by Rachel's difficulties with nursing and her failure to recognize the extent of her children's dependent needs, as well as their problems dealing with sibling tensions. Conflicts over family and career needs are an ongoing problem for modern women, and solutions always entail significant compromises. Rachel often found her children difficult, frustrating, even maddening. But she never felt they were monstrous. The monstrousness was hers. She would project blame onto her husband and children, but the projection never worked and was usually taken back with increases in guilt and anxiety. Denial and paralysis of action often resulted, but loving feelings prevailed in Rachel's struggle with ambivalence.

Other women are not as fortunate. Despite disruptions and dif-ficulties in the mother-daughter relationship between Rachel and Hannah, Rachel always wanted children and did not fear pregnancy, childbirth, or raising her children. Despite the frustrations and exhaustion of two small children and working, she never felt that her children were out to thwart or harm her. And although Rachel had defensively distanced Hannah and dismissed her as not very liber-ated or courageous (neither really true), she still consciously loved and unconsciously emulated her in many ways.

With two exceptions, the patients I described in chapter 5 also serve as examples of women who tended to take responsibility for their failures, that is, to internalize blame. In these two exceptions, Sarah and Phyllis, there were strong elements of projection of blame—in Sarah's case, into an unborn infant; in Phyllis's, into a child. (We shall see as we go on that they were far from being on the most disturbed end of the ambivalence spectrum.) Rebecca, on the other hand, turned out to be a very loving and concerned mother of three children. Amanda, Sandra, Sybil, and Priscilla did not have children, but I am convinced that if they had they would have managed in a relatively healthy and responsible fashion. Amanda might have had trouble with a baby, because of her own early history but also because her husband was not supportive of the part of her that *did* want a child and seemed to have no interest in helping her. But she would have done very well with older children and did in fact have a very good relationship with her niece and nephew. Sandra, too, had an affectionate relationship with two nieces, from their infancy on, as did Sybil with her nephew and Priscilla with her many nieces and nephews. Whatever fears these women had about what their wombs might produce and about their capacity to mother, they would not have taken it out on their babies. Their good ego strength would have helped them to deal rationally with the hidden side of motherhood.

CHAPTER SEVEN

Whose Fault Is It?

The Externalization of Ambivalence

Rachel felt that her negative feelings toward her children were all her fault. If she were a different, a better, person and mother, her children would have been spared all their anxieties and insecurities. She minimized the role of their genetic endowment and temperaments but *did* recognize their differences. She understood that some sources of difficulty are inborn, but like so many mothers with perfectionistic expectations, she felt that she should be able to rise above the troubling impact of their temperaments and personalities on her own inner states of mind. No matter what they did, what they were like, she should *not* be ambivalent.

In contrast to Rachel are those women whose responses are paranoid, who use blame as a means for handling maternal ambivalence. Viewing their angry and disturbed feelings as the child's fault, they feel rage more than guilt, and they don't hold their feelings inside. They express them in aggressive behaviors, and they see their inner problems as residing in their children. For these women, monstrous children are always, at least in part, maternal projections.

In chapter 5 I spoke of Phyllis, a mother who struggled with negative feelings about her son, Josh, a charming and inquisitive child but prone to fits of remarkably stubborn behavior. Toilet training him had been a nightmare, and if he was not ready to leave the playground when she was, wild horses could not move him. Phyllis feared that Josh was a replica of her demanding and intrusive mother. She felt he was abnormally difficult, that his behavior was doing something *to her*. "Why is he doing this to me? I'm not imagining it. Other people have noticed he's stubborn, too," she told me. She wondered what she had done to deserve his behavior, which she experienced as a punishment.

As far as I could tell, Josh was a bright, imaginative, strong-willed child whose problems resulted from struggles with his concerned but controlling mother and worries about his loved and loving but passive and physically ill father. Because he was worried, as children tend to be, that he was responsible for his father's illness, he had problems separating from his parents and, therefore, relating comfortably to other children. In reaction to his concern that his aggression had hurt his father, he behaved omnipotently and clung to compensatory fantasies, all in the service of denying his fears of punishment, loss, and bodily vulnerability. "I can do it all myself; I can do whatever I want; I'm not weak or frightened."

Josh did not really understand the nature of his father's illness and physical preoccupations, which were due to a rare immune disorder with many vague symptoms. The whole situation made him very anxious. Phyllis knew this and felt quite badly about some of her thoughts and feelings toward the boy. She wanted to love him. In fact, she did love him more than she could let herself know; generally she warded off awareness of *all* her needs for closeness. But she could not rid herself of the feeling that her mother's worst features, with which she sensed she was unconsciously identified, had been passed "genetically" into her son. Features and behaviors the child did have became so inflated in her mind that she couldn't see him for who he really was or might become. Just as Phyllis's mother was unable to support her daughter's autonomy, Phyllis could not see her son free of what she projected into him—her own most feared and hated parts. And, as so often happens, Phyllis's failure to recognize Josh's need to be his own person increased the struggles between them and intensified his stubbornness.

Women who need to put the blame for failures in parenting onto their children do not, in my experience, seek therapy directly for their parenting problems. Their psychological equilibrium depends on keeping the blame outside of themselves, and they address problems with mothering fearfully. They have difficulties seeing their children as separate from them, as people with their own minds and feelings. Therefore, they cannot think about the child's behavior from the point of view of the child's characteristic methods of coping. This was certainly true for Phyllis. She knew she had problems in her marital, family, and social relationships, as well as problems with achieving success at work, but she was resistant to seeing problems with her son as part of *her* difficulties. "Whose fault is it?" is a very troubling question to women like Phyllis. They are ruled by a rigid and unforgiving superego, the psychoanalytic term for that part of the mind we usually call the conscience or moral sense. In these women good and bad qualities in themselves and others are seen in all-or-nothing terms, where imagined punishments are severe and real forgiveness is rare.

However, although Phyllis could never admit her role in Josh's difficulties, she recognized he was in trouble and accepted the recommendation that he have some therapy. This relieved much of

Josh's anxiety, and as he grew older and more mature his relationship with Phyllis improved, partly as a result of both of them being in treatment.

FOUR CASE STORIES

I have been deeply impressed with several illustrative case stories from novels in which the unconscious appeal of the narrative has everything to do with the compelling but forbidden issue of child hatred. These novels, as I read them, all demonstrate marked degrees of maternal ambivalence but with different configurations of culpability between mother and child and different solutions to their problems. These children are all experienced unconsciously by their mothers as a punishment. They represent, in different ways, the mother's most repudiated parts, usually involving some form of aggression, greed, or ruthlessness. Whether the authors had such issues consciously in mind does not matter for my present purpose. The vividness of their depiction of the dark side of motherhood is what interests me.

All four novels are, explicitly or implicitly, horror stories. What makes them horrible is the theme they share, in one way or another, of unloving mothers and unlovable children. Lurking beneath our difficulty accepting maternal ambivalence is a strongly held conviction about motherhood: All children can be lovable if they have *the right mother,* and any woman can love *the right child.* The reality that this is not true in some situations is frightening to face. What these four novels have in common—why they appear together in this chapter—is that each of the "monster" children they depict represents some denied or dissociated truth about the mother's psychological makeup. The degree of aggressive disturbance in the mothers, mirrored in their children, represents a spectrum that worsens as it moves from externalization and projection of the mother's problem *(The Fifth Child, We Need to Talk about Kevin)* to psychosis *(Rosemary's Baby)* to dissociation based on severe early trauma *(The Bad Seed)*.

Maternal and Fetal Ruthlessness: The Fifth Child

Doris Lessing, an author who does not hesitate to deal with difficult relationships and painful psychological states, has written a remarkable novella, *The Fifth Child,* that may be read both as a morality tale in which ruthless and greedy mothers beget ruthless and greedy babies and as a metaphor for how psychotherapeutic treatment works. Most likely, this metaphor was *not* Lessing's intent. The book jacket of the copy I own describes the novel as "a vivid reflection of society's unwillingness to confront—and its eventual complicity in—its most brutal aspects."

This is a sociopolitical reading. Accepting the postmodernist position that there are as many readings as there are readers, I choose to discuss this novel from a psychological point of view. I see the fear of a monstrous child as a reflection of certain disavowed and disturbing states within the mother. The novel's narrative line and central events bear certain similarities to an important aspect of the psychotherapeutic process. Specifically, I am referring to the projection of unacceptable parts of the self into others (in this case, the child) and the return and metabolization of these parts as an aspect of the painful coming to know and accept oneself that is integral to successful therapeutic treatment. In Lessing's book, the mother's greed and ruthlessness appear in a monster infant of whom she attempts to rid herself, unsuccessfully. A psychological dilemma is posed by questions about where the boundaries between mother and child lie. Whose greed and ruthlessness does the "monster" represent, and how can it be managed?

The Fifth Child is the story of Harriet and David Lovatt, a young couple drawn together by their disapproval of the selfishness, greed, and sexual license that permeates English society in the late 1960s. They share a longing to raise many children, to live a responsible, natural, old-fashioned life centered on loving family relationships. They marry soon after meeting and buy an enormous old home in a suburb of London. In this house, a maternal symbol described in loving detail by Lessing, four darling and lovable children are born in six years. Harriet gives birth at home in the big master bedroom with an attached nursery, the fertile nest she and David have created. There she nurses all her babies. Relatives pour in for the holidays and sit around the table in the large, hospitable kitchen, eating, talking, laughing, and playing with the children.

> Happiness. A happy family. The Lovatts were a happy family.
> It was what they had chosen and what they deserved.... It had
> been hard preserving their belief in themselves when the spirit
> of the times, the greedy and selfish sixties, had been so ready to
> condemn them, to isolate, to diminish their best selves. (21)

This is what David and Harriet consciously feel. They have fulfilled the goal of so many young parents these days. They have done parenthood perfectly. But those around them become disturbed. For, from the beginning, the young Lovatts have been unable to afford either the house they buy or the children they rapidly conceive. Their wonderful home is paid for by David's wealthy father, and much of the household work is done by Harriet's widowed mother, Dorothy, who seems to represent the unheeded voice of reality in

Harriet's psyche. It is Dorothy who senses the baby greed that drives her daughter and son-in-law and cautions them to slow down. "Think about it," Dorothy says. "I wish you would. Sometimes you two scare me" (16). Later she summarizes her concern more clearly: "The trouble with Harriet is that her eyes have always been bigger than her stomach" (26). David, too, is implicated. He despises his father's wealth but accepts the financial help without which his wonderful household could not manage. The families on both sides unite in insisting that David and Harriet stop having children, at least until they are better able to afford them. Nobody directly addresses the issue of the emotional problems posed for the existing children by endlessly arriving babies.

At first Lessing is subtle in her references to the ruthlessness that lies behind David and Harriet's behavior. The early part of the book, which describes the making of the home and the birth of the four children, is a crescendo of nurturant, evocative images—Harriet as a more than "ordinary devoted mother." The references to greed, stubbornness, and duplicity are few but disquieting, as a sense of uneasiness creeps in. This uneasiness represents the first breakthrough in the Lovatts' mutually reinforced denial of the omnipotence and greed—baby greed—that first drew them together and that they have been living out.

When, despite precautions, Harriet finds herself pregnant for the fifth time, the tone of the novel becomes dark, ominous, and unsettling. For this fifth pregnancy, this fetus and this fifth child are something *very* different. Lessing's painstaking description of Harriet's pregnancy illustrates the entire panoply of fears about monsters and monstrous births that I elaborated in chapter 4. Fantasies of the fetus as a parasite, of mutilation and death in childbirth, and of an endlessly insatiable and unlovable infant are all elaborated. These passages describe *exactly* the kind of baby Amanda feared she would have. The good humor and hopefulness that Harriet and David have always shared during her pregnancies is replaced by tears, anger, and unspoken recriminations. This pregnancy is an unconscious rebellion against having to give up greedy and omnipotent wishes (we can *have* and *do* it all), and the Lovatts' uneasiness represents a barely acknowledged recognition of the punishment in store for them.

And punishment it is, for this fifth pregnancy is a nightmare. The fetus kicks hard, continually. Harriet spends her days in pain, either drugged or walking, running, and working furiously to distract herself, in battle with the "monster" (as she thinks of it) inside her. Her appetite is insatiable, her mood fearful and unstable. She feels alone in her ordeal and becomes morose and suspicious of those around her. A paranoid explanation, Harriet's first line of defense, is already in place. Something is being done *to* her.

> Phantoms and chimeras inhabited her brain. She would think,
> When the scientists make experiments, welding two kinds of
> animal together, of different sizes, then I suppose this is what
> the poor mother feels. She imagined pathetic botched creatures,
> horribly real to her. (41)

Fearing that her fetus is trying to kill her and that she won't survive the battle, Harriet appeals to her doctor to induce the baby. The doctor does not see that this pregnancy is different. Harriet thinks, "It's because you don't want to. It's not you who is carrying this— She cut off monster, afraid of antagonizing him" (47). She wonders what she will see when the baby is born. Insisting on a hospital delivery with anesthesia, at eight months she is delivered of an eleven-pound baby boy, Ben. Harriet and David are both dismayed at his appearance.

He was not a pretty baby. He did not look like a baby at all. He
had a heavy-shouldered hunched look, as if he were crouching
there as he lay. His forehead sloped from his eyebrows, to his
crown. . . . He opened his eyes and looked straight up into his
mother's face. . . . She had been waiting to exchange looks with
the creature who, she had been sure, had been trying to hurt her,
but there was no recognition there. And her heart contracted
with pity for him: *poor little beast, his mother disliking him so much.*
(48–49; emphasis mine)[1]

This baby is feared and pushed away, before birth and after. The
bonding that Winnicott has so movingly described never takes place.
Harriet feels Ben does not attach to her, and she cannot attach to him.
He doesn't smile or respond to his mother's voice or other attempts
to engage him. He never cries but rather roars with rage and nurses
voraciously and cruelly, biting his mother's nipples. Harriet soon gives
up nursing. Her kindly pediatrician is dismayed at her bruised breasts
but does not seem to see that there is anything wrong with the baby.
He tries to tell her, reassuringly, "It is not abnormal to take a dislike
to a child. I see it all the time. Unfortunately" (54). The pediatrician
says what women like Harriet, who pride themselves on their capacity for motherlove, want to deny—that some mothers cannot or do
not love some children. Harriet feels the pediatrician is blaming her,
implying that the monstrous behavior is hers.

Although Harriet cannot love this baby, she tries to hold him, to
cuddle him, to make him ordinary. He bites her, breaks toys, hurts
animals and people. He is like an animal himself, who needs to be
tamed, rather than a child who needs to be loved and socialized.
Everyone becomes frightened of him. The family begins to shun the
Lovatts, and again, Harriet feels blamed. Unconsciously, she experiences Ben as a punishment.

"As if I were a criminal!" she raged to herself. Even David, she believed, condemned her. She said to him, "I suppose in the old times, in primitive societies, this was how they treated a woman who'd given birth to a freak. As if it was her fault. But we are supposed to be civilized." (60)

Sarah, Harriet's younger sister, has a Down's syndrome child. Harriet feels that Sarah's unhappy and quarrelsome relationship with her husband has "attracted" the afflicted child. Ironically, she resists the idea that anything about herself or David has "attracted" Ben. Rather, she sees him as an invader, a creature—"that he had willed himself to be born, had invaded their ordinariness, which had no defenses against him or anything like him" (58). What she is really talking about when she thinks the phrase "anything like him" is the intensity of Ben's needs and hungers, the unrelenting quality of his aggressive pursuit of satisfaction. After all, Harriet's pursuit of satisfaction ("eyes bigger than her stomach") has led to Ben.

Soon the rest of the family confronts Harriet with the need to institutionalize Ben, to send him away for good. He is having a negative effect on her other children who have virtually lost their mother. This is an example of maternal ambivalence in a hidden and rationalized form. All Harriet's attention goes to her "monster" child and away from her healthy, responsive children. Her rationalization is that she is protecting them from Ben, who is still dangerous, but if so, wouldn't sending him away protect them even more? Harriet knows it must be done, but she protests, "He's a little child. . . . He's our child," and David replies, "No, he's not . . . Well, he certainly isn't mine" (74). Agonized and torn, Harriet nevertheless agrees. When Ben is sent away she feels enormous gratitude and relief. Her other children turn to her as if she had been ill or had gone away and is now home among them. Peace returns to the family.

The novel could end here, but it doesn't. For Harriet rescues Ben. *Why?* She does not miss him and does not love him, but she feels guilt and horror and suffers from bad dreams. David and the family are furious. Suddenly Harriet has a realization that is psychologically germane to the issue of where the monstrosity in Ben lies. She wonders "why she was always treated like a criminal. Ever since Ben was born it's been like this, she thought. Now it seemed to her the truth, that everyone had silently condemned her. I have suffered a misfortune, she told herself; I haven't committed a crime" (78). This, she feels, is how she is seen—*she* the mother, *not* David the father. She rescues him because sending him away does not ameliorate the issue of what Ben represents in Harriet's own psyche. Symbolically, the rescue represents a step in coming to terms with the *Harriet-in-Ben*. When she decides to take Ben home, the attendants, who fear Ben, look curiously at her as if she and Ben were part of the same phenomenon.

When she brings Ben home, David feels Harriet has dealt the family a mortal wound. The other children are frightened and withdraw from their mother. The three oldest ones leave for boarding school as soon as they can, and the youngest, Paul, remains at home, clingy and disturbed. If children must be protected at all costs, why doesn't Harriet protect Paul? In a sense, she now has committed a crime. The baby greed that drove her to have and then rescue Ben leads her to suggest to David that they should have more children. He is appalled and asks if the four they have don't count.

Harriet takes Ben to a child psychiatrist who admits something is wrong but can do nothing about it. Although this doctor gives Harriet what she wants, confirmation that Ben is outside the human pale, it does not relieve her. Harriet moves painfully from the conviction to which she tries to cling, that Ben is not human and therefore not her fault, to a feeling that she and David are being punished for wanting and taking too much, for their greed and exploitation of others. As she comes to terms with her responsibility in this problem, Ben, now an adolescent and the leader of a gang of truant, delinquent boys, drifts out of their lives and disappears.

. . .

A central issue implicit in the fear of monstrous births is suggested by Lessing's compelling work. This issue, with which Harriet is struggling, is culpability. *Whose fault is a child like Ben?* Where does the monstrosity lie—in a fatal genetic mutation, a trick of the genes, or in the mother whose worst, most secret parts have been passed into her child? Or is this a punishment for the mother who cannot love her child?

The experts see Ben as a sturdy, not very bright child, who tries hard and whose mother does not like him. They view Harriet with disapproval, although they deny this, and, reading between the lines, also with horror. Their failure to see is puzzling—after all, so much is wrong with Ben—but this failure may be understood as a defensive idealization of the child, the tabula rasa on whom the parents inscribe themselves. If they, in particular, the mother, can love him, he will thrive; if not, he will wither and go bad. Clearly, in the eyes of society to not be able to love a child is a heinous crime, not just a misfortune for both parties.

Harriet sees herself, in the eyes of others, as the guilty party, and she struggles with dreadful inner conflicts. For a long time she feels that Ben is not human, not a real child at all. She sees her sister's daughter, Amy, as a real although damaged child, whose birth defect was caused by the sister's unhappy and quarrelsome marriage. Amy, retarded, odd-looking, but loving, is manageable, and her mother can therefore tolerate the "blame" of having given birth to her. Ben, in

Harriet's eyes, is not a real child but rather a troll, an alien, a Neanderthal baby. Odd-looking and nonloving, he cannot be a reflection of anything within her. Harriet feels it is dreadfully unfair that others blame her. ("I have suffered a misfortune. . . . I haven't committed a crime.") If, however, Ben is *really* not human, why can't she let him go? Why does she destroy her family to save him? Harriet's denial of her responsibility for Ben and of her attachment to him (ambivalent and warped as it is) does not work. Impossible as he is, he is her child. Harriet believes children are sacred and much to be desired, and she cannot let him die. However, if she lets him live, the family as a unit dies, her marriage dies, her cherished dreams and ideals are shattered. It seems an impossible dilemma.

If, however, Harriet's dilemma is viewed as an inner psychological problem, it begins to make more sense. We have seen that David and Harriet are greedy for offspring and ruthless in their determination to procreate. They are warned and counseled against additional children but remain stubbornly committed to doing as they wish. Ben can be seen as the personification of the greed and ruthlessness his parents will not control in themselves. Do Harriet and David want more children to *love* them or to *have* them?

From the outset Harriet dislikes her fifth pregnancy, her fetus, and ultimately her baby. She feels immediately the pregnancy is very wrong (the fetus is poisoning her) but does not even consider an abortion. This child is not something of which she can rid herself, but at the same time he is something she does not wish to own as part of herself. For Ben, as fetus, infant, and child, is a pure culture of aggression and greed. He is like a horrible, exaggerated caricature of the hidden corruption in his parents. Harriet is Dorothy's greedy baby. She exploits Dorothy for maternal care as she accumulates babies of her own.

The pediatrician and child psychiatrist see Harriet as an unloving mother, and the attendant at the institution, as well as the psychiatrist, view her as if she and Ben are part of each other. They clearly see Harriet as the problem. Why is the culpability seen as Harriet's when David too is implicated? Or perhaps, why does David rid himself psychologically of Ben so much more easily than Harriet?

Ben is Harriet's problem. If we view Ben as an intrapsychic presence *in* Harriet, he is the repository of those parts of his mother that she cannot bear to see in herself. We may say that she has projected them into Ben and that the projection doesn't work. She has not rid herself of her unacceptable impulses and behaviors by giving them to Ben, for now she feels she has to control them *in him*. In psychoanalytic terms we are really dealing with a projective identification rather than a projection. For if a projection is successful—*they are the bad guys, not us*—the problem is solved. The projected feeling, wish, behavior, fantasy, or quality of character is seen as residing totally in the other person and therefore ceases to be troubling. I suspect successful projections are more infrequent than we think and are, more often than not, projective identifications. This term describes a kind of *putting-something-bad-into-the-other,* which doesn't work because we continue to be worried and involved with the issue we have put there.

Harriet's rescue of Ben, the wrenching turning point of the novel, marks the beginning of inner shifts. Unconsciously, she can no longer put him, or the parts of herself that he is, away. She shifts back and forth from angry, paranoid feelings about the rest of the world that leaves her alone to deal with Ben to an increasing sense of regret, sadness, and tragedy as she acknowledges her own greed and ruthlessness. Of course, this process takes time. Even after Ben returns from the institution and the family is shattered and dispersed, Harriet fantasizes about having more children. At this point Harriet has retreated temporarily into a magical solution where a normal child would prove to her that her insides are not poisonous or her personality warped, that she can ignore this "mistake" that is Ben and continue to have other normal children. But, in the end she gives up this wish. She tells David, "We are being punished for presuming ... we just wanted to be better than everyone else. ... We thought we were" (117–18). Implicit in this is the admission that she wanted it all.

I see what Harriet has gone through as a kind of mourning. She comes to see and own the Ben inside herself, and as she does so, she no longer needs Ben as a repository. This is why he disappears. The answer to my question about why Harriet rescues Ben is that Ben represents, not himself, but something inside Harriet that must be worked out, lest she produce more Bens.

As Ben's father, David doesn't agree with Harriet's guilty and regretful conclusions. Although he "grows up" and becomes financially responsible for his family, he sees Ben as an alien, not any part of himself. Fathers, too, must fear that their offspring will be monstrous reflections of themselves. Perhaps it is part of every father's fantasy life during his partner's pregnancy. I believe, nevertheless, that the fear of a monstrous outcome is more of a problem for the mother in whose body the baby grows. And it is her problem in the eyes of the world also.

All children come from mothers; monster children are no exception. Emotionally, culturally, and artistically, the mother-child bond is the most deeply cathected of all human relationships and one that inspires awe, longing, envy, fear, and sometimes horror. Longing and awe are easy enough to understand; gestation and birth are amazing creative events, inspiring and redemptive. And, as we have seen in Winnicott's observations, the very survival of the baby, its essential humanity, is shaped by the relationship with a mothering person.

It is not difficult to understand envy of the capacity to create and bring forth a living being from one's own body. Dr. Frankenstein certainly struggled with such envy. And since we envy that which we can't have, perhaps all men envy women's reproductive capacities. Fear and horror, on the other hand, are reflections of our feelings about the dark or hidden side of maternity. We wish to see, to believe in, a giving Madonna and a blissful child, not an angry witch and her greedy monster offspring.

Concerning the cultural bias against seeing the dark side of maternal feelings, two aspects of the mother-child relationship trouble us deeply, its exclusivity—which inspires jealousy—and its drivenness—which inspires fear. Implicit in the concept of monstrousness is the idea of *too much*, of behaviors and feelings that are unmodified, uncontrolled, unsublimated.[2] Ben, like Frankenstein's monster, like Count Dracula, like the creature in *Alien*, is inhumanly strong and driven. His drivenness is acquisitive and ruthless. It is the need to eat (Dracula and his vampires, Ben, Harriet's insatiable appetite in her pregnancy with Ben), to breed (Ridley Scott's *Alien*), to have *more*. It is not the drive to find others and to attach and relate to them, so crucial to human development. Ben imitates his siblings and learns from his mother, in order to better provide for his own needs, but he never forms identifications with anyone or anything human.

But it is not just the monster baby Ben that inspires unease. It is his mother, too. There is something about the relationship of mother to child that cannot be questioned. It is crucial to our survival (so, of course, Harriet had to rescue Ben), but it is also a bond from which others are excluded, and this exclusion breeds resentment.

In Toni Morrison's *Beloved* Sethe kills her child to prevent her from being taken back into slavery (see chapter II). She is arrested by the lawmakers but not executed. If a black slave woman had killed anybody else, she would have been hung. Sparing her life is not mercy on the part of her captors but horror and avoidance. On an unconscious level we feel Sethe has a right to do this because the child is part of her, once part of her body, now inextricably attached psychologically. You don't get punished for cutting off your own leg, although you might be sent to a mental hospital. In reality, of course, women *are* punished for murdering their children, but in Morrison's fantastic and psychologically brilliant work the disbelief and guilt that surrounds this crime shapes the behavior of Sethe's captors. There is a hidden fantasy that because the child is part of the mother's body, it belongs to the mother, who can do with it as she wishes. This fantasy, as part of our unconscious life, may account for some of the incredible difficulties in separation between mother and child that often lead people, both mothers and their children, to seek psychotherapy. The guilt of the lawmakers in *Beloved* may connect to a feeling that they are trespassing on unlawful or forbidden territory in disrupting Sethe's ability to protect her children.

Reproduction in a species that can think and fantasize must seem awesome and magical. The mother-child bond is a crucial element in religious imagery, not just as Madonna and child, but in the conception of deities of all sizes and shapes that have magical powers to protect and destroy. Contained in this imagery of protection and destruction are both the redemptive and destructive aspects of maternity.

Malevolence and Vengeance: We Need to Talk about Kevin

While writing this book I was on vacation in Canada, where one of the pleasures I enjoyed was listening to Canadian Public Radio. As I drove onto a ferry that would take me back to the United States, I heard a brief discussion about a recent book that had horrified both broadcasters. As one of them put it, "This novel deals with a very taboo subject—women who can't love their children. It's about a monstrous child whose mother can't love him." Oblivious to the honking cars behind me, I grabbed a pencil and wrote down the name Lionel Shriver—the female writer who had written the disturbing novel in question, *We Need to Talk about Kevin.* After reading it, I, too, felt very disturbed—more disturbed than I had felt reading any of the other literary case stories. I think the source of my feeling of disturbance is the novel's insistence on hopeless, unremitting, and incurable mother-child hatred, every mother's worst fear.

The elements of this case story are similar to those in *The Fifth Child* in some ways but with less of the sense of redemption and resolution that characterizes the latter. Shriver's is the story of a reluctant mother, Eva Khatchadourian, and Kevin, her very disturbed and unloving child. It raises several especially difficult questions: What is a mother to do when she finds herself with a child she *cannot* love, a child she fears and hates? What is a child to do who cannot love his mother and knows she cannot love him? Can such a situation ever be resolved or remedied?

Eva (so unlike Harriet) is uncertain from the start that she wants children. She finds them dull and doesn't experience

> that overriding urge I'd always heard about, the narcotic pining
> that draws childless women ineluctably to strangers' strollers
> in parks. . . . When I hadn't gone into maternal heat by my
> mid-thirties, I worried that there was something wrong with
> me, something missing. (27)

Eva is not comfortable with not wanting children, but this seems more a reflection of her difficulty tolerating any weakness or failure in herself—"something missing"—than a real conflict of desire, and she accedes to her husband's wishes and becomes pregnant. Her pregnancy is not difficult, but she feels that people are revulsed when they look at her.

> Ever notice how many films portray pregnancy as infestation, as colonization by stealth? *Rosemary's Baby* was just the beginning. In *Alien*, a foul extraterrestrial claws its way out of John Hurt's belly.... I'm sorry, but I didn't make these movies up, and any woman whose teeth have rotted, whose bones have thinned, whose skin has stretched knows the humbling price of a nine-month freeloader. (58)

These are not the feelings of a woman who looks forward to her baby but rather of one who already dreads what she is carrying.

One of Eva's most striking qualities of character is her counter-phobic reaction to danger. Her mother, a survivor of the 1915 Turkish genocide against the Armenians, is agoraphobic; she never leaves her home. The last thing Eva wants is to be like her mother. She takes on things that frighten her all the time, and motherhood is high on that list. She refuses an epidural during a difficult delivery: she "wins" if she can do it without anesthesia. But the pain overwhelms her, and she says, "In the very instant of his birth, I associated Kevin with my own limitations—with not only suffering, but defeat" (76).

Eva expects, despite these fears, to love her baby instantly. But from the moment he is born, she feels he rejects her. He won't take the breast, not only at that initial moment (when many babies are too exhausted by childbirth to nurse), but forever after. He won't take milk from her in any form; he will only take a bottle of formula from his father. Says Eva, "He could smell it. He could smell me.... I shouldn't have taken it personally, but how could I not? It wasn't mother's milk he didn't want, it was Mother" (86).

Interestingly, recent infant studies reveal that infants do know the smell of their mother's milk from the beginning. When two pads soaked with breast milk, one from the infant's mother, the other from another woman, are placed on either side of the infant's head, the infant turns toward the pad with his mother's milk.[3]

Not surprisingly, Eva becomes depressed. Postpartum depressions are often related to ambivalence about the baby, to feeling overwhelmed, to being too judgmental about not living up to one's expectations of maternal behavior and feeling. But most women recover from them and often go on to become very loving mothers. Postpartum depression is a sign that something is wrong but not necessarily a harbinger of a hopeless relationship.

Eva feels that nothing she can do will soothe or satisfy Kevin. He cries constantly when he is alone with her, a cry of outrage and wrath, and only calms down when his father feeds or holds him. Ben, who was also filled with rage and spite, did accept his mother's milk— and, to some degree, her mothering, when it took the form of teaching him how to survive in the world. Neither of these two "unusual" children seeks a loving relationship with its mother, or anyone else for that matter, but Ben seems more an animal in need of taming, whereas Kevin is all too human and clever in the worst sense of the word. He seems malevolent, resentful, and vengeful from birth. If a baby could be born a psychopath, Kevin is that baby. He is chilling in his lack of emotion and his cruelty.

How does a child get to be this way? Is initial maternal ambivalence that destructive? Or is this the way his guilty and unhappy mother, who cannot love him, needs to see him? With sadness, Eva describes her inability to love him; she pleads guilty of emotional malfeasance. But she also can't tolerate failure, so is this an inability to love, or has Eva given up trying?

Eva's husband, Franklin, loves Kevin and sees nothing wrong with him. The problem, Eva feels, is that Franklin loves the idea of having a son and ignores the reality of the son he has. Eva sees a child who tortures her by refusing to use the toilet well past school age, who won't eat anything she cooks, who puts purple ink into his squirt gun and sprays her newly decorated study, who hurts and humiliates other children. Her husband, Franklin, sees him as a mischievous boy, whose mother blames him constantly. This kind of disconnect between parents' views of a troubled child can interfere seriously with any attempts to solve the problem, professionally or otherwise. In this case a disconnect is in the appraisal of who is at fault, Eva or Kevin.

Eva insists on having another baby to find out if her inability to love Kevin is specific to him or a real inability on her part to love *any* child. She forms a strong, mutual, and positive attachment with her second child, Celia, a very different baby, passive, sensitive, and loving. Celia even loves Kevin. But Kevin returns no one's love, neither his father's nor his sister's, and his rage and vengeance mounts as he enters adolescence. He blinds his sister in one eye, and finally, a few days before his sixteenth birthday, he commits a mass murder at his high school, killing eight students and one teacher. All his victims share the "crime" of having the capacity to love and enjoy something in their lives. This is a capacity Kevin does not have but clearly envies and wishes to destroy. The last two murders in the killing spree are those of his father and his sister.

Eva blames herself. But neither she nor the reader (at any rate this reader) can explain how Kevin *became* so hateful. After all, many women have children reluctantly or hate their pregnancies, only to eventually fall in love with their babies. A good friend of mine told me adamantly she never wanted children, fearing she would be like her cold, critical mother. She married and reluctantly decided to have a child, for her husband's sake. Several months after the birth, I received a letter describing her amazement at how deeply involved she had become with her wonderful baby, how much she loved him and how she'd love to have lots more. At last count, she had three. She was a woman who loved animals and children, a teacher who taught handicapped children. What she feared was having a child of her own, lest unconscious identifications with her mother prevail over her own positive maternal capacities.

Another friend described her first reaction to her second child: "The moment he was born he looked like an angry turtle. I thought to myself, Omigod! What is this?" The child was difficult, stubborn, and argumentative from the beginning. My friend was very clear that she found her daughter more lovable "from day one," but she remained connected to her son and concerned about his well-being. Basically, she *wanted* to love him, and their relationship, though difficult, improved considerably over the years as the son grew older and more mature.

The experiences of these two friends were normative ones in the spectrum of ambivalent reactions. It is not unusual for a mother to prefer one child to another, although many mothers guiltily deny this, considering it a crime. Nor is it unusual for mothering to become pleasurable to a woman who has had many reasons, based on her own childhood experience or troubled familial identifications, to initially dread it. What *is* unusual is for a child to take such a dislike to a mother from the start. The opposite is really the case. Children need to love their mothers and will often love notoriously awful parents and, sadly, sometimes grow up to emulate them. But Kevin defeats his mother over and over. "I beg you," Eva says,

> to understand just how hard I'd been trying to be a good mother.
> But trying to be a good mother may be as distant from being a

good mother as trying to have a good time is from truly having one. Distrusting my every impulse from the instant he was laid on my breast, I'd follow a devout regime of hugging my little boy. (195)

Her behavior is to no avail. She is pretending, and Kevin knows her attempts are hollow. Eva admits that "real love shares more in common with hatred and rage than it does with geniality or politeness" (195–96). In fact, when Eva does show her rage and hatred, Kevin respects her. He doesn't believe in faked or forced love, which is what he usually gets from his mother and, in a way, from his clueless father, who loves the image of his own masculinity reproduced in his son, not the son himself.

One clue to this horrifying situation is that maternal-child love develops; it is not inborn. True, maternal and infantile instincts exist from the beginning and lead the way. By two months infants reward their mothers with a smiling response, which by most reports makes it all worthwhile. In normal situations most mothers don't remember difficult childbirths, and they forgive early problems with lactation, fussy babies, and sleepless nights. And as infants settle down from their first month or two of physiological disorganization, a feedback loop of positive interactions helps to develop strong positive attachments.

John Bowlby, founder of attachment theory, has said, "Just as the baby needs to feel that he belongs to his mother, the mother needs to feel that she belongs to her child and it is only when she has the satisfaction of this feeling, that it is easy for her to devote herself to him."[4] Sometimes the attachment between mother and child is more clinging than it should be or more detached than it should be, or more disorganized than it should be, but between Kevin and Eva the attachment is based totally on negative valences. He trusts only her hatred, and she comes to trust only his. What is so horrible about this story is that Kevin, unlike other babies and children, does not give his mother a chance to become a better mother. It is every woman's worst nightmare—a child who will not love you, no matter how hard you try. Eva is certainly easily defeated, which she finds intolerable and cannot forgive, but right from the beginning it appears to be too late. Furthermore, Kevin keeps her ambivalence alive by tormenting her cruelly. A horrifying example of this torment involves his blinding of his younger sister. He uses lye to wash out Celia's eye when she gets a piece of dirt in it. Later, after he kills Celia, he removes her glass eye, and, in prison, he shows it to his mother, as vengeance for her preference for her daughter and out of the need to hurt her deeply.

I posed some questions earlier. What does a mother do when she cannot love her child? What does a child do who cannot love his mother? I have some thoughts but no final answers to these very painful questions. In real life some women in this dilemma would seek help, for themselves and their child, but as I pointed out earlier, the crime of not loving your child, or of not being loved by him, is often too heinous and shameful to admit, especially in our current culture of child worship. Eva's husband feels she should "get some help," but Eva refuses to consider psychotherapy. She reaches a partial solution, though, by taking responsibility for Kevin. She pays with her guilt. Eva admits that she, like Kevin, never gave the relationship a second chance. And, although he has killed the two people she loves most, her husband and daughter, she won't abandon him completely. She visits him in prison regularly and vows to make a room available for him in her home when he is released. She, like Harriet, takes responsibility for the outcome of her mothering, but in this story I am unable to offer the interpretation I did in *The Fifth Child,* where Ben's ruthlessness and greed was seen as a projection of a disavowed part of Harriet. In *We*

Need to Talk about Kevin the malevolence and vengeance *seem* so truly to belong to Kevin that there is no sense that Eva has worked something through in herself.

Yet, like Dr. Frankenstein's creature, Kevin still clings to his rejecting mother. When he shows her Celia's glass eye, Eva tells him that if he *ever* does that again, she will stop visiting him permanently. And she means it. At their next visit, Kevin gives her a tiny wooden coffin he has made, containing the eye, and asks Eva to bury it. It is his way of saying 'don't abandon me completely—even a hateful and disturbed relationship is more important than none at all.' Hatred is often the result of disappointed love and given the nature of human attachment, particularly between mother and child, *anything* is preferable to total indifference. And, regardless of how disturbed their relationship is, Eva and Kevin are very far from indifferent to each other.

Peripartum Madness: Rosemary's Baby

Eva mentions *Rosemary's Baby* as "just the beginning" of a wave of monster movies in which a baby infests and drains its mother. I would put forth *Frankenstein* and *Dracula* as earlier novels—then films—that dealt with such themes in more disguised and sophisticated forms. However, whatever one may think about the literary merits of *Rosemary's Baby*, it took off like wildfire with the public, as both novel and film. It heralded a rash of similar movies, for example, *The Exorcist,* in which children appeared not as the good and hopeful Shirley Temples or Little Lord Fauntleroys of the world but as demonic figures, the agents or sexualized victims of evil forces. Perhaps in this postnuclear and post-Holocaust world, where the reality of mass death and destruction has become traumatically imprinted on human consciousness, the unthinkable is more real. The "unthinkable" to which I am referring, in this instance, is evil and malevolence in children. Why does this theme have such a grip on modern audiences? It would seem that by disguising "ordinary" demanding babies as devilish monsters, it is more acceptable to dislike and fear them, or to dislike the drain and conflicts that their demands may produce in a mother.

For a woman as desirous of a baby as Rosemary is, her pregnancy gets off to a very unpleasant start. The plot device that explains this circumstance has to do with Rosemary's selfish and ambitious husband, Guy. He makes a bargain with two neighbors, members of a Satanic cult—a bargain that his wife will bear the Devil's child for them—in return for *his* guaranteed professional success.

If we take this plot at face value, it is a silly but engrossing horror story. Seen through the psychoanalytic lens I am focusing on maternal ambivalence, it makes more sense if we turn the plot 180 degrees. Then we are dealing with a fantasy of a pregnancy complicated by both prepartum and postpartum psychotic states. Rosemary can now be seen as a frightened and ambivalent woman who projects fear of her own destructiveness into her unborn baby and then onto the outside world. Consciously, she longs for this baby and will protect it at all costs. Unconsciously, she fears its monstrosity and her own. No explanation is offered for this fear, but then the author is writing a thriller, not a psychological novel.

The pregnancy causes Rosemary unremitting and inexplicable pain; she loses her appetite and craves salt and raw meat.

> The pain grew worse, grew so grinding that something shut
> down in Rosemary. . . . Until now it had been inside her; now
> she was inside it; pain was the weather around her, was time,
> was the entire world. Numbed and exhausted, she began to
> sleep more, and to eat more too—more nearly raw meat. (141)

In the middle of one night Rosemary finds herself eating a raw chicken heart, her mouth and fingers dripping with blood. She begins to vomit. This passage describes an inner state. Rosemary feels as if she has been taken over by a fetus she fears as destructive. Furthermore, she fears it is creating monstrous behaviors and desires in *her*, which she tries to vomit out and expel. The degree to which she becomes involved in these fantasies, so that she is now *inside the pain* that was previously inside her, suggests a loss of boundaries, dissociation, and pathological withdrawal, states symptomatic of psychotic functioning.

When, at four months, the pain stops and the baby begins to move, Rosemary seems to recover. But according to the 180-degree rereading I am suggesting, this only marks a shift in symptoms. Now, instead of seeing the destructive impulses in her fetus, or herself, she sees them in the outside world. She discovers the "plot" that is being carried out against herself and the baby, now allies. The witches want to kill the baby and use its flesh and blood for their perverted rituals. They are the cannibals, not Rosemary herself, eater of raw chicken hearts. She becomes increasingly paranoid. Everything fits; everyone is involved in the effort to steal and destroy her baby.

Rosemary tries desperately to escape but goes into labor and is delivered at home after having been given an injection. As she lapses into unconsciousness, she apologizes to the baby for not having it naturally. Later she is told the baby died and that she has had a prepartum psychosis. She is drugged and her breasts are pumped at regular intervals. She doesn't know what becomes of the milk. Since I am assuming that the Devil baby fantasy is part of a peripartum psychosis based on the mother's fear and ambivalence, I read these passages differently. Rosemary represses all experience of the birth and nurses a baby to whom she can't relate or, as happens more often in these conditions, refuses to nurse.

The rest of the novel can be read as a gradual recovery from her postpartum psychotic state. After about a month Rosemary begins to hear a baby crying, and when she hears this her breasts begin to leak. She becomes convinced that the baby is alive. Her maternal urges begin to prevail. She tells herself that while he may be part Devil, he is also part of her and therefore good. Roman Castavets, the ringleader in her paranoid fantasy, now encourages her, pointing out that the baby responds to her voice, that she is a good mother. What he is really saying is that she *can* be a good mother, that the negative side of her ambivalence has not *permanently* damaged her child.

LESLIE

Leslie, a thirty-year-old pregnant woman, came to see me for brief psychotherapy. She had a history of clinical depression successfully treated with medication. Because of her pregnancy she had stopped taking antidepressants and had become anxious and volatile. Her central worry was that she would develop a postpartum depression and be unable to care adequately for her baby.

Leslie was a bright, accomplished woman but had been a "problem" adolescent. Uncomfortable with her female body, she became very rebellious, making up for what she viewed as her lack of beauty by acting out with drugs and alcohol. She had interrupted her graduate career to become pregnant and feared she might resent the baby's interference, but even more she feared failure in this feminine life task. She felt that her parents and siblings did not have much confidence in her in this area, that they viewed her as damaged.

Childbirth and early lactation were difficult for Leslie. The baby took quite a long time to develop a reliable sleep cycle, and Leslie's husband, although concerned and loving, was of limited help. She and I met several times a week during the end of her pregnancy and the early months of motherhood. When the baby was three months old, Leslie and her husband moved out of the area (a preplanned move) and we had to discontinue our work. By that time Leslie had the baby on a livable sleep cycle and was no longer worried that she would become depressed and fail.

An important reason for the success of the treatment was that I did not approach Leslie with an expectation that she would mess things up, as she felt her mother did. Of course, Leslie's concerns about her mother's reactions may have been projections of her own worries about her feminine adequacy. The chance to have an older maternal substitute (me) who insisted she look at her feelings but also had confidence in her abilities ensured Leslie a fate very different from Rosemary's.

Early Trauma and Dissociation: The Bad Seed

Three mothers, Harriet, Eva, and Rosemary, wrestle with the problem of highly problematic offspring, but they function at different levels of psychological awareness. Harriet struggles with denial of the greedy desires that she has projected into her child but comes to a conscious recognition of the problem within herself and with this achieves a more realistic, albeit sad, solution to her problem. Eva, on the other hand, does not recognize or work out her internal conflicts but accepts her hatred as a more genuine response to her vengeful son. Furthermore, she takes on the responsibility of not abandoning him, hoping to use his highly ambivalent attachment to her as a means of controlling his vengeful behaviors. Both mothers function on the level of reality.

Rosemary seems more in the grip of something frightening and magical, and her transformation from psychotic, rejecting mother to good and loving mother is equally magical. It is a psychological fairy tale in the sense that no motivation for Rosemary's behavior is really suggested or obvious. In the text of Levin's novel, Rosemary is a perfectly loving and accepting mother-to-be, at the mercy of outside forces. As author, Levin joins in his character's paranoid views, then reverses them (as Rosemary accepts her baby) without giving or suggesting any evidence that inner conflict has been worked out.

William March, author of the posthumously published best-seller, *The Bad Seed*, was interested in psychoanalysis. He had been in treatment himself, and his novel describes the roots and vicissitudes of Christine Penmark's maternal ambivalence in a psychologically convincing way. *The Bad Seed* is a story about a mother who has suffered a severe early trauma. This trauma—witnessing the murder of her siblings by her mother—has resulted in dissociation and repressed memory, as such situations often do. Christine's conflicts surrounding aggression and her "survivor guilt" play out in her relationship to her own child, Rhoda, resulting in a tragic outcome.

This kind of psychic numbing, which is Christine's response to unbearable early trauma, interferes seriously with her ability to relate to her child in a live way, exemplified by her inability to see how disturbed the child really is. I include Christine as an example of an ambivalent mother because her numbness and lack of emotional awareness, despite good maternal "behavior," speaks to a serious kind of maternal absence, worse in a way than hatred, in which something is at least *alive* between mother and child.

Rhoda has always been something of an enigma to Christine.

Neat, orderly, and disturbingly self-sufficient, she seems to have no affection for her mother or anyone else, nor does she seem to care that she doesn't. What she does care about is acquiring appealing toys, jewels, and prizes, using charm, manipulation, and murder to achieve her ends. The story opens with a school picnic at which Rhoda murders Claude Daigle, a child in her class, to obtain a penmanship medal that she feels should have been hers. By the end of the novel she will have murdered the janitor, Leroy, out of fear that he will expose her murder of Claude.

Rhoda is a caricature, a non-three-dimensional creature motivated by greed. She has no guilt, no anxiety—unless threatened with exposure—and no visible needs for human relationship. (She does experience rage, when thwarted.) Yet when she achieves her goals, her capacity for enjoyment seems muted and perverse. When she wants something, she is driven to ruthless actions to obtain it, but because she remains unrelated to others, she doesn't experience any real joy. There is no one to share or reflect back her pleasure.

Christine's friend, Monica Breedlove, notes Christine's fear of violence and thinks it is because she is unconsciously fascinated with the subject. The janitor, Leroy, Rhoda's soul mate in meanness and greed, sees Christine as a passive, masochistic victim of whom he would like to take sexual advantage. In their own ways, both Monica and Leroy are right about her. Inside Christine there is some violence and some compulsion to surrender, about which she does not wish to know.

It is Rhoda's indifference to Claude's death that breaks through Christine's entrenched denial and forces her to pay attention to the shadowy intuitions and ominous questions she has always had about both Rhoda and her own past. Events in the novel unfold to reveal Rhoda as a habitual killer, while Christine wonders whether she herself has been adopted and, if so, who her real parents were.

The premise of the novel is that Rhoda's warped nature is genetic, the result of a "bad seed." As Christine attempts to understand her daughter by reading about other habitual murderers of the past, she comes across the name Bessie Denker and realizes that this woman was her mother. Gradually, through dreams and recovered memories, she puts together her own disturbing history.

Bessie Denker, after a lifetime of murdering for profit, was found out by a cousin. In an attempt to frame the cousin and prove her innocence, she murdered all her children except Christine, who managed to run away and hide. Christine is the survivor of a family holocaust and the carrier of the "bad seed." Rhoda is Bessie Denker's incarnation.

Christine's reactions to her discoveries are complex. At first she is relieved to no longer be hiding from what she has always unconsciously known, to finally be conscious. In my opinion *The Bad Seed* is not really about Rhoda. Written from her mother's vantage point, Rhoda is more an element in Christine's inner struggles than a flesh-and-blood character. How could Christine not have noticed how much is missing in Rhoda and from their relationship? She is neither stupid nor unobservant, but she seems like a sleepwalker, dissociated from the horror around her. At first she blames herself and feels she must protect Rhoda. "It was her duty to protect her child. What kind of a monster would she be if she betrayed and destroyed her own child?" (149). She alone is responsible as the "bad seed" carrier, not her husband and not Rhoda.

Christine tries desperately, in a kind of last-ditch denial, to love the little girl and elicit some affection from her. But soon "the sense of guilty tenderness she felt for the child had worn itself out. She regarded her daughter now with uncomprehending, chilly distaste" (183). Christine watches Rhoda constantly to protect others around them, but she doesn't know yet what she will do.

Viewed psychologically, Christine cannot tolerate her guilt as sole survivor of her entire sibship. This guilt is a result of the normal infantile wish to have one's mother all to oneself, to get rid of the other children. For Christine, this wish has come true and is unbearable, so she projects her unacceptable murderous impulses into her child. For Christine, who has always been too nice, too passive, and too unaware, any aggression is unacceptable. Projected into Rhoda, her aggression becomes monstrous. I read this book with the assumption that one of the meanings of Rhoda's two-dimensional caricature-like qualities is that, psychologically, she is Christine's unconscious fantasy, Christine's projected bad self.

Christine's anxiety about aggression and violence produces dissociated states.[5] She has, in fact, *lived* in a dissociated state in relation to Rhoda. When Rhoda decides to kill Leroy by setting his bed on fire, Christine sees her take the matches. She is very close to knowing what will happen but is unable to let this realization become conscious and therefore to take action. When she sees Leroy fleeing in flames, she becomes dissociated; she hears someone screaming and only later realizes that the person screaming is herself. Leroy's death is a repetition in which Christine witnesses murder and is helpless to do anything but hide. The horror of her own mother's murderousness, the loss of her siblings, and her ambivalence about her survival cannot be digested. Her overwhelmed ego goes into a dissociated state, as it did when she was a child.

When Christine recovers she is able to make her final decision. The witnessing of another murder tears away her dissociation and permits action. She will kill Rhoda with sleeping tablets and shoot herself. Her plan is only partially successful. She dies, but Rhoda is saved.

The ending of the novel is intended to be ironic but is in fact tragic. Christine has been traumatized by witnessing the deaths of her siblings and by her knowledge that her mother would have killed *her* had she not escaped. Dissociation, flatness, and denial are typical for a traumatized person struggling to keep memory repressed. For many survivors of extreme conditions (the Holocaust, for example), children are viewed as saviors or as reparative replacements of those lost, but for Christine, her child is her punishment and a living monument to her guilt. In killing Rhoda, Christine attempts to kill the *bad* parts of herself, but since she cannot live with the idea of murdering her own child, as her mother did, she must also kill herself.

. . .

Three solutions to maternal aggression projected into monstrous offspring—realistic, magical, and tragic—conclude these novels. The realistic ending of Lessing's novel reflects psychological processing by Harriet into a mature sadness, as does Eva's story to a lesser degree, while Rosemary solves her dilemma in a kind of quasi-religious, magical manner. Christine cannot do what Harriet and Eva can because she has been damaged too early. Her immature ego retreats into primitive defenses, extreme denial, and dissociation, and she cannot know about her desires, past or present. Harriet and Eva desire too much, Christine too little. All their offspring reflect the characters of their mothers in these more general ways. Ben is full of greedy desire in an active, striving way; Kevin must win in a battle of hatred and malevolence; Rosemary's baby is a fairy-tale devil, and Rhoda, though monomaniacal in her greed and the actions she takes to satisfy it, is curiously flat. She's horrible, but psychologically she's not very interesting. "Larvated" is a term Christine's friend, Monica, uses, and by this she means unhatched, undeveloped, and unknowing. When this term applies to Christine, it represents the stunting of emotional development that accompanies severe trauma. In Rhoda, Christine's projection, this stunting leaves her fixated at the level of oral greed where one can only take in but never really give back.

The disturbing fantasy of child murder pervades all these novels in one way or another. Each of these mothers deals, consciously or unconsciously, with the question of whether or not to kill their children. For Harriet, sending Ben away is tantamount to murdering him. Seeing him as the source of all misery, a complete drain on society and the family, a murder disguised as necessary custodial care is painfully tempting. Because Harriet is able to see her complicity in Ben's monstrousness, he can become psychologically integrated and concrete murder is no longer a necessary solution. Eva's form of murder would be to abandon Kevin completely, something she cannot do. Rosemary, like Andrea Yates, is trapped in a psychotic state, in which the baby, as the carrier of all her bad, psychotically distorted impulses, must be eliminated. In the grip of hormonal imbalance, as well as religious and societal attitudes that permit no real forgiveness for maternal aggression, both Rosemary and Andrea Yates can envision only one solution—stop the devil before he spreads. For them, the child as dangerous is all too real. Christine can only see the fault as hers. She survived what others did not, and she does not deserve to live. Rhoda, the murderer, is disembodied in a way. She is closer perhaps to the "creatures" in the *Alien* series than are the other monster children I have described because of the mechanical and unconnected quality of her relationships. Where the creatures have a drive to reproduce, she has a drive to acquire; and in neither case is there *any* hint of a drive to relate to the maternal figure. Perhaps this unrelatedness is why she produces in Christine a sense of chilliness and deep dread rather than the heated fear with which Harriet, Eva, and Rosemary struggle.

The situations depicted in these novels are admittedly extreme. I have seen nothing this severe in my clinical practice. Yet their popularity as novels suggests that they speak to fears deep within us about our capacities for aggression and, in particular, our fears and fascination with maternal aggression.

CHAPTER EIGHT

When Fears Are Realized

Therapists who work with children see maternal ambivalence as a serious problem for the child, sometimes as *the* problem. The problem it creates for the mother takes second place. Even in the mother's psychotherapy, the therapist's concern about the child may compromise empathy for the mother's conflicted situation. Women's reluctance to talk about hatred—the negative side of their ambivalence—has a real basis in society's idealization and protection of children. At the same time, the strains of raising a difficult child tend to be left mostly at the mother's door. Think about Harriet in *The Fifth Child*. Her husband doesn't recognize Ben as his child. Nobody believes Harriet when she claims that Ben is a monster. Nobody believes or rescues Eva either. Her husband represents society's idealization of children, and this is reflected in his failure to recognize that any of the wickedness and malevolence between Eva and Kevin is the child's fault. If the mother sees the child as monstrous, it is *her* problem, her distortion. Nobody believes Rosemary. Nobody shares with Christine her horrifying knowledge of Rhoda's true nature.

The psychological dilemmas of these four unfortunate mothers dominate their case stories. Their children are presented as fantastical caricatures, so they don't arouse much empathy in the reader. But the child has a story, too. There are many instances in which maternal ambivalence can be very damaging, and it is important to not lose sight of this in an attempt to understand the mother's point of view. This chapter and the next one focus on an important consequence of maternal ambivalence, the *child's experience* of being seen as monstrous and hateful. In my clinical work I have encountered three situations that are relevant to the child's experience of being hateful—the deformed child and the mother's response, the child who develops a hateful identity to solve certain extreme needs of his or her own, and the child who is made monstrous to satisfy pathological needs of the mother.

I begin this chapter with the dilemma of the deformed child. The word *monster* comes from the French verb *monstre*, "to warn" or "to display or show."[1] In connection with the centuries-old fantasy that the monstrous (i.e., deformed) child was the product of the mother's imagination or behavior, something is revealed to the world that the mother would rather keep hidden. Therefore, the deformity may be experienced by the mother as her shame, fault, or punishment. There was something she failed to do, or should not have done.

Is there ever a pregnancy in which the mother does not worry about whether her child will be normal, even if she has already had normal children? "Is he okay? Does he have all his fingers and toes?" A friend, pregnant with twins after two normal births, saw her obstetrician for her final checkup prior to delivery. He commented casually, even a bit humorously, that the head of the first baby was well engaged in the pelvis and that this definitely ruled out the (admittedly rather remote) possibility of Siamese twins. Although she had plenty of other anxieties about a twin birth, my friend had not consciously worried about Siamese twins, so she was amazed at how relieved she felt on hearing the obstetrician's comment. Fortunately, in the majority of cases a mother's fears turn out to be unfounded. But what happens when they are not?

Mothers often blame themselves for their child's deformity, and some experience this misfortune as a punishment. Maternal guilt feelings about a child's deformity and maternal worries that the deformity represents punishment are actually psychologically sophisticated reactions to abnormality. A more primitive response connects deformity to evil forces and sees the child, too, as evil. Women accused of witchcraft were executed in Salem, Massachusetts, in the late seventeenth century for "causing" miscarriages, stillbirths, and malformations—for doing the Devil's work.[2] The mother who blames herself for her child's deformity attempts reparation; those who see the deformity as evidence of evil, of something being done to *them,* reject the child, in their minds if not in reality. I don't think there is any way that a child's deformity cannot produce feelings of ambivalence in the mother, and as in other situations that induce such mixed feelings, there are both internalizing (guilty and reparative) and externalizing (angry and rejecting) reactions.

Not all deformities "show." A psychologically troubled and troubling child may be experienced as deformed, certainly as abnormal. A child may have a genetic disorder—for example, a cardiac malformation or juvenile diabetes—that does not necessarily affect appearance or behavior but leads to a compromised and shortened life, requiring special care. On the other hand, a deformity that shows, say, a cleft palate or a large birthmark, may be less troublesome if the family is accepting or the condition surgically correctable. The degree to which the child's deformity impinges on the lives and needs of the rest of the family determines how problematic it is.

Now, what about the *child's* fantasies and reactions? A central, albeit unconscious, fantasy in the mind of a deformed child is that the mother has caused the deformity. This resonates with the child's conviction of its mother's omnipotence and also with the ages-old idea of birth defects being caused by the mother's "imagination" or behavior during pregnancy. The idea that a mother cannot love a deformed child is consciously accessible to the child; after all, even where there is nothing physically or cognitively wrong, children worry about their naughtiness and extreme behavior. If you lose your mother's love because you have behaved badly, you can make it up to her, but if you have a permanent illness or defect, you cannot.

Less consciously accessible is the fantasy of maternal causation—that is, if my mother *had* loved me, *had* wanted me, I wouldn't be this way. Paradoxically, children often protect their mothers, who are so desperately needed, by remaining unconscious of this fantasy. It is actually something of a breakthrough when a child can access his feelings of blame toward the mother; it is a step on the way to not blaming themselves. An even further step is the realization that nobody is to blame, tragic as the situation may be. In loving and well-balanced families or in the context of very good therapy, this final step can often be achieved.

Here's an example of this more fortunate outcome. I know a woman who gave birth to a child, Larry, with Down's syndrome. The woman had three other children who were normal, two younger than Larry. Her husband held himself to blame, as he had been working with radiation during the time his wife became pregnant. This family was unusually accepting and noncritical of all their children, and

Larry was no exception. He was included in all family activities, his siblings were kind to him, and the general atmosphere in his home was one of remarkable patience. Later in his life he was sent to a very good institutional program near home, where he learned some skills that enabled him to do a menial job. As Larry got older and became increasingly aware of his limitations, he became depressed. This turned out to be harder for the family to deal with than his being "intellectually challenged." As a family they tended to minimize negative affect; this was a characteristic of their "family culture." This made Larry's depression, which developed despite all their kind efforts, even more difficult for them. Ironically, their total acceptance of Larry may have made it harder for him to deal with less charitable responses in the outside world.

I feel a comment is in order here about our current need to make the appellations of deformity more acceptable. We no longer say "Down's syndrome"; we say "learning differences" or "special needs." While I agree that expressions such as "mongoloid" are racially tinged and implicitly insulting and marginalizing, I don't think that using politically correct, albeit more respectful, expressions helps in any fundamental way to alleviate the pain of being different or the ambivalence it engenders in afflicted families.

A deformed child is not always seen as monstrous, as is evident in the case of Larry. Some parents accept deformity better than others. These parents do not just tolerate but enjoy the care of such a child, especially if the deformity, illness, or retardation is not too severe. Their afflicted children may become very special, the ones who will never leave home, the ones who give their parents a sense of mission and meaning. Such an adjustment is not necessarily pathological. However, sometimes it becomes so.

I am thinking of the phenomenon of "super-families." The parents in these families usually have children of their own as well as adopted and foster children, sometimes as many as eighteen or more altogether. Often some of the children are handicapped. The conscious motivation of these parents is charitable and reparative, but the way in which these children have to be raised is reminiscent of an army camp. It is hard to believe that any of them get anywhere near an optimal amount of parental attention, and I suspect that the underlying sibling tensions are both disturbing and forbidden. In *The Fifth Child* Harriet's normal children deeply resented Ben and left home because of him, although Harriet seemed unable to digest this. Parents driven to rescue *so* many children are often dealing with a hidden ambivalence that they overcome with massive denial. (This seems to be the case with Nadya Suleman, the mother of octuplets.) This ambivalence may relate to *their* childhood deprivations. Raising children evokes the memory of earlier states and experiences in the childhoods of the parents. Rather than become aware of the envy that is aroused in them by what their own children are getting, these parents take on more and more, denying their envy with charitable acts and ultimately, paradoxically, reproducing their own experience of deprivation in their children.

Sometimes parental "acceptance" of deformity is achieved by denying its severity or by overcompensating, in a guilt-driven way, at the expense of other children or spouses. For instance, I once treated a man, Donald, who was extremely distressed about his younger sister, although this was not the reason he sought psychotherapy. The sister had two children, a normal girl and an extremely retarded younger boy, a child so retarded, in fact, that at the age of nine he was still in diapers, without speech or even minimal motor skills. He could lift his head, but he couldn't sit or walk. The boy was cared for at home, without help, by his parents, at the expense of his older sister, who suffered from emotional neglect and guilt over her resentment of her brother.

Donald felt that his sister was sacrificing her own life and that of her daughter to her deformed child. A gay man, he felt himself marked as the deviant one in his conventional midwestern family. He was both troubled by his nephew's abnormality and identified with his niece's sense of being left out and not understood in the "culture of the abnormal" represented by *her* family situation. In this family the healthy were sacrificed to care for the needy, as in *The Fifth Child*. My patient's niece had a double dilemma. She was implicitly punished for resenting her mother's attention to her brother, and she was not appreciated for her skills and intellectual abilities in part because they contrasted so painfully with her brother's lacks. The mother could not *see* her, for to do so was to acknowledge the enormous gap between her two children; then she would have to see how hopeless and bizarre her own choice was.

I did not know enough about Donald's sister to understand her conflicts and motivations, but I imagined her as suffering from a powerful sense of guilt at having produced such a damaged child. Her inevitable unconscious hatred of the child would have fueled this guilt. In this extreme situation there was no evidence of the possibility of a real relationship with the afflicted child other than a fantasied one in the mother's mind. Harriet, too, had no possibility for a real relationship with Ben, but she was realistic about his limitations. She did not imagine, as my patient's sister may have, that she could make him well or that she would, one day, be deeply rewarded for her sacrifice. The need for reward suggests that my patient's sister may have unconsciously experienced the boy as a punishment.

A mother may be unable to accept a deformed child because the latter is a blow to her self-regard—How could I have produced a child like this?—or because the reinforcement of her sense of maternal worth falls far short of the efforts involved in taking care of such a child. These issues contributed to the emotional situation between Ben and Harriet in *The Fifth Child* and also to that between Kevin and Eva in *We Need to Talk about Kevin*. These women finally gave up; they just didn't get enough back. Harriet overcompensated by spending too much time and emotional energy on Ben, but this was not entirely in the service of repairing her injured narcissism at failed mothering. She did not want to admit her own baby greed because she had had too many children. Eva could not deal with *any* failure in her life.

Since I did not see Donald's sister as a patient, I have had to conjecture what her motivations may have been. The case of my patient, Diane, illustrates the afflicted child experienced as a punishment more clearly. Diane had a normal older daughter and a son, Danny, who was neurologically damaged from birth. He had a mild form of cerebral palsy, along with learning difficulties. As he entered adolescence, he developed very serious behavioral problems. Outside care had been suggested by many specialists, but Diane was unable to accept this solution. Yet she and her husband had the funds to provide such care, and they found Danny exhausting and infuriating to deal with at home.

Diane's younger sister had been stricken with serious polio as a child. As an adult the sister had made substantial physical recovery but remained extremely dependent on her parents, more than could be accounted for by her residual motor difficulties. Diane grew up feeling that her mother had babied her younger sister unnecessarily, and at her emotional expense. Diane's mother was a passive and very masochistic woman who spread her suffering and incompetence over the rest of the family like a suffocating web. In reaction to her mother, my patient prided herself on her upbeat attitude, self-sufficiency, and capacity for realistic action. Danny was a blow to her sense of herself as a competent mother, and there was little pleasure in mothering him. Yet she could not place her son outside of the home, where she knew he would have been better off.

Diane's puzzling behavior had several roots. She had had a stillborn daughter a year before Danny was born. She viewed Danny as a punishment, her "cross to bear," for her resentment of and murderous wishes toward her own sister, unconsciously equated with the stillborn child. That is, unconsciously she felt she had caused the stillbirth. And, though competent and realistic, she was still deeply identified with her own mother who had suffered taking care of Diane's "crippled" sister all those years. This combination of guilt and identification with a masochistic mother made liberating action impossible.

A second patient, Mary Anne, was able to deal with a child with cerebral palsy differently, and it is interesting to think about why this was so. Mary Anne's afflicted daughter, Lana, was institutionalized. Her severe illness, worse than Danny's, had played no small part in Mary Anne's earlier divorce. There were two younger sons. All three family members visited Lana about every three weeks, watched her participate in Special Olympics activities, and took part in other institutional celebrations and activities.

Clearly, this was a less masochistic solution than Diane's, as Lana did not impinge on family life daily. Yet Mary Anne herself was a much more masochistic and self-depreciating person than Diane. The hidden issue in this family was that nobody, including the two younger brothers, could express *any* resentment. (Diane's family could.) Even in her psychotherapy, Mary Anne was unable to admit any resentment about Lana. All direct aggression was forbidden, and herein the hidden ambivalence was to be found. Mary Anne punished herself and her two sons by not allowing or accepting any expression of hatred, which could have provided some relief. That way, Mary Anne could hold onto the fantasy that she was endlessly patient and good and that it was in everybody's best interest that Lana be institutionalized. It seemed as if putting Lana in outside care took care of the problem; nobody had any right to resent her for the time and attention she took, for her special position in the family. Mary Anne's ambivalence was taken out on her two healthy children who were forced to partake in endless institutional visits without being allowed the relief of complaining.

It is no surprise that Mary Anne herself felt unloved in her own family. As with the super-parents, she had to see herself as a model parent to conceal resentment about her own childhood. Paradoxically, although Diane could not act to alleviate her distress about her unmanageable son, she could use therapy to understand and accept her ambivalence and therefore that of others in her family. Mary Anne, able to take action, could never look at her real feelings. Her sons suffered, whereas Diane's daughter did not.

Another painful situation is that of children who feel that their deformities cause harm to their parents. I have encountered this fantasy, in a subtle form, in several patients whose mothers were depressed during their childhoods. These patients felt their mothers' conditions were brought on or worsened by their excessive energy and needs. Some of them dealt with their mother's depression, as children and adolescents, by repressing and undercutting their own energies and abilities, by failing in one way or another—scholastically, creatively, and socially. Children always worry about harming their parents and being left without caretakers, but actual physical and emotional problems in the mother intensify this fear, which is now rationalized by reality. "I have exhausted and hurt my mother because of who I am."

A poignant literary case story of a child who takes responsibility for her own deformity, in order to protect her mother, is that of Trudi Montag, the heroine of Ursula Hegi's novel *Stones from the River.* Trudi is an achondroplastic dwarf.[3] Her deepest wish is to be physically normal, loved and accepted as part of the ordinary world. Her body is stunted, but she has some unusual talents: a beautiful singing voice and an uncanny ability to see into people. They don't hide their secrets from her because, being little and deformed, she doesn't count. She gathers these secrets as ammunition for revenge but also to weave into stories, the expression of her creative powers. She is a complex character, full of life and courage. Her loving father, Leo, tells her she is perfect the way she is. He means she is perfect in her essence, but Trudi feels he is lying to her.

Trudi cannot believe Leo's reassurances because of disturbances in her early relationship with her mother, Gertrud. "For months after Trudi Montag's birth, her mother wouldn't touch her at all. . . . [H]er mother had taken one glance at her and had covered her face as if to shut out the image of the infant's short limbs and slightly enlarged head" (11). Three days after Trudi's birth the mother flees. Gertrud is mentally ill. Her illness preceded Trudi's birth, but Trudi doesn't believe this. Both she and Gertrud hold themselves responsible for the deformity. Gertrud feels Trudi is her punishment for an extramarital liaison. Trudi feels her birth has driven her mother mad. In her desperate need for Gertrud, she reverses the generations and becomes her mother's caretaker. "To lead her mother by both hands from the dark—it was the one thing Trudi could do to offset her guilt that her mother had crossed the line to insanity because of her" (22).

Trudi has a second source of guilt. When Gertrud becomes pregnant again, the parents put sugar cubes on the windowsill to show the stork where to bring the baby. Trudi doesn't want a brother or sister because he or she might be normal and then her parents won't want her anymore. She gets up at night and eats the stork's sugar. When her mother miscarries, she is sure she has killed the baby.

Despite Trudi's valiant efforts to save her, Gertrud deteriorates and has to enter a sanitarium many times. The last time she goes, Gertrud tells Trudi that people don't die if you love them enough. "When I get back, things will be better between us" (40). But Gertrud never comes back. Trudi wonders if this, too, is her fault, if she has not loved Gertrud enough. She fears her mother has seen something in her, "that wicked part Trudi hated and nurtured in order to survive" (86). "If you lived in a freak's body long enough, though you didn't feel like a freak inside—what could you do then to make sure your body wouldn't *turn all of you into a freak?*" (126; emphasis mine). Trudi *is* vengeful, storing up people's secrets when she is rejected; so this worry about her wicked part is to some extent based in reality. She feels that inside she is just like others, but they can't see it. Instead they feel disgust, and this disgust "fused her to them with an odd sense of belonging. . . . [T]hat disgust—it nourished her, horrified her. She would have done anything to be loved by them, and since she could not have their acceptance, she seized their secrets and bared them" (159).

This is an example of how the narcissistic injury of deformity leads to the envy of "normal" others and feeds vengeful omnipotent fantasies. These omnipotent fantasies deny dependency on others, a dependency that is both intensified by the deformity and feels doomed to inevitable disappointment. Part of this disappointment has to do with the feeling that the parent has no choice but to take care of the "cripple" and does not do it lovingly or willingly, so that the increased dependent needs consequent to disability are not *really* gratified. The vengeful destruction of others both proves they are not crucial and inflicts a sort of talion—eye-for-an-eye—revenge by injuring, killing, or deforming them in fantasy. This revenge is often directed at normal siblings, seen, as in Trudi's case, to be preferred by the parents.

Like Trudi, a child may fear that physical deformity is a punishment for evil thoughts, wishes, and fantasies. Furthermore, they may fear that the deformity goes through and through and makes them entirely evil. Trudi feels "the power of being different, the agony of being different" (9). The power offsets the agony, but for Trudi it doesn't really work. For her, revenge is a poor substitute for love. Trudi has a loving father, and later in life she meets a man who loves her for who she is, not for how she looks. This enables her to compensate for the maternal ambivalence and loss from which she has been suffering. It allows her to relinquish her vengeful hatred. She is finally able to mourn her mother's death and move to self-acceptance. "Everyone had something to battle—something that could either destroy you or strengthen you—and what she had battled was maybe not all that bad."

Trudi goes from protecting her mother, by turning her hatred on herself, to allowing herself to hate a mother she *unconsciously* blames, a mother who abandoned her, to forgiveness and an acceptance of her misfortune. I think of this novel as a "therapeutic narrative" because it parallels the steps that an afflicted patient, in a successful psychotherapy, would go through to reach relief and self-acceptance.[4]

CHAPTER NINE

From the Child's Point of View

Some children adopt a monstrous or negative identity, as a whiny brat, perhaps, or an unremitting troublemaker but basically as a needy and demanding person who can never be satisfied. Such people, as patients, usually prove to be caught up in a desperate bid for parental attention that was inadequate earlier in their lives and was often accompanied by a disruption in attachment. This bid can have a vengeful underside in the form of a stubborn claim that the problem can never be repaired. *Monstrous* may seem an extreme term; perhaps I think of it in this way because several of the literary monsters I deal with in my case stories are all angrily attached to their "parents" and endlessly vengeful. They can neither separate nor forgive. I have in mind Dr. Frankenstein's monster, Count Dracula and his vampires, Kevin and Eva, and, as we shall see below, Oskar Matzerath in *The Tin Drum*.

A patient, Brenda, had deep-seated reasons for needing to see herself as monstrous. The first of three children, she suffered a disruption in the relationship with her mother when she was nine months old. At this time her mother's older sister died suddenly and unexpectedly, leaving several children of her own and a family torn by grief and crisis. Although Brenda was not separated physically from her mother when this catastrophe happened, it is very likely that the mother was preoccupied and depressed for some time. It is reasonable to assume that the patient, at nine months, would have been very sensitive to what she later described as a "sense of abandonment." The second half of the first year, six to twelve months, is when stranger anxiety tends to appear. By now the child recognizes her mother as someone crucially important, unique, and irreplaceable, and she reacts intensely to separations, actual or emotional.

As Brenda grew up, her early feelings of loss and disappointment became entangled in a constant and rageful struggle with her mother about her weight and appearance. The patient felt her mother wanted her to be thin and attractive, like her two younger sibs; she wanted to feel she was loved, even if she was "fat and ugly." What was striking about Brenda was her exaggeration (in my opinion) of the extent of both her weight and her ugliness. True, she was somewhat overweight and not beautiful by conventional standards, but she was neither obese nor repellent in appearance. She had lovely brown eyes and, when she chose to, dressed in a unique artistic style. But her need to see herself as ugly was a reflection of her rage, envy, and disappointment in a world perceived as unreliable and unloving, that is, an ugly world, which she turned into an inner conviction of her own physical ugliness. She used this self-perception to test her mother, friends, and analyst. They could do nothing right. To agree that she was fat and ugly was to insult her. To deny it was to take something away from her.

Unconsciously, she didn't want to change her situation because to do so was to lose the means of maintaining an intense, but disavowed, dependent connection to her mother, and then she feared she would have nothing. An endless, punishing, sadomasochistic battle went on between Brenda and those who cared about her. Like many compromises, it was very unsatisfactory. She felt guilty about hurting friends and family members who tried to help her but also frightened about giving up her investment in being and looking "monstrous" because she feared it was all she had. I suspect this pattern developed because as a child Brenda surmised correctly that appearance *was* very important to her mother and her mother's family. The early disruption in her attachment to her mother made her desperate to find something that she could count on getting a reaction to, and, indeed, she found it. It was my impression that Brenda's mother was an anxious person, concerned about having her mothering criticized and therefore always on the defensive with her daughter, whom she feared and to whom she catered. The catering was the "secondary gain" in Brenda's development of a negative identity.

It is not unusual for insecure children to assume that their sibs are loved more because they are smarter or prettier or more obedient. There is often an element of truth in these assumptions. Maureen Dowd, in her book *Are Men Necessary?* addresses the issue of women's obsession with beauty and perfect bodies: "So it shouldn't be surprising to learn that parents have the same beauty bias. Still, a 2005 headline in the *New York Times* was jolting: 'Ugly Children May Get Parental Short Shrift'" (220). Dowd goes on to describe an observation from a group of Canadian researchers about parents buckling their children into shopping carts. Pretty children were buckled in 13.5 percent of the time, in contrast to homely children, who were buckled in only 4 percent of the time. A casual study of supermarket behavior is hardly an exhaustive scientific study, but it is suggestive. Does anyone ever say, with loving enthusiasm, to a child, "Oh my, what a plain little girl you are!"?

Brenda's fantasies about her relationships with others were all or nothing. That is, either she got exactly what she needed and wanted or she would take nothing. She had the skills and power to get people to keep trying to relate to her, but to accept a relationship on any basis that involved compromise was unacceptable. Compromise meant growing up and dealing with the difficulties of imperfect and autonomous living. Consciously, she denied her dependence on her parents, especially her mother. She did not want to see how her other relationships were shaped and compromised by these attachments. She both clung to others and rejected them.

The case story of Oskar Matzerath, the "hero" in Günter Grass's Nobel Prize–winning novel, *The Tin Drum,* has some striking similarities to that of Brenda. I am referring specifically to his adoption of a negative identity in order to remain connected to early figures in his life and to avoid the dangers of growth and autonomy—and to the vengeful fantasies that led both Brenda and Oskar to punish those who had deeply disappointed them.

THE TIN DRUM

The Tin Drum is a dark, surrealistic novel with many complex meanings, from which I am teasing and elaborating a single strand. Oskar, the stunted three-year-old who will never grow up, is a representation of the Third Reich, the monstrous and stunted society into which he was born. The noises of drums, shrieking voices, splintering glass are the background sound effects of his terrible story. But the thread I am pursuing is that of Agnes, an ambivalent mother who dies, and Oskar, the child who tries to possess her forever.

Oskar is born "claudirient," already with full knowledge of the world. At his birth he hears his father say he will be a grocer when he grows up. Agnes says that when he is three, she will give him a toy drum. Oskar, creative and special from birth, does *not* want to be an ordinary person, a grocer. At age three, having obtained his drum, he throws himself down the cellar stairs, to allow the grown-ups to "explain" why he won't ever grow any bigger. He tells us, "I remained the precocious three-year-old, towered over by grownups but superior to all grownups, who refused to measure his shadow with theirs, who was complete both inside and outside, while they, to the very brink of the grave, were condemned to worry their heads about 'development'" (54). In other words, I am already perfect.

Oskar drums incessantly and throws tantrums if his drum is taken away from him. His voice can shatter glass, and he uses it to do so, frequently, when thwarted. He is fixated on omnipotent fantasies and claims, as if saying, "I won't grow up, I can and will do as I please, I am a realer Jesus than Jesus, I am Satan in disguise, the rules don't count for me, I respect neither the passage of time nor generational boundaries." Monstrousness, in the sense of unbounded expression of destructive and aggressive impulses, characterizes Oskar's dealings with the world, but unlike the evil, deformed society his dwarfed body symbolizes, he is vulnerable to suffering and the longing for human connection.

For Oskar is desolate without his tin drum, a transitional object. He uses up one drum after another, depending on his mother, or mother substitutes, to provide him with replacements. The drums are all lacquered, red and white, and they must all look, feel, and sound the same. Like the more usual transitional object, the teddy bear or blanky, which must also always look, feel, and smell the same (one washes it at one's peril), the tin drum is a substitute for Oskar's mother. Agnes was a nurse before she married, wearing a white uniform with a red cross on her bosom, and the tin drum stands for her and comforts Oskar in her absence. Oskar, unlike most children, who give up their transitional objects, remains obsessed with his tin drum and sexually obsessed with nurses, or nurselike women, throughout his life.

Oskar's feelings of superiority are reinforced by his vision of the adult world as corrupt, filled with lies and deceit. Oskar's mother is in love with her cousin, Jan Bronski, who is, in fact, Oskar's real father. Agnes, her lover, and Matzerath, her husband, live in a tense menage à trois from which Oskar feels completely excluded. He sits under the table as the three adults play cards, watching Jan secretly put his foot under his mother's dress; nobody cares if Oskar sees. Although little, he is not protected from adult sexuality as an ordinary child would be because the adults unconsciously sense he is not really innocent. Oskar feels that he is not protected because he doesn't really count. His tragedy is that he fears his mother doesn't love him, can't love him, and he protects himself against these feelings by pretending to himself that he does not need her, only the drums that connect him to her.

The death of Agnes, when Oskar is fourteen, reveals his most troubling fantasies about his relationship with her. At this time Agnes is pregnant with a second illegitimate child. In torment over the incestuous triangle in which she is living, she eats herself to death with fish that poisons her. Oskar tries to see her as dying to save Jan, who is Polish, from Matzerath, who has become a Nazi and could harm him. But what he *really* feels is that he has killed her (*and* her fetus). Shortly after her death he encounters the dwarf, Bebra, who has been a mentor to him and who, in the following passage, functions as his "psychotherapist."

"My mama has died," I tried to explain. "She shouldn't have done that. I can't forgive her. People are always saying: a mother sees

everything, a mother forgives everything. That's nonsense for
Mother's Day. To her I was never anything but a gnome. She
would have got rid of the gnome if she had been able to. But
she couldn't get rid of me, because children, even gnomes, are
marked in your papers and you can't just do away with them.
Also because I was *her* gnome and because to do away with me
would have been to destroy a part of herself. It's either I or the
gnome, she said to herself, and finally she put an end to herself.
The gnome drummed her into her grave. Because of Oskar she
didn't want to live any more: he killed her."

    I was exaggerating quite a bit. . . . Most people blamed
Matzerath and especially Jan Bronski for Mama's death.
Bebra saw through me.

    "You are exaggerating, my good friend. Out of sheer jealousy
you are angry with your dead mama. You feel humiliated because
it wasn't you but those wearisome lovers that sent her to her
grave. You are vain and wicked—as a genius should be." (162–63)

Bebra is only partly right. Yes, Oskar is jealous and humiliated,
but beneath that he is desolate and guilty. He feels that he has punished his mother and driven her to her death, but he also feels that
she has rejected and deserted him, partly because he is a projection
of her worst parts: "Mama would throw me out with the bath water,
and yet she would share my bath" (154). Agnes is orally and sexually greedy. Oskar, like his mother, cannot control himself, cannot
control his drumming, his rage, and his vengeful behaviors. He feels
he has driven her mad. Yet to the degree that he is part of her, identified with her, and a projection of her poorly controlled greed and
impulsivity, he cannot help it. Furthermore, she has never really
discouraged his excesses (since they are part of her), and this makes
her desertion even crueler in Oskar's eyes.

    Oskar is deeply concerned about the monstrosity of the society outside of him (which gasses dwarfs and other freaks), the monstrosity within him (which longs incestuously for mothers and drives them to their deaths), and the monstrosity of women whom he sees as greedy, desperately needed seducers and abandoners. As the book ends, Oskar, reminiscing about his life, is preoccupied with a childhood jingle that runs through his head: "Where's the witch, black as pitch?" The mother who deserts, the mother he can neither forgive nor relinquish, is the black witch.

Brenda resembles Oskar. She chose a monstrous identity in which she saw herself as physically grotesque and behaved in ways that were emotionally controlling. In holding on to this view of herself she ensured she would remain attached to her childhood objects and would never have to give up these attachments for more mature and less omnipotently configured relationships.

CHILDREN MADE MONSTROUS

Brenda "chose" her negative identity because it suited her emotional needs. She couldn't imagine another way to be. In the next situation I describe, children sense that their parents need to *use* them as receptacles for unacceptable parts of themselves. This is a bit different from those instances in which the mother projects parts of herself into the child and blames the child for *what she cannot accept in herself.* In the kind of situation I am now talking about, the mother uses the child as a container for unacceptable impulses of her own, which she secretly values and *does not wish to relinquish.* In her mind she and the child are one, and the child's behavior satisfies her psychological needs. (This kind of mother is closely related to the vampyric mother that I address in the next chapter.)

Emily was the youngest of four children, by many years, born into a highly achieving family. For many reasons she was unable to keep up socially or intellectually with her older siblings. Marital problems between her parents led her to side with and identify with her mother, an intelligent woman who maintained a very appealing and functional social appearance that masked chronic envy and conflicts about real professional or creative accomplishment. Moreover, during her adolescence, Emily developed the first symptoms of a mood disorder. As a result of early misdiagnosis and the difficulty this high-achieving family had accepting such a mental disorder, Emily was not adequately treated during a crucial developmental stage.

Moreover, from early childhood, inadequate limits were set on her overexcited and rebellious behavior. Emily was asked, not told, what to do, often bribed and cajoled, indulged rather than regulated. Like her mother, she never saw herself as someone who would *have* to work. Nevertheless, she graduated from college, worked for a while, and eventually married a man who was very dependent and dysfunctional. They managed to get along, however, with considerable family help, and did adequately with their first child, Alan, a sensitive and compliant little boy.

Their second son, Robby, was a lively, active child with a mind and will of his own. His babyhood was easy, but from toddlerhood on, he reacted to the chaos in the household and the lack of needed and reassuring parental discipline. By the age of four he was very difficult to manage. His parents were unable to set limits with him, which led to more and more testing on Robby's part, just as it had during Emily's childhood. When the marriage fell apart a few years later, he became almost impossible to handle. With intensive psychotherapy for Robby, the situation became more manageable, but serious problems still remained.

Emily indulged her children as she had been and still wished to be indulged. In her unconscious mind, they were three children together, not a mother and two children. She projected into Robby, who for temperamental and psychological reasons "took" the projections, her wishes to do as she pleased. Tacitly, she encouraged his disruptive behavior, using it to get back at those she envied and feared, especially her family members, who were quite upset about the situation. Robby expressed the chronic anger Emily felt, and Emily enjoyed this arrangement. Alan, her older child, was more depressive and repressed in nature. He was a caretaker; he defended his mother and took over some of her responsibilities. He also suffered from psychosomatic symptoms, his way to express the anxiety and resentment engendered in a situation marked by the failure of parental competence and reassurance.

In the sense that they both "chose" negative identities, Brenda and Emily resemble Oskar. But Emily, like Agnes (Oskar's mother), expressed her own unruly and vengeful impulses through her son. Her inability, or unwillingness, to provide a sense of reality in the form of ordinary and reasonable limits made him constantly test and torment others, and this unconsciously gratified her, because they were not really psychologically separate.

Another literary case story of a child made monstrous, this time by being preferred to a spouse and overindulged, is depicted in Booth Tarkington's novel *The Magnificent Ambersons*. Isabel Amberson, the daughter of the most important family in town, is a delightful but proud young woman. She spurns her suitor, Eugene Morgan, whom she loves, because of his rowdy behavior while he is serenading her. She does so not because he was drinking at the time but because he was disrespectful. Her pride and sense of self-importance lead her to marry another man, whom she does not love. They have one child, Georgie. When Isabel discovers she cannot have another child, she pours into Georgie the kind of indulgent maternal "love" that turns him into a little monster that no one can control. He is, to use the old-fashioned term, thoroughly spoiled.

Isabel does not see herself as proud and self-centered, nor does she see these qualities in her son. Unlike Emily, she is not making Georgie the receptacle for parts of herself she secretly values. Rather, she uses him to make up for her disappointments in love. He becomes both son and "husband" to her. When, years later, Isabel's husband dies and Eugene Morgan resumes his courtship, Georgie interferes in a way that drives Eugene away and hastens his mother's death. Georgie knows he is more important to his mother than *anyone* else, and it is a knowledge that ruins him.

This kind of indulgent behavior toward a child is often the result of disappointment in the mother's emotional and erotic life. Her relationship with her child is not explicitly incestuous, but it takes on an importance that is both age-inappropriate and, paradoxically, depriving to the child who needs both discipline and guidance. There is a hidden form of maternal ambivalence in this kind of misuse of a child, and it is not uncommon. Because of marital strife and unhappiness, a child, boy or girl, is preferred by the parent of the opposite sex and sometimes used openly to cause jealousy in the spouse. This preference may be very gratifying to the child, but it inevitably leads to guilt and self-destructiveness when the child grows up, in the formation of adult relationships with the opposite sex. A mother (or father, for that matter) who was truly unambivalent about parenthood would not burden a child with too much stimulation and gratification and thus engender crippling conflicts later in life.

CHAPTER TEN

Vampyric Mothering

From Stage Moms to Invasive Moms

The spectrum of maternal ambivalence extends, as we have seen, from the normal occasional hatred of a demanding, inconsolable baby, a baby one otherwise feeds with pleasure, through various degrees and forms of maternal-child disturbance. At the end of this spectrum is vampyric mothering, which I consider to be, in its extreme forms, maternal ambivalence at its most destructive. I conceptualize this kind of mothering as having two divergent but frequently overlapping characteristics. The first is a feeding *from* the child to obtain gratifications the mother is unable to obtain in other ways. In its milder forms, this is the overly involved mother (the stage or soccer mom) whose narcissistic needs depend so much on her child's accomplishments and attachment to *her* that love of the child is always somewhat conditional on the mother receiving this kind of feeding. The second, more ominous form of maternal vampirism is a forcing of "food" *into* the child—food in the form of ideas, behaviors, allegiances, and beliefs, in particular, beliefs about the nature of human relationships—to a degree that may totally co-opt the child's autonomy, defeat creative effort, and lead to a paranoid view of the world. ("The only people you can trust are your blood relatives," or "The only person you can really trust is me. I know what the world is really all about.") This can lead to a level of emotional abuse in which the child's most basic needs and sense of reality are disregarded. Such mothers can literally drive a child crazy by invading their minds and wills, a form of poisoning. I assume the reader understands that these behaviors are found in fathers as well as mothers, but I feel that in fathers they are not viewed as *quite* so dangerous (perhaps erroneously) because of the mother's larger formative role in the child's early developmental life.

I refer to such behaviors as "vampyric" rather than as faulty or unempathic parenting because of the parent's need to *literally survive* psychologically through the child. Neglectful, obtuse, misguided parenting of any kind is damaging, but in such cases parental conflicts and motivations may lie elsewhere than in psychic survival, for instance, in split loyalties between child and spouse or between work and home, in powerful identifications with misguided parents of their own, in immaturity and developmental failure and a host of other phenomena. Vampyric mothering is more subtle and harder to recognize as it so often masquerades as special love and concern: "Nobody loves you the way I do, and therefore you must love me more than anyone else, even to the total exclusion of anyone else."

Emily's behavior resembled vampyric mothering in some ways but was not quite the same thing (see chapter 9). She did not particularly control her children's activities and accomplishments. While she wanted them to do well and to reflect well on her, she lacked the kind of unfulfilled ambition to achieve *on her own* that is often a factor in stage mothering. Emily did want her sons to share her views of other people but not obsessively—only enough so that they would not criticize her failures in mothering and in mature functioning. She was more interested, unconsciously, in encouraging their expression of envious and rebellious feelings, so like her own. In the sense that she gave her children the message that their maturation would be threatening to her, she compromised their development, and in this respect her behavior is an example of vampyric mothering.

BENIGN VAMPYRIC MOTHERING:
CAROLINE AND ELAINE

Caroline was a patient who illustrated the more benign kind of vampyric mothering—the soccer mom—in which the mother feeds from her child's accomplishments. A married woman in her forties, she came for treatment because she couldn't love her husband, had poor relationships with her family of origin, and had few friends. The one person she loved was her only child, Josie.

Caroline was born to parents whom she experienced as mean and withholding. As far back as she could remember, she had felt insufficiently fed and unloved. As a child she was overweight and obsessed by having enough food, which she would often steal. As an adult, she continued to steal and cheat in other, subtler ways. There was never enough of anything. Others were always getting what she felt she should have, so she felt justified in taking what she could. She felt mistrustful and envious, and she was aware of a wish to spoil the pleasure of others, a wish about which she was not happy. She had a hair-trigger sensitivity to any perceived criticism of herself or Josie.

Caroline felt her mother harbored crazy and magical ideas about food. She was always going on idiosyncratic, faddish diets and trying to get Caroline to reduce. Caroline felt that her mother attempted to control her body and viewed it as damaged and flawed. From

Caroline's point of view, the most painful flaw was the lack of love between her mother and her.

Her father was a disappointed and spiteful man who criticized and spoiled the pleasures of other people. He favored Caroline over her older brother, but she was terrified of any expression of love or intimacy with him. Perhaps she feared her mother's jealousy and the further erosion of their relationship that closeness with her father would produce. She carried these fears of intimacy into her marriage and her treatment. She denied any conscious need for her husband and for me, but it was clear that the opposite was really the case.

The one source of real pleasure and satisfaction in Caroline's life was Josie—"the best thing that ever happened to me," she said. Caroline lived through Josie. On the one hand, she devoted a great deal of interest in and support to Josie's every endeavor—in fact, to her every wish. On the other hand, she was constantly on the look-out for evidence of Josie being cheated, which she experienced very acutely as a wound to herself. Josie thrived on Caroline's interest but felt uneasy and pressured when her mother crossed the line from encouragement to anger and disappointment at any failing in scholastic or athletic accomplishment, or in obtaining popularity and power. When this happened, I suspect Josie felt she was depriving her mother more than herself. Caroline *was* concerned about her daughter's difficulty making and sustaining relationships with other children but was unable to acknowledge that either she or Josie had any role in this difficulty, which was intensified by Caroline's jealousy of others and Josie's sense of entitlement.

Caroline sought treatment because she was alarmed at her own anger, and she recognized that her attachment to Josie, at the expense of her marriage, was not healthy. She feared that her behavior might lead to a rupture with her husband, whom she needed, and—an even more disturbing thought—with Josie herself. Although she was very possessive of her daughter, she was genuinely concerned about Josie's welfare and development. She knew it would be damaging to Josie to not have a good relationship with her father. It would be a repetition of *her* unhappy past. Moreover, though she sometimes envied Josie's success, she didn't wish to spoil it but rather to fill herself up by feeding from it. She could, for instance, allow Josie her own ideas and choices. In the spectrum of vampyric mothering, Caroline's was not a pathological case. Although Josie would always be the emotional center of Caroline's life, she could see her daughter as a whole, other person and allow her enough autonomy to keep their relationship viable.[1]

In contrast to Caroline, who participated adventurously in Josie's life and thoroughly enjoyed her participation and Josie's pleasure, are those women who control their children's life in a *constrictive* way. Elaine was a woman in her late forties who sought therapy because her husband was losing interest in her. His waning interest was directly related to her overinvolvement in her ten-year-old child's life. Elaine had suffered repeated miscarriages before she was able to conceive her only child, Ilana. She felt her body had let her down, for she had wanted several children and it was now too late. It would not be unusual for a child so longed for to be very special to her mother, but Elaine's anxiety and overprotectiveness reached painful proportions. Rather than encourage Ilana's accomplishments at school and wish to participate in after-school activities, she was always supervising her, keeping her close to home, filling her with anxieties about the dangers of the outside world. Even the neighborhood swimming pool, a few blocks from home, with a lifeguard present, was not safe. During this period of Ilana's life, when peers are so important, friends were not encouraged.

Not surprisingly, Elaine had been an only child whose unhappily married mother kept *her* closely tethered. She recognized how much she had disliked her mother's overprotectiveness, which encouraged passivity and withdrawal from the world, but unlike many women who consciously strive to be different from their own mothers, Elaine ended up being much like her. Perhaps her mother had so thoroughly succeeded in frightening her about the dangers of autonomy that she could not do otherwise than repeat her mother's pattern. This kind of anxious overprotection is a subtle form of ambivalence in which the mother does not want the child (often a daughter) to have more than she had. This kind of mothering is more insidious and tinged with envy than stage mothering; the latter is so right out there that the child can recognize it and rebel. The message stage mothering conveys is "be active, succeed," not "stay home, be passive." However, neither of these two kinds of controlling motherhood is anywhere near as harmful as the form of vampyric mothering that I take up next.

MALIGNANT VAMPYRIC MOTHERING

This second and more disturbing profile of vampyric mothering is well portrayed in case stories from Bram Stoker's horror classic, *Dracula*, and from two modern novels, *Anywhere but Here* by Mona Simpson and *Other People's Children* by Joanna Trollope. I am proposing an interpretation of *Dracula* from the perspective of mother-child relations. Many *Dracula* interpretations emphasize the Count's perverse sexuality—his intense and ruthless orality—and the issue of possession, that is, the state of being undead—with its accompanying loss of identity and personal boundaries. I would like to add another reading that accounts, I believe, for much of the novel's horrific resonance. Implicit in Stoker's story are disturbing representations of the dark side of maternity in the form of greedy, monster babies and enthralling, vampyric mothers.

Unlike Dr. Frankenstein's monster, Count Dracula is feared not so much for how he *looks,* how he exaggerates, caricatures, and aborts the human form, but for the utter desperateness of his needs, to which both he and his victims are totally in thrall. *Dracula* addresses universal psychological concerns about basic survival, the fear of what happens when mothers cannot be counted on to provide what is needed, when it is needed.

Certain features of Bram Stoker's life suggest the imaginative origins of his novel. He spent his first eight years as a bedridden invalid, cared for by his mother, whose favorite child he was. The nature of his illness is not clear, but after eight years he apparently recovered and was able to become strong and active. As a long-invalided child, Stoker would have struggled with conflicts over weakness, passivity, dependence, and surrender, a surrender that may have taken on sexual meanings as he reached the Oedipal phase of development. Pleasure in these yearnings to surrender, as well as terror, could have permeated his feelings toward a mother who both cared for and saved him while she frightened him with stories about others who succumbed to contagion, weakness, and death (in the cholera epidemic she had witnessed during her own childhood in Ireland). Moreover, since children hold their mothers responsible for their bodily vulnerabilities, Stoker may have had the fantasy that she caused his illness and kept him weak. Fears of an overpowering, intrusive, and controlling woman are an undercurrent in *Dracula.*

In his twenties Stoker met Sir Henry Irving, a well-known and charismatic actor, described by friends as a "bloodsucker." Stoker was very taken with Irving, whom he described in the following words, suggestive of his later description of Count Dracula: "The awful horror of the blood-avenging sprite—eyes as inflexible as Fate—eloquent hands, slowly moving, outspread, fanlike."[2]

Eventually, Stoker became Irving's personal manager and spent the next twenty-seven years of his life serving him. He was clearly in thrall to the actor, but I suspect this situation allowed him to develop a compromise that seemed to work for him. There is no evidence that their relationship was homosexual, but it seems that Irving protected Stoker from women, the real danger. Stoker could gratify his unconscious wishes for surrender to a powerful and incestuously charged mother by transferring them to Irving and living them out in disguised form.

While the reality-based inspiration for the figure of the Count may be Henry Irving, I propose an earlier developmental theme in this novel—the Count as a condensation of vampire mother and vampire baby. But why vampires? What is it that is so fascinating about beings that survive by forcefully drinking the blood of living others, beings that are themselves "undead"? And what does it mean to be undead? I think this book is about desperate needs to become and stay alive and the quality of forcing into and taking, that is, *possessing*, where *willing* feeding is not expected. *Dracula* emphasizes over and over the need to eat and sleep for strength, states of weakness and recovery, and fears of contagion and contamination (as metaphors of possession), and these are certainly the concerns of a sick child but also the concerns of anyone in a vulnerable state of mind where basic survival is an issue. This level of vulnerability, of course, includes babies.

My view of the vampire fantasy as a condensation of mother-child bonding gone wrong begins, in a sense, with the blood that first nourishes the fetus through the placenta. At birth that blood becomes another warm, isotonic fluid—milk—that nourishes the infant who wakes at night and feeds. And the infant's urgent feeding may be experienced as ruthless, especially if exhaustion and inner conflict increase maternal ambivalence. Dracula, viewed as a monster baby, never moves beyond the stage of infantile ruthlessness, where desperate need leads to possession.

As a monster baby, Dracula makes women into bad mothers. When he vampirizes women he turns them into nonmaternal, sexual predators. When he vampirizes Lucy Westenra, a sweet, loving young woman, he turns her into the Bloofer Lady, who, as a vampire, now feeds *on* children, draining their life's blood. However, Dracula's ruthlessness may also be understood as a *projection* of maternal aggression *into* the infant. In the throes of maternal ambivalence (always present to some degree but most marked in postpartum depressive and psychotic states) infants are spoken of as mean and spoiled creatures, as bloodsuckers and parasites. In a way the infant's need and total dependence on the mother suggests that we may look at *Dracula* as a paranoid fantasy on the part of the *baby,* one whose function is to protect against maternal unavailability by ruthless pursuit. In this fantasy the baby is empowered to empty the mother whenever he can. Unlike a healthy mother-infant relationship in which the mother responds to the child's needs as they arise, the life of the vampire is restricted. His survival is not easy. He can feed only at night; he must work to find a victim; his fragile being must be protected during the day by consecrated earth. These arcane symbols of vampirism represent an uncertainty about nurturance that engenders defensive fantasies of omnipotence and ruthlessness. Count Dracula's unusual physical strength and supernatural powers of corporeal transformation illustrate these fantasies during his active nighttime state. During the day he is undead, and he makes those he needs undead, too. The undead don't age, don't die, and don't really live. It is a state of endless dependence and possession by another, a state that has to do not just with passivity and surrender but also, more specifically, with the inability to choose, change, individuate, and relate. The term *undead* describes, somewhat theatrically, the dangers of being possessed and controlled by a mother who both feeds *from* and puts poison *into* her child.

Several famous passages from *Dracula* will serve to illustrate the dual themes of vampire babies (the mother's view) and vampire mothers (the child's view). I start with the vampire baby. The Count in his undead daytime state is seen twice by his prisoner, Jonathan Harker, in his coffin of earth. Here is Harker's description of the first sighting:

> He was either dead or asleep, I could not say which—for the eyes were open and stony, but without the glassiness of death—and the cheeks had the warmth of life through all their pallor, and the lips were as red as ever. But there was no sign of movement, no pulse, no breath, no beating of the heart. . . . I saw the dead eyes, and in them, dead though they were, such a look of hate, though unconscious of me or my presence, that I fled from the place. (53)

This look of hate that terrifies Harker is that of a sated but passive and enraged child whose hatred is generated by his lack of power and control and is directed at all who are alive and necessary for his survival. Dracula, perpetually disappointed in his need for control over his sources of attachment and feeding, seeks refuge in vengeance.

In Harker's second sighting of the Count in his coffin, he is filled with a different kind of horror and loathing.

> There lay the Count, but looking as if his youth had been half-renewed, for the white hair and moustache were changed to dark iron-grey; the cheeks were fuller, and the white skin seemed ruby-red underneath; the mouth was redder than ever, for on

the lips were gouts of fresh blood, which trickled from the cor-
ners of the mouth and ran over the chin and neck. Even the deep,
burning eyes seemed set amongst swollen flesh, for the lids and
pouches underneath were bloated. It seemed as if the whole awful
creature were simply gorged with blood. He lay like a filthy leech,
exhausted with his repletion. (56)

Harker's reaction this time is more one of disgust than fear. Dracula has drunk deeply and rests peacefully, a caricature of infantile
satisfaction and bliss: rejuvenated, replenished, but seen as an ugly
engorged leech, as a monster. Here the earliest image of pleasure, the
sated baby, is depicted as a greedy corruption. Not dribbles of milk
but "gouts of fresh blood" run from his mouth. His cheeks are full
and rosy, but the feeling is unhealthy, unnatural—"the whole awful
creature," "a filthy leech."

I conjecture that Stoker's disgust was directed at himself, the
sickly child lying in his bed, fed and cared for but helpless and dependent on his mother, but this disgust goes further. The infantile bliss
of satisfied feeding is the first paradise lost. As infants mature they
are expected to be able to wait, to tolerate disappointment and discomfort. Disgust at what one once was, or what one once wanted, is a
powerful ally in defending against the wish for impossible pleasures
that can never be fully relinquished. Much as we may wish it, we
cannot be babies forever. In this second passage it is the regressive
infantile wishes carried to an extreme that Harker defends against
with disgust; in the first passage it is the fear of being rendered helpless in satisfying these wishes. In these coffin scenes we are shown the
"psychologically real" Count behind the powerful active figure he
shows to the world.

The third passage deals with the vampire mother, in the person of
Lucy Westenra. Lucy's story illustrates the tension between female

sexual desires and maternal yearnings, a subject of much concern to the Victorians who were the first readers of this novel. When we are introduced to Lucy, she is young, beautiful, innocent, admiring of men and engaged to be married. She is only dimly conscious of her sexual yearnings and flirtatiousness as she awaits her wedded state and, presumably, the maternity that will follow. As Lucy becomes a vampire, she also becomes blatantly seductive. When she seems to be dying she invites her fiancé, Arthur, to kiss her "in a soft, voluptuous voice" such as he "had never heard from her lips" (176).

Shortly after Lucy's death, reports begin to appear in the newspapers about missing children who wander away at night and later talk of meeting a Bloofer (beautiful) Lady. Some of the children have bite marks on their throats. Lucy's empty coffin is revealed, and she is seen vampirizing a child at night.

> A dark-haired woman, dressed in the cerements of the grave . . .
> bent down over what we saw to be a fair-haired child. There was
> a pause and a sharp little cry, such as a child gives in sleep. . . .
> [W]e recognized the features of Lucy Westenra . . . but yet how
> changed. The sweetness was turned to adamantine, heartless
> cruelty, and the purity to voluptuous wantonness. . . . [O]n Lucy's
> face we could see that the lips were crimson with fresh blood,
> and that the stream had trickled over her chin and stained the
> purity of her lawn death-robe. (230)

Upon seeing her fiancé, Lucy's eyes

> blazed with unholy light, and the face became wreathed with
> a voluptuous smile. . . . With a careless motion, she flung to
> the ground, callous as a devil, the child that up to now she had
> clutched strenuously to her breast, growling over it as a dog
> growls over a bone. . . . There was a cold-bloodedness in the
> act which wrung a groan from Arthur. (232)

Here is the idea of maternity perverted by sexuality that was so horrifying to the Victorians, and not to them alone. It is a more universal uneasiness with the intensity of unbound female sexuality, seen as totally incompatible with maternity. But it is also a horror at a maternity turned monstrous, one that feeds on children rather than feeding them, the mother as vampire.

The final passage I wish to quote involves the vampire mother again, this time in the person of Count Dracula. In this passage the most ominous aspect of vampyric mothering is shown in the forcing of "food" into the possessed child, in this instance Jonathan Harker's wife, Mina.

> On the bed beside the window lay Jonathan Harker, his face flushed and breathing heavily as though in a stupor. Kneeling on the near edge of the bed facing outwards was the white-clad figure of his wife. By her side, stood a tall, thin man, clad in black. His face was turned from us, but the instant we saw, all recognized the Count. . . . With his left hand he held both Mrs. Harker's hands, keeping them away with her arms at full tension: his right hand gripped her by the back of the neck, forcing her face down on his bosom. Her white nightdress was smeared with blood, and a thin stream tricked down the man's bare breast, which was shown by his torn-open dress. *The attitude of the two had a terrible resemblance to a child forcing a kitten's nose into a saucer of milk to compel it to drink.* (311–12; emphasis mine)

Later, Mina, describing her experience, admits, "Strangely enough, I did not want to hinder him. I suppose it is part of the horrible curse that such is, when his touch is on the victim" (326). The Count tells Mina that once she drinks of his blood, their minds will be in contact, and he will always know where she is. They will be merged. This merging is the most primitive and frightening level of anxiety expressed in this story, representing an annihilation of the self, of the sense of agency, cohesion, and autonomy.

When the Count forces Mina to drink from his breast, he becomes the vampire mother who forces her milk *into* the child. The child may experience withholding by the mother, or separation from her, as a persecutory experience; likewise, the sense of being forced, of having mothers who don't recognize their children's separate needs and wishes. Their milk is poison, a source of both longing and terror. In Mina's statement, "I did not want to hinder him," we see the conflict and confusion over a needed yet poisonous substance that makes it so difficult for the child to fight for autonomy.

An equally ominous profile of vampyric mothering, in a modern setting, is portrayed in Mona Simpson's chilling 1986 novel, *Anywhere but Here*. In this novel motherhood becomes the template for the expression of a disturbed personality. Adele August is a divorced mother with a teenage daughter, Ann, whom she uses as a twin, an extension of herself, a means of gratification, and a partner in crime and fantasy. On the surface *Anywhere but Here* is a sort of female road novel. The critic Walker Percy refers to the two women as "American originals" and to Ann as a "new Huck Finn." But I found this novel a dark and disturbing tale of vampyric mothering masquerading as "real total love" and "emotional closeness." Using these words, Adele, in the closing sentence of the novel tells us about Ann, "She was the reason I was born" (530). What this means for Adele is that Ann is as much her *mother* as her daughter. She feeds *from* Anne, denying her a separate emotional life or the opportunity to live successfully in the real world.

Adele sees Ann as an extension of herself, of her childlike, needy parts. She veers between inappropriate and intrusive "closeness" and sadistic indifference, keeping Ann from gratifying her teenage needs for privacy, friendships, a relationship with her father, even a stable home with normal furniture (her own bed, a desk at which to do her homework) and regular meals. During the long road trip that makes up most of the novel, Ann and her mother sleep in the same bed and eat the same food. "The thing about my mother and me is that when we get along, we're just the same," Ann says (9). They *have* to be the same; Adele is threatened by any manifestation of Ann's independence.

Ann tries desperately to love her mother and to see her as a reliable parent. Her painful ambivalence is expressed when she tells us, "Even if you hate her, can't stand her, even if she's ruining your life, there's something about her, some romance, some power. She's absolutely herself. No matter how hard you try, you'll never get to her" (17). Certainly, there is admiration in this observation, but Ann also means that Adele, in her need to have someone to merge with, doesn't really hear her daughter, doesn't acknowledge her daughter's needs and separate personality. "I didn't like being just with my mother all the time. You were alone but she was there. My mother must have felt that too, but I think it was one of the things she liked about having a daughter. You never were all alone" (31). Adele cannot be alone, and she cannot let Ann be alone either. She consistently spoils Ann's efforts at scholastic success and dating, and while this is bad enough, the most disturbing aspect of their relationship is Adele's incursions into Ann's private bodily life. In a harrowing scene Ann describes Adele giving her a back rub to help her get back to sleep. This is an experience that once was pleasurable but not anymore.

> The night my mother pushed my pajama top down off my
> shoulders and felt the soft hair under my arms, I became
> less than a baby, a blob, a primitive living thing she could do
> anything to as long as she fed me with tickles. She liked to pull

off the sheet, push down my pajama pants and pat my buttocks,
they clenched at her touch. She wanted to look at me and blow
air on my tummy with the full price of possession. She kissed me
on the lips and I shirked. When her hand reached down to the
elastic of my pajama pants, I stiffened and bucked away from her.
"Don't."

"I don't know why not," she said. "Why won't you let me look,
you've got such a cute twussy little patutie. Can't I be proud of
your little body that I made?" When she stared at me like this, it
seemed she could take something, just by looking. (344)

This abuse stops short of actual incest, but Adele uses Ann's body
as if it *were* her possession. Count Dracula needed to keep his objects
with him by merging with or invading them repeatedly, and this is
what Adele does to Ann, out of her own desperation and neediness.
The vampyric quality of Ann and Adele's relationship is symbolized
by their mutual fixation on certain foods—bloody meat and sweet
milk. Adele *must* have an ice cream cone nightly; both women crave
rare steaks and order them whenever they can. Eating big dinners,
with dessert, feeling satiated, obsesses both mother and daughter.
Furthermore, Adele's need to keep Ann from growing up, from moving on, from making choices is a way to keep her one of the "undead,"
robbed of her own life and living in thrall to her mother.

In another distressing scene, Ann is watching TV in the base-
ment. Adele becomes upset that she isn't watching upstairs with her.
She has a sudden psychotic moment when she accuses Ann (who is
about ten years old at that point) of moving her hips. "Did someone
fuck you?" she asks, becoming excited and persecutory. Desperately,
Ann runs into the bathroom and crouches in a corner, going into a
temporarily dissociated state. She is so invaded by Adele's excitement

and anxiety that she becomes paralyzed with fear and rage. After this violent encounter is over, Ann thinks about Adele as follows:

> She hates you. She hates you more than anything she is and she's tied up until she kills you, it's that deep in her. She will stay. And you know you have to get up. You want to close your eyes and be dizzy, let this blur dark, tasting the blood in your mouth, like a steak, and let her come back to you and touch you softly, lead you to your bed, tuck you in, care for you. (418)

Ann is describing the experience of being vampirized, the seduction of giving in. But she now knows that what passes for maternal devotion is really Adele's need to get what *she* wants through her daughter. And she also knows that Adele is envious and needs to spoil, destroy, and possess, as Count Dracula did with his vampirized victims.

When I describe Adele as a borderline personality, I am highlighting certain features of her mind and character. She is not psychotic (except temporarily, when her rage and anxiety become overwhelming), but her view of herself and others is suffused with totally unrealistic idealizations and devaluations. She splits her world into good and bad people, and people into good and bad parts that are never brought together and experienced as part of a whole person. Ann is either an evil monster or her mother's savior; she is never just a child with strengths and weaknesses, needs and vulnerabilities.

Adele cannot deal with ambivalence, the holding of mixed feelings toward herself or others inside herself with the understanding that both kinds of feelings can exist without destroying anyone. Adele longs for omnipotent power and the attainment of endless wealth and romance. Her sense that something is lacking inside herself fuels a neediness that is monstrous in its proportions. Adele cannot help

Ann grow up because she herself does not feel safe; her inner life is primitive and driven by fantasies of rescue by powerful parent figures rather than by a sense of her own abilities and resources.

Ann is eventually able to leave her mother. She has had very healthy and supportive relationships with her grandmother and her aunt, relationships that allow her to develop alternate internal models of adult womanhood on which to rely. Once she gets away, she is able to have some empathy for Adele: "The thing I keep thinking when I remember my mother, is how young she was" (491). In fact, Adele was not just young but emotionally unequipped to mother a child. In that sense she really did her best. Her overinvolvement, distorted as it was, was preferable to total disinterest or neglect.

What the outcome will be for someone like Ann, in later years, can only be imagined. I can see her struggle with the problem of her unconscious identifications with Adele, identifications that may lead to repetitions of her own experiences when she becomes a mother. But consciously, I would guess, she will try to be like her grandmother or her aunt. Like Rachel, who tried to be more like Rivke than Hannah, Ann, like many women, will have her struggles with the dark side.

In Joanna Trollope's *Other People's Children,* the mother, Nadine, keeps her children poor, cold, deprived, and indifferently educated as an act of revenge against their father and his new wife, who live in a comfortable and hospitable home. Nadine's three children are faced with the knowledge that their mother will consider them disloyal and damaging to her if they love their father or develop a positive relationship with their stepmother. Nadine knows she cannot manage without her children, but she maintains the illusion that they can't manage without her. When any of them confront her with her unwillingness to get a job, to live in a better place (she has *some* money), she flies into frightening rages in which the threat of her harming them, or herself, is always implied, although unspoken. She then bribes them with treats and protestations of their importance to her and of her importance to them. Like Adele with Ann, she treats them as if they are everything to her, or nothing—ungrateful, disloyal wretches. Her split inner world is filled with idealized figures and villains. The children become part of that world, for Nadine does not have the emotional capability to see them as children, to see what they need and how she deprives them.

Although there are differences between Adele August and Nadine, they both function at a disturbed level. Intense, changeable enthusiasms in the form of new projects, hobbies, and ambitions are their ways to recover from disappointments and deny their own failures, and to hold onto a fragile sense of who they are. Basic childhood needs for privacy, bodily care and comfort, stimulation and learning, friends and a dependable social environment are sacrificed to the mother's need to deny the difficulties of reality and to live in a fantasy world dominated by her own power. And in both cases the child (in Nadine's case, her eldest daughter, Becky) is the one who sets the limits and who refuses to sacrifice her life to her mother's needs. Another similarity in these two stories is that both Ann and Becky have a strong figure in their lives who, when allowed, provides good parenting. For Ann, it is her grandmother; for Becky, it is her father. After an especially searing fight with Nadine, Becky struggles not to have

> thoughts of her father, and how she wanted him to be there and how she kept remembering times when he was there, bringing with him a sense that not only were some things in life to be relied upon but that there were other things to be aimed for, striven for, which would bring mysterious and potent reward.

Without her father there, Becky had lost a sense of the future, a sense that round the next corner might be something other than just more of the same. (108–9)

Rescue through a relationship or identification with a sane and loving person can be lifesaving, in a psychological sense, for children such as Ann August and Becky. Vampyric mothering is a subtle form of child abuse. Usually, no real physical harm is done, but the erosion of the child's sense of self, sense of reality, and self-confidence can be devastating.

CHAPTER ELEVEN

The Darkest Side of Motherhood

Child Murder

Accompanying *Newsweek*'s July 2, 2001, shocking headline, "'I Killed My Children': What Made Andrea Yates Snap?" was a photograph of a smiling family: Andrea, her husband, Rusty, and their four young sons. At the time this photograph was taken, Andrea was pregnant with her daughter, Mary. On June 20, less than a year later, Andrea Yates, exhausted and suffering from postpartum depression and psychosis, drowned all five of her children.

The front page of the *San Francisco Chronicle* of Thursday, October 20, 2005, carried a story about Lashaun Harris, a twenty-three-year-old single mother who threw her three sons, ages six, three, and one, off a pier into the cold waters of the Pacific the afternoon before. All three drowned. Lashaun was suffering from untreated schizophrenia. In 1994 Susan Smith shocked the nation when she confessed to drowning her two sons in a South Carolina lake.

Child murder is big news. In these three cases all the deaths were by drowning. Of course, not all child murders are done in this way, but it strikes me that these mothers, totally unable to cope with mothering—in their lives, at that time—"chose" to return their children to a "womb," albeit a cold and deadly one. In their deranged and deadened states of mind, they could not care for the children but did not want to let them go, so they symbolically "reclaimed" them.

It would seem that child murder is the most extreme and shocking manifestation of maternal ambivalence we can imagine. Yet, curiously, it is more understandable and *perhaps* less terrifying than extreme vampyric mothering, where the mother survives by possessing her child's mind and will, creating a death-in-life. For, if we look at case histories, we can see that child murder is almost invariably the result of maternal despair about conditions in which it is impossible to raise children, at least, *for that particular mother, at that particular time.*

Child murder, especially infanticide, is as old as human society and found in all cultures. In a recent study of mothers who kill their children, Cheryl Meyer and Michelle Oberman emphasize that the crime of infanticide "is committed by mothers who cannot parent their child under the circumstances dictated by their unique position in place and time."[1] Historically, according to Meyer and Oberman, the factors attributed to infanticide have included poverty, illegitimacy, and femaleness, as well as maternal madness. By the twentieth century mental illness has moved to the forefront of causality as it has become clearer that child deaths occur where *both* social and intrapsychic conditions make mothering and parenting unbearable or impossible.

Newsweek used the occasion of the Yates tragedy to run a long article on postpartum depression in the same issue. This was followed by Quindlen's Last Word column, "Playing God on No Sleep," in which she talked about how mothers who would never resort to murder can still understand Yates's breakdown. Quindlen spoke of what all mothers know: "the love that is fraught with fear and fatigue and inevitable resentment" (164).

Three weeks later, in the July 23 issue, *Newsweek* carried fourteen letters from readers (selected from a much larger group) about their own experiences with motherhood and depression, expressing their understanding of Yates's dilemma and thanking the editors of *Newsweek* for bringing this widespread problem to public attention. The gratefulness of these readers, finally speaking their piece, is a reflection of the shame that surrounds postpartum depression. It is viewed as an aspect of maternal ambivalence and as such is surrounded by guilt and shame. *Good mothers don't become depressed.* But in fact they do, and their guilt and shame may prevent them from admitting the seriousness of their condition and getting treatment.

In 1922 England passed the Infanticide Act, creating a separate criminal category carrying a lesser charge—manslaughter—for women who kill their infants of less than one year. This act recognizes that infanticide is connected to the impact of pregnancy and birth on the mother's mental status and that this impact is a mitigating circumstance.[2] Hormonal and other biochemical changes, predisposition to depression, underlying personality difficulties, and difficult life conditions are all contributants to postpartum depression and its more serious manifestation, postpartum psychosis.

In discussing *Rosemary's Baby* I speculated that Rosemary suffered from a peripartum psychosis in which she saw her baby as the Devil. Women suffering from such psychoses may kill their children because they fear them as fiendishly monstrous and dangerous, but beneath this they may really kill to save the child from their *own* projected aggression and its potential damage. These latter killings are experienced by the mother as altruistic—with *me* as a mother, my child would be better off dead—and they are often accompanied by maternal suicide. This was Christine's fantasy in *The Bad Seed*. Christine's guilt doomed Rhoda, the personification of her own murdering mother. Then she doomed *herself,* first for carrying the bad seed and then for murdering her child. She saves others from Rhoda's ruthlessness—this is the altruism—but feeling deeply responsible for the death of her siblings, she cannot permit herself to survive either.

Andrea Yates's killings may have been partially altruistic. She certainly contemplated, and even attempted, suicide and indicated that she had been haunted by inner orders to kill her children, who (I believe) she felt were tainted by her own badness and hatred. As I think about her case, it seems to me such hatred was almost inevitable.

Andrea was the youngest of five children, a good girl and over-achiever, the daughter of a much-loved father who had high expectations of her. She married Rusty, another high achiever. Reading between the lines, he sounds demanding and rigid. For Andrea, motherhood represented another task in a lifetime of perfectionistic expectations. She not only had five children under the age of seven, but she home-schooled them, leaving no time for her own needs. Without help or much of a support system, this family was more than nuclear; it was totally insular. Furthermore, Andrea, a nurse by training, spent a substantial amount of time taking care of her elderly father, who suffered from Alzheimer's disease. He died in March 2002, shortly after Andrea's fifth child was born. She had suffered a serious postpartum depression after the birth of her fourth child and had been advised not to have any more children. Apparently, neither she nor her husband took this advice seriously. If God sent them more children, they would care for them. Andrea felt she could, or *should,* be able to do it all. Although trying to look functional on the surface, Andrea, already depressed, began to slip further after her father died. She became haunted with ideas about hurting her children and finally did so.

In her sensitively written book *Down Came the Rain,* Brooke Shields talks about her experience with postpartum depression. Shields, also a perfectionist (by her own admission), was deeply disappointed in herself for her difficulties becoming pregnant and for a less than flawless delivery. When she became depressed, she criticized herself further for not being the perfectly bonded and attuned mother she had anticipated she would be. But it was her beloved father's death, a few months before her baby was born, that pushed her over the edge. Astutely, Shields later came to recognize the role of incomplete mourning—a guilty preoccupation with the departed—in her failure to "fall in love" with her baby. In this situation, therapy and appropriate antidepressant medication led to a fortunate outcome.

Not so with Andrea Yates. In my opinion, more than loss of a beloved parent was involved. Andrea's efforts to care for her father, in the face of other overwhelming responsibilities, may have represented an intense and driven attempt to deny her hatred of him and of her five children, *all* of whom she experienced as making endless and implacable demands on her. Since these demands were also coming from *within,* they could never be fulfilled. Unconsciously, she must have wished for her father's death, and unconsciously, she felt responsible for it. Therefore, did the murder of her children contain elements of self-punishment (I don't deserve to have children)? Could unconscious incestuous wishes, which in her psychotic state became realities—that is, that the children were incest babies—have led her to murder the products of a guilty *imagined* liaison? Such ideas are too uncomfortable and unacceptable to ever find their way into a trial or a news story, but viewed psychoanalytically, when a mind *cannot* distinguish unconscious fantasy from reality, the results may be shattering.

I do not mean to minimize the element of isolation in Andrea Yates's life. It was extreme but also self-imposed. She and her husband both pursued ideals of self-sacrifice and self-sufficiency (bolstered by religious beliefs) that must have been hard for those around them to question. As Quindlen clearly points out, society expects mothers to do it all, and mothers come to expect it of themselves. And the right of a couple to have as many children as they like, whether or not it is good for the children, is never questioned. In *The Fifth Child* Harriet is punished for her child greed. In an even more tragic way, so is Andrea Yates.

MOTHERING IN TRAUMATIC CIRCUMSTANCES: TONI MORRISON'S *BELOVED*

I have never treated a child murderer in my practice, or anyone (to my knowledge) who ever seriously considered murdering a child. But I have certainly seen many women who feared they might hurt their children. Rachel, whose case I discussed in chapter 6, is an example of such a woman. Other women express anger at offspring with murderous words: "I could have killed her!" "I felt like hitting him over the head with a baseball bat!" And they mean it. But they don't do it.

In fact, I have treated patients who have lost children to illness and accident. It is the worst loss imaginable to the parent and to the therapist of that parent as well. Guilt is extreme. "I couldn't, didn't protect her"; "If only I hadn't let him go to that party"; "I should have seen the symptoms sooner, then maybe someone could have helped." The depression seems, at first, unyielding: "I will never recover from this." Parents who lose children do recover, but it is described as a loss unlike any other. For the child has not had a chance to grow up. The sense of thwarted possibilities seems cruel beyond words. In Anne Tyler's novel *The Accidental Tourist*, the protagonist, Macon, who has lost a son in a random shooting, is only able to come to terms with his loss when he imagines the son, Ethan, growing up in heaven, having those possibilities fulfilled *somewhere*. If the death of a child that could not be helped produces such suffering, what must it be like for mothers who murder their children?

If we factor out, for the moment, untenable social conditions, what are some of the *psychological* motivations and conflicts that lead to child murder? Newspaper and magazine articles tend to report on social conditions and maternal illness but cannot, for a variety of reasons, really do in-depth reporting. For one thing, these mothers are often very ill; for another, they are often imprisoned or in the hands of the legal system; and for a third, many readers do not really want to know. The response to *Newsweek*'s story about Andrea Yates was largely in terms of gratitude to the editors for their exposure of postpartum conditions and the suffering they cause.

Once again, literary case stories provide a rich field for the exploration of these extreme psychological situations. Of the many possibilities I have chosen two: *Beloved*, by Toni Morrison, and *Medea*, by Euripedes. Both dark and disturbing stories, they are, nevertheless, very different narratives. And in both stories, as in all cases of child murder, real or literary, there has been a traumatic rupture of the mother-child bond under circumstances of severe psychological distress and trauma.

I approach Toni Morrison's Pulitzer Prize–winning story with some trepidation. A stunning novel, mythic in quality, fantastical yet psychologically sophisticated, it deals with the murder of a child that seems so "justified" by conditions of external evil that analyzing it in terms of the dark side of motherhood feels like treading on sacred ground. For *Beloved* is primarily a novel about slavery and the emotional sequelae of a shameful national crime that damaged, debased, and humiliated African Americans for four hundred years, disrupting familial bonds and ignoring basic human needs in ways that still cripple its descendants. This novel, uncompromising in its exposure of the traumas resulting from slavery, is based on a true story.

Sethe, the mother of the baby girl called Beloved, is born into slavery. Her mother works in the rice fields and only nurses her for two or three weeks before having to turn her over to the black wet nurse, Nan, who feeds her after "the whitebabies fed." When Sethe's mother is killed, Sethe is sold to Mr. Garner, the owner of a small plantation in Kentucky called Sweet Home, where she is treated with relative kindness. At Sweet Home she cares for Mrs. Garner and at the age of fourteen "marries" Halle and has four children in rapid succession. When Mr. Garner dies, the plantation is taken over by his brother-in-law, Schoolteacher, a cruel man who humiliates and mistreats his slaves until, in desperation, they make a plan to escape. The plan goes badly awry, but Sethe is able to send her three children, Howard, Buglar, and Beloved (ten months old), ahead to freedom while she, pregnant and on foot, follows behind. During this harrowing trip her fourth baby, Denver, is born, but Sethe manages to get to Ohio, to the home of her loving mother-in-law, Baby Suggs (herself bought into freedom by Halle, her only surviving son), where for the first time in her life, she is free and has a "mother" to take care of her and her children.

One month later Schoolteacher and three other men (pursuing the infamous Fugitive Slave Act) come to take Sethe and her children back into slavery. In a state of hysterical desperation, perhaps even psychotic dissociation, Sethe attempts to murder her children to keep them from being taken. Beloved dies, and the other three children survive.

As the novel begins it is eighteen years later. Baby Suggs has died, Howard and Buglar have run away to fight in the Civil War, and Sethe and Denver live alone in a house haunted by the ghost of the murdered baby. Paul D., the only other survivor of the six slaves at Sweet Home, finds Sethe and banishes the "ghost," who then reappears in the flesh, as a strange eighteen-year-old woman who acts and talks like the baby she was when she died.

As Sethe gradually realizes that this young woman is Beloved, she vows to repair the terrible tragedy that has engulfed them both. But her attempts at reparation, which take the place of true mourning and recovery, do not work. Beloved cannot forgive her mother. She becomes more and more monstrous and demanding, draining and almost killing Sethe, until Denver and the women of the town drive Beloved away. Then Sethe, able to mourn, may take up the threads of her previously frozen and shattered life.

This is a selective synopsis of a very complexly layered narrative. I would like to speculate psychologically on some aspects of this story that concern traumatic destruction of the mother-child bond: the nature of Sethe's relationship with her own mother and its impact on her relationship with her own children, the way in which the murder illustrates the dark side of motherhood, and the place of mourning and resumed development in both Sethe's and Denver's lives.

Sethe's love for her children is powerful. Both Morrison the storyteller and Sethe herself, in confessions to Paul D. and in her inner soliloquys, insist on this "basic" truth about her. Her babies are all she has, her "best thing." She is not really allowed to marry Halle but rather to have babies with him, babies who will grow up and be sold away from her, although unconsciously Sethe denies this reality. Her babies belong to *her*. There are many references in *Beloved* to female slaves who refuse to become attached to their children, knowing they will lose them. Sethe's mother has had several babies (by white men) who she has "thrown away"—or refused to nurse. Sethe's father is black, and her mother loves him, so Sethe is cared for by her mother briefly and then by the wet nurse. So while her own mother cannot directly care for her, she looks out for her. Baby Suggs, once she is free, becomes a mother to Sethe and her entire community, but she cannot, or will not, remember her first seven children, all of whom were sold. Only Halle, her youngest, remained with her. In both real and symbolic ways, the mother-child bond among slaves was regularly and ruthlessly murdered.

Because the Garners are relatively compassionate slave owners, Sethe *is* allowed to take care of her own children, although she still has to work hard in both house and field. She is, in this sense, privileged but with the serious limitations of being entirely on her own in her mothering and of not being able to keep her children from being sold away. She later tells Beloved there was no woman to braid her hair or to help her learn to take care of a baby. Her children were backward in developing, but she is able to nurse them well, and this is of enormous importance to her. She was nursed herself, although there was never enough. "I know what it is to be without the milk that belongs to you; to have to fight and holler for it, and to have so little left," she tells Beloved (200). It is a source of great pride to Sethe that she is able to escape and get her milk to her baby girl, now safe with her grandmother. And when she arrives at Baby Suggs's home a few weeks later, Beloved has already learned to crawl, suggesting that with adequate time and maternal attention, everyone, Sethe *and* her children, will finally flourish.

It is not only an external mother that Sethe longs for but a good internalized mother-child image. She may "know" (having been told) that she is the only one her mother kept, but she has not *experienced* an ongoing relationship with her mother, one that would allow for the formation of a good inner sense of self and others that is based on more than fantasy. She tries to find a maternal relationship by nursing the ill Mrs. Garner as she would have nursed her own mother "if she needed me. If they had let her out the rice field, because I was the one she didn't throw away" (201). Sethe, in a sense, is like Beloved, clinging to her children as Beloved clings to *her* because safe and adequate mothering has not been possible to pave the way for further development. In Sethe's case, this further development would mean a mature relationship with Paul D. and the relinquishing of her children (Beloved, in fantasy; Denver, in reality) to their own lives. When Sethe says, in her soliloquy after she recognizes Beloved, "Oh, but that's all over now. I'm here. I lasted. And my girl come home," I read that as her longed-for reunion with the mother she knew about but never really *had*. And after a month of Baby Suggs's tender care (unconsciously another maternal reunion) the threat of recapture and the repetition of her original loss are so unbearable, so traumatizing, that Sethe breaks. She tries to murder the children to keep them from being retaken.

This brings us to the tragedy at the heart of the novel, the murder of Beloved. It is not even revealed until the novel's halfway point, but, in retrospective readings, it is implied from the beginning. The event that pulls together all the disparate and confusing pieces of the plot, it leaves the reader shocked—but not totally—as if the secret that must explain all this suffering has finally surfaced. The murder leaves *everyone* shocked. Sethe's neighbors, former slaves, all aware of the fragility of family relationships, the dangers of attachment, the stories of mothers letting babies die, cannot justify Sethe's behavior. Baby Suggs takes to her bed in grief but thinks to herself that despite Sethe's incredible courage and suffering in bringing herself and her children to safety, the men came into her yard anyway, and she "could not approve or condemn Sethe's rough choice" (180).

This murder seems especially horrifying because Sethe has had her children with a man she loved, who was recognized as her partner, even if not a legal spouse. She knew and loved them all; they were her source of greatest pride. They were not the product of shameful forced couplings with white men or black. Even more puzzling is that Sethe feels somehow she had a *right* to do what she did. Although shocked and grieved, she does not apologize, and it is for this pride (or seeming pride) that her community cannot forgive her.

Sethe says two things that make her decision to kill clearer to me as a reader and an analyst. The first is this: "I took and put my babies where they'd be safe" (162). And the second: "My plan was to take us all to the other side where my own ma'am is" (203). To the degree that such desperate behavior could have a plan, Sethe's was that of a murder-suicide that would free them *all* from slavery and reunite them with her mother. Her second statement comes as a response to Paul D., who, shocked when hearing of the murder, tells her that there *must* have been another way, that she has two feet, not four. Sethe thinks that

> though she and others lived through and got over it, she could never let it happen to her own. The best thing she was, was her children. Whites might dirty her all right, but not her best thing, her beautiful, magical best thing—the part of her that was clean. (251)

In these statements, Sethe is talking about two different wishes, her fantasy of safety and reunion with a *lost* object, her own mother, and her need to save her children, her *present* objects, from unbearable humiliation.

I see both these wishes as long-term denizens of Sethe's unconscious life. This must have been true for most slaves. (Spirituals, the musical heritage of slavery, are filled with themes of reunion with a powerful, mothering God, who will heal the body and free the soul, who will revenge the sufferer.) Sethe has found her mothering God in Baby Suggs, who represents both a lost maternal object and freedom from humiliation. Baby Suggs is a powerful figure in her community, dedicated to healing and the restoration of self-love and respect to her flock, and Sethe, as her daughter-in-law, has "the full benefit of Baby Suggs' bounty and her big old heart" (157). It is this bounty that earns Sethe the envy and resentment of her neighbors, who, in their lives of deprivation, also long for the mantle of protective mothering that has fallen on Sethe. To lose something one has longed for and finally obtained is more unbearable than never having had it at all. Sethe's fantasy of getting to the other side to her own ma'am is a means of restitution that nobody can *ever* take away again.

It is also an omnipotent fantasy. It gives Sethe, in her own mind, the right to kill her children (albeit in order to save them), and it is this claim that really drives others away. When Paul D. finds out about the murder, he thinks, "This here new Sethe didn't know where the world stopped and she began. . . . [M]ore important than what Sethe had done was what she claimed. It scared him" (164). Omnipotent fantasy is, among other things, an attempt to protect oneself from humiliation or even the possibility of it. In the sense that slaves were *really* powerless, what else but fantasy could they have? Yet what Paul D. wrestles with is the question of what right Sethe had to protect her children from humiliation *at the cost of their lives.*

This question leads me to consider, once again, the dark side of motherhood. One of the themes in this novel is the narrow and shifting border between maternal love and protection and maternal possessiveness and unconscious aggression. Sethe feels she *owns* her children, perhaps as she was owned, that their lives are hers. In her mind they must stay children forever, and she will love them forever. That way, perhaps, they will never be sold and she will never have to experience the loss that comes with their growing up. It would seem to be a case of too much love but a love that possesses and controls. In fact, what Sethe can't face is that she doesn't own her children, even in the ordinary sense that a free mother would. The murder is partly an attempt to omnipotently deny the reality of her total helplessness.

But there is more to the meaning of this murder. What Sethe cannot *consciously* experience is her anger at children who trap her and who get a love from her that she herself never had. Her desperation to get her milk to her baby girl is an attempt both to make up for her own deprivation and to prove that her children cannot survive without her, that she really loves them, and that she has some power and agency in her life.

Furthermore, Sethe had a mother, about whom she knows, a courageous and strong woman who nevertheless murdered her other babies by neglect and, in Sethe's experience as a neglected infant, abandoned *her*. As we saw in Mary Shelley's novel about an "abandoned child," self-blame, fear, and the need for revenge prevail. Sethe identifies with her mother, in fantasy, as one who murders and turns to her unconsciously, in her terrified and traumatized state, as one who saves. (Frankenstein's monster, too, identifies with the callousness of his abandoning parent, yet follows him to the ends of the earth, committing suicide when the doctor dies.)

One of the puzzling features of this novel is how marginalized the two older male children are. Sethe's mission is to reunite with Beloved. Although she talks about the boys, somehow they don't feel very important. Fearful of Sethe, after her attempt on their lives, and fed up with the spiteful and desperate antics of the "ghost," they disappear into the army and are not heard from again. I think the meaning of this marginalization lies in Sethe's deep identification with both her daughters, although she is preoccupied with Beloved. I see Beloved's anger as a projection of Sethe's rage as an abandoned, deprived child and a humiliated slave. Sethe, in her reparative attempts, cannot deny Beloved anything, cannot limit or discipline her, but can only indulge her.

In the absence of any maternal limits (a common form of ambivalence) Beloved becomes a monster-baby, a vampyric child, filled with rage, spite, and greed, and utterly devoid of concern for a mother who she now vengefully drains and almost kills: "Sethe was trying to make up for the handsaw. Beloved was making her pay for it" (251). Denver later comes to believe that Beloved was more than a ghost, implying that she was something evil. And as the victim of unconscious maternal hatred, masquerading as maternal love, Beloved *has* become monstrous.

But there is more to Beloved than a need for vengeance. She comes back as an eleven-month-old burdened by dreams of exploding (fragmentation) and of being swallowed (merging). She has not yet achieved any psychological separation from her mother, being too young. In her reincarnation she grows, but hers is a stunted growth in which she continues to feel she owns Sethe and is part of Sethe, but all the bad parts are *in* Sethe. It is Sethe's badness, not her own, that has led to the murder.

Perhaps Beloved's destructive seduction of Paul D. is also a desperate effort to separate and grow. She pleads with him to touch her on her inside part and call her by name. For Paul D. seems to represent growth, survival, and moving on, the possibility of a separate identity. He has withstood terrible suffering himself, but he wants to make a new life with Sethe. He immediately recognizes the sadness in the house created by the ghost and drives it away. He takes Sethe and Denver to a carnival, out into the world, and it is on the return from this outing that Beloved reappears. Sethe is not ready to let her go.

This brings us to the issue of pathological mourning, which is much of what this novel is about. Sethe tries desperately to not think about Beloved, to stay dead inside and not remember, but she fails. Beloved is always in her mind. In normal mourning, the lost person is relinquished bit by bit, and the sufferer, while not forgetting, gradually gives up the attachment and accepts the reality of the life she has following the loss. Sethe has not done this, nor has she let Denver move on with her life. They are both frozen in time. It is only when the townswomen drive the voracious and pregnant Beloved away that Sethe becomes truly depressed and real mourning occurs, freeing her to move on to a life with Paul D. Sethe has been seeking an impossible forgiveness from Beloved; now she has to forgive herself.

Denver, too, is now freed. She has been murdered in a symbolic way by Sethe's prevention of her growth and individuation. For years she has wished for her daddy's return. Unconsciously, she welcomes Paul as the agent of her freedom. When, as a child, she finds out about the murder, she is frightened of her mother and suffers from "odd and terrifying feelings" and "monstrous and unmanageable dreams" (102). Yet it is really Denver who saves Sethe, and herself. While Sethe, in her guilt, must think of Beloved as "her best thing," it is really Denver who is her best part. Denver has Sethe's courage, but having had a mother who raised her, however compromised the relationship, she *is* able to leave. Unlike Sethe, she relates to a live mother, not a fantasy, and unlike Beloved, she has developed enough to be able to long for separation and growth.

Mourning and moving on is an issue for all the characters in Morrison's novel (as it is for all women struggling with the dark side of motherhood). Their suffering has been terrible, and as former slaves, in 1873, it will continue, for generations. It is the horror of the murder and her own defensive pride that isolates Sethe and makes mourning, which in most situations has a strong social component, so difficult. For Sethe, the rallying of her neighbors to save her from Beloved, as well as Paul D.'s return, is crucial to her recovery.

. . .

I titled my discussion of Morrison's novel "Mothering in Traumatic Circumstances" to emphasize that breakdowns in mothering severe enough to result in murder, either "soul" murder or body murder, are the result of *unmanageable disruptions* in the conditions of mothering. Although in this work I am emphasizing psychological breakdowns in maternal functioning, traumatic social conditions contribute strongly to such disruptions. Under unbearable social conditions, some people are driven to acts of madness and extremity while others are able to endure, however great their suffering, without violating societal boundaries. In *Beloved* it is made clear that letting an unwanted baby die is an acceptable behavior in the face of forced sexual couplings and the inevitability of family breakups as part of life under slavery, but active murder, even if meant to "save," is not.

SPITEFUL MURDER: *MEDEA*

Horrifying as the murders discussed above are—although rationalized by "altruism" in the minds of unhinged mothers—the Medea myth arouses even more horror. Murder of one's children to punish a partner who has inflicted a narcissistic injury is the issue in the Euripedes play based on the myth. Medea, struck by Cupid's arrow, falls in love with Jason against her will. She is an enchantress and may fear the loss of her female power and independence in the state of being in love. At the cost of her brother's and father's lives, she helps Jason obtain the Golden Fleece. With their two sons, she and Jason flee to Corinth. Here Jason, in order to protect himself and his children, abandons Medea and proposes marriage to Creusa, the daughter of Creon, king of Corinth. Filled with rage at her abandonment, Medea causes the death of both Creusa and Creon. But this is not revenge enough. Despite her pain and grief and her own wish for death, she kills her two sons to punish Jason. She has been offered protection by Hegens, in Athens, but she neither avails herself of that protection nor chooses suicide. Calling the murder of her "dear sons" an "unholy deed," she tells the chorus, "But worst of all is to be laughed at by one's own enemies"(45).[3] Wounded pride and the need for omnipotent revenge overpower maternal feelings. "Rage will bite through reason's curb—how useless to know / that the worst harm comes to us from heedless wrath" (57).

The horrifying story of Magda Goebbels, who at the end of World War II murdered all six of her young children, is both an illustration of revenge and an illustration of murder under catastrophic circumstances, echoing the themes of *Medea* and *Beloved*. Magda was married to Joseph Goebbels, Hitler's minister of propaganda, who was a notorious sadist and philanderer. Although she was a dedicated

Nazi, she could not bear living with him, and in 1939 she attempted to escape from Germany, with her children. She was prevented from doing so by Hitler, who feared the negative publicity that would ensue from the failure of this "model" Nazi family.

As it became clear that Germany would lose the war, Goebbels and Magda decided to murder their children to prevent them from falling into the hands of the Allies, as the Russians advanced on Berlin. Apparently, Joseph changed his mind once the whole family was hidden in Hitler's bunker. Others had volunteered to protect and raise the children (all under the age of sixteen), but Magda, out of narcissistic rage at her husband's cruelty and infidelity, poisoned all six. Then, her revenge complete, she and her husband committed suicide. Like Medea, she had been offered protection for the children, but revenge was more important. Unlike Sethe, Magda's children would have been taken care of in a humane way, but like Sethe, she felt her children were part of herself, and in the face of the hysteria that prevailed as the Allies invaded Berlin, she took them with her.

Perhaps an unconscious need for revenge was a factor in Andrea Yates's situation also. Powerless to fight her own sadistic and demanding superego, frightened of the disapproval of her husband and his psychological predecessor, her father, she punished these two parental figures while destroying children into whom she had projected her own sense of badness. Yet with Andrea Yates and Sethe, both of whom slaughtered the innocent, there is not the *same* sense of horror as with Medea and Magda Goebbels. Perhaps sense of evil would be a better way to put it. Their losses were overwhelming, but *conscious* vengeance was their most powerful motivation, replacing mourning. Both knew they had choices that would save their children but wanted so desperately to punish their husbands that humane judgment was irrelevant. I do not think Andrea Yates or Sethe were capable, in the

204 / The Darkest Side of Motherhood

extremity of their suffering, of making a sane choice, and this is why, despite our horror, we sympathize with them.

A German psychoanalyst, Marianne Luzinger-Bohleber, has written about the Medea fantasy as an unconscious determinant in certain cases of psychogenic frigidity and sterility. She discusses a number of women who entered treatment with a fear of sexual passion and of bearing children. All these women had mothers who were depressed during their early years, and all reported disturbances in their relationships with their fathers during their Oedipal phases of development. All feared intimate relationships (like Medea resisting Cupid's bow). Sexual passion was associated with the danger of fusing with their love object, that is, of losing their separate identities. If deceived and abandoned, they were then, in their minds, disempowered and left at the mercy of aggressive impulses threatening to themselves and others. These women feared that out of female destructive rage, they would kill their children. Psychogenic sterility and frigidity became desperate solutions to their dilemma. Interestingly, successful outcomes in these cases were associated with *acceptance* of these disturbing aggressive impulses.

Luzinger-Bohleber feels that knowledge of the shadow side can stabilize female identity and the maternal function. An important factor in my treatment of Amanda was my nonjudgmental acceptance of her fantasy of babies as monsters (see chapter 4). The outcome in her case was not that she went on to have children but that her very demanding superego, a function of her identification with her father, was modified, allowing greater satisfaction in many other areas of her life. The monstrously demanding babies were really a projection of this punitive and demanding part of herself. Harriet Lovatt, in accepting Ben's monstrousness as a projection of her own greed and ruthlessness, was able to reach some peace of mind. I am in strong agreement with Luzinger-Bohleber that integration of the dark side of maternity into one's identity, as *an inevitable part* of the psychological experience of motherhood, is essentially therapeutic, reducing guilt, the need for self-punishment, and further fear, desperation, and rage.

The psychologist Susanne Chassay describes a chilling case of the failure to overcome maternal ambivalence in two generations, that of the patient toward her own mother and, later, toward her child.[4] This case is essentially a Medea fantasy with a perverse twist. The patient, Anne, was the only child of a depressed and controlling mother. Like Andrea Yates, Anne was depressed, passive, and enraged her whole life, despite outwardly good and dutiful behavior. She married a man for whom she had no passion and was unable to get pregnant, even with repeated attempts at in-vitro fertilization. She left her husband and traveled in Nepal, where she became pregnant during a casual liaison.

Anne was chronically suicidal, but during her pregnancy this symptom subsided and she began to write and feel some hope about her life. At first she was delighted with her baby boy, partly because he *was* a boy and not a devalued girl but also because of his lively personality and robust development. Mother and child did well during his infancy, and she was able to nurse him with pleasure. But when he became a toddler (and stopped nursing) she began to find him unmanageable, and things began to slip. She moved back in with her mother, and in the wake of the inevitable regressive feelings stirred up by this move, she rapidly went downhill. Escalating depression and psychosis ended in her suicide, exacting a terrible revenge on her own mother and leaving motherless the child she could not (in her mind) separate from herself.

This is a form of child murder in a woman suffering from what I referred to in chapter 1 as the psychosis of early child rearing. Anne suffered from psychogenic infertility. When she left her husband and mother behind, she became pregnant easily. When her child was the age she had been when she needed, and didn't get, maternal support for her own separate development, she became psychotic and killed herself and (unconsciously) her child. In reality, for a child this young to lose his only parent is to suffer an incalculable loss *akin* to being murdered. Infertility had protected Anne and her unconceived children from her envy, rage, and vengeance. A self-murder, unconsciously designed to punish both her mother and her guilty self, became the psychic slaughter of her innocent and abandoned son.

As I previously mentioned, the term *psychosis of early child rearing* is not an actual diagnosis in any formal sense. It is a term my husband and I developed to try to describe the experience in mothers (and fathers) of disturbing feelings stemming from their own early lives, stirred up by their empathic identification with their children, at different stages of development.

A less disturbing example than that of Chassay's patient came to my attention from a patient of mine, a husband describing his wife's breakdown when their second child was about four months old. His wife, also a second child, had endured a separation from her mother when she was four months old, due to the mother's illness and subsequent depression. She could not, of course, remember this period of her life, but she "remembered" it through her depression when her child reached the same age.

It is possible that many child murders are done in the grip of these kinds of disturbing feelings, which seem to come out of nowhere because the original traumatic events cannot be remembered. Are these murders an attempt to kill off the dangers of unbearable feelings that are breaking through? Is this part of what may have happened to Andrea Yates and Lashaun Harris? In their psychotic states were they unable to differentiate present feelings from those of the past, their own feelings from those of their children, or those of their mothers? I think it is possible.

ABORTION AND CHILD ABUSE

Abortion is felt by many to be a kind of child murder. I have never looked at abortion in this way but rather as an unfortunate necessity in many cases, lest something worse happen. When I was in college and medical school, abortions had to be obtained illegally. They were often dangerous, sometimes fatal. I knew such things happened, but it was still a pretty distant issue for me. During my fourth year in medical school, I was present at an emergency hysterectomy performed on a forty-two-year-old married mother of four who had become unexpectedly pregnant for a fifth time. This Italian Catholic woman, with few financial resources, had gone secretly to an illegal and probably disreputable abortionist.

A day later she started to run a fever. She was examined in the hospital Emergency Room and told to return if her fever spiked above 100.4 degrees Fahrenheit. Somehow, being frightened and feverish, she did not get these directions clear. She only returned to the hospital when her temperature was already above 104 degrees. By this time she was dehydrated and septic. Hydration and antibiotics were useless, and within a few hours she was having surgery and died on the operating table. Her family knew nothing of this disaster and had to be called in and notified. She left four children, not yet in junior high school, behind.

In my mind, this was not the murder of a child but of the child's desperate and overburdened mother. If abortions had been legal in

Connecticut at that time, this tragedy would not have happened. Certainly, this woman was ambivalent about the pregnancy—perhaps she had been ambivalent about some of her other pregnancies. She probably did not have access to birth control, or perhaps, as a Catholic, at that time, she felt it would be sinful to use it. If she had had this child, she might have been a loving mother, but the odds are she would have been overburdened and exhausted and highly ambivalent. Those who claim that abortion is the murder of a baby do not consider the fact that the ambivalence engendered by an unwanted birth may lead to a much more serious outcome.

For a year or so after my psychiatry training was finished, I did some abortion counseling as part of my private practice. Most of the women I saw were consulting me about their first pregnancy. They were young, unmarried, and, in some cases, without steady boyfriends. Generally, they opted for abortion. But I clearly remember one woman who could not bring herself to terminate her pregnancy, and I did not attempt to convince her to do this. I never attempted to convince women either way, just to hear them out and ask questions when I felt there were issues they needed to consider. Lucy was an artist, she was on her own, and she didn't have much money, but she decided to have the baby. Fourteen months later she came to see me with her delightful eight-month-old daughter. She was raising her alone, and they both looked very happy together. She brought me something she had made—a beautiful, celebratory, batik banner in yellow, orange, and purple. It looked for all the world like a giant vulva! Lucy's was a happy outcome.

The recently released movie based on Richard Yates's 1961 novel, *Revolutionary Road,* ends in a different key. In this tragic story the wife, April Wheeler, causes her own death by performing a self-abortion during her third, unplanned pregnancy. She is unwanted, the only child of a flapper and a playboy who divorced before April was a year old. She was raised by two aunts, neither of whom she loved or felt loved by. Having little in the way of good mothering experiences, April keeps her children clean, well dressed, and polite but shows very little evidence of being able to understand them or relate to them. Her ambivalence is largely unconscious and very profound. What little mothering these two children get comes from their father. The abortion, in this instance, is a suicide.

The most disturbing form of child murder, in my eyes, is that of children who die as a result of chronic abuse—starvation, beatings, exposure, neglect. The media thrive on these stories. Often the father or boyfriend is involved. A mother's pathologically strong dependence on a jealous and sadistic partner may erode her fragile positive connection to her child. Alcohol and drugs may play their part in loosening controls. Maternal immaturity, uncontrollable maternal aggression, and impulsivity all contribute to a form of the dark side of motherhood that, to me, is even more horrifying than are murders carried out in a state of psychosis or dissociation. Child Protective Services may rescue a certain number of these children, but far from all. And rescued or not, their suffering is long and tragic—children abused and neglected by the parents they depend on or separated from parents whom they love and need, despite their abusive behavior. As I have emphasized throughout, mothers need to be able to forgive themselves and move on, and children need to be able to forgive their parents as only human, but at this, the darkest end of the dark side, forgiveness may be impossible.

CHAPTER TWELVE

What Happens Later

The Fate of Maternal Ambivalence

I have explored the spectrum of ambivalence in motherhood from the bright to the dark side by looking at many examples, both clinical and literary. What is the fate of maternal ambivalence in the whole life cycle, childhood and beyond? What happens to mothers when children grow up and gain independence, leave home, develop careers, go to work, get married, and have children of their own? In this chapter I want to review some of the changes that can occur in the mother-child relationship in the more or less "normal" course of development. I emphasize both positive opportunities for growth and reparation and unfortunate outcomes of fixation within the mother, where development does not lead to a lessening in the negative side of ambivalence.

As we have seen, individual mothers struggle differently with the various stages of childhood. Some mothers have trouble with infancy, others with toddlerhood, still others with latency or adolescence. Toddlerhood and adolescence seem to be the most difficult.

Babies in the first year or two of life tend to be so delightful, friendly, and programmed to connect to their mothers that once the difficult, sleep-deprived early months are over, most mothers can relax and enjoy their offspring. Ambivalence is probably at its lowest ebb during this time, but it is *not* absent. For first-time mothers life as they have previously known it is turned upside down. Even when babies are deeply desired, the adjustments are challenging. Being confined to the house by the schedules of infants and babies may be trying for women who have been previously active in the world outside of the home. Career modifications are necessary but difficult to arrange, and marital strains are very frequent. Additional children increase the strains on mothers, although experience and familiarity with the needs of children tend to mitigate some of the difficulties. Hormones abound, creating unstable moods (baby blues) and, for some unfortunate women, full-blown postpartum depressions.

Postpartum depressions are a powerful and disabling threat to a mother's feelings of adequacy. Often a manifestation of an underlying mood disorder, they also occur in women whose confidence about their ability to mother has been derailed by disturbances in their early relationships with their own mothers. Perfectionistic expectations and the need for control make some women more susceptible to depression. Sometimes these conditions are precipitated by a serious loss in the mother's life during her pregnancy (e.g., Brooke Shields and Andrea Yates). Fortunately, postpartum depressions and psychoses (a more ominous situation) are treatable. Shields, who accepted treatment, recovered, developed a loving relationship with her child, and had a second child, without complications. Yates, who did not have treatment, had repeated postpartum depressions, ending in a drastic outcome.

Toddlerhood is a very difficult time for some mothers, in two ways. Those mothers who have treasured the warmth, gentleness, and dependency of infancy and babyhood may have difficulty tolerating the baby's independence as he or she now walks, explores, and destroys instead of cuddling. Other mothers find infantile dependence exhausting and draining. They are relieved when their children become able to navigate and play by themselves. However, this second group of mothers may have trouble when their "independence-seeking" children lapse into dependence and the need for reassurance, a typical occurrence during the "rapprochement" phase of separation, as elaborated by Margaret Mahler, Fred Pine, and Anni Bergman in *The Psychological Birth of the Human Infant.*[1]

Maternal ambivalence in early childhood is often "cured" by children's progress into later stages of development. For example, if a mother finds nursing onerous or fears she is inadequate as a feeder, her child's growth and ability to move on to eating solid food may release her from these anxieties. If more widespread underlying issues—disturbed body image, need for control—are at the root of the nursing problem, they may surface in different forms at later phases of the child's life. For instance, Phyllis, whose neatness and cleanliness contributed to anguished struggles with her son over toilet training, was not finished with control struggles as he grew out of toddlerhood (see chapter 7). The content of their struggles changed during latency and adolescence, when the battlegrounds were school performance and independence from his parents. Phyllis had been so much under her mother's thumb as she went through childhood that she could barely imagine another way to be. She had internalized the relationship with her mother and was now the dominating and controlling mother herself.

For many other mothers, latency, the period when children are in elementary school, is easier as children tend to be industrious and cooperative during this time. However, issues of achievement and competition are especially problematic for modern mothers, especially those of the middle and upper classes, who strive to enrich their children's lives in so many ways that neither they nor their children have much if any time for relaxation, imaginative free play, and woolgathering. Moreover, when the mother's unfulfilled ambitions are channeled into her children, their failure to perform adequately may be a source of maternal resentment and disappointment. Latency is also a time when peer relationships become very important, and there are mothers, like Elaine (see chapter 10), who are threatened when their children turn away from them to their friends. These mothers tend to be controlling, overprotective, and critical of the other children in their children's lives, and this resentment does not necessarily end when their children grow up.

In contrast to latency, adolescence is almost universally more difficult. Many parents cannot tolerate the rebelliousness and experimentation of adolescence, to say nothing of the mixed messages of separation and dependence. In these ways toddlerhood and adolescence have some commonality. Both phases of development are characterized by swings, back and forth, from dependent clinging to defiant separation. The difference is that in adolescence the dependency tends to be denied. Adolescents become difficult and critical of their parents. They act in a variety of ways that are disturbing, dangerous, and frightening. To complicate matters, they deny their needs for parental closeness and guidance, and there are many parents who believe that they mean it. It may lead to a kind of giving up on the parents' part, which is not what adolescents *really* want, no matter how loudly they protest otherwise.

Adolescent sexuality can be a major challenge to both parents. Pregnancy, rape, and drug use are the most obvious sources of anxiety. A more insidious problem, for mothers in particular, is that of the daughter's development into a mature woman. Some mothers do not handle their daughters' puberty well. These mothers tend to be women who have not been comfortable or fulfilled in their own sexual lives, or mothers, like Elaine, who are globally overprotective of their daughters and don't want them to grow up.

The first menstrual period is a major event in the lives of young women, and the impact of maternal envy and disapproval may be intense. I have treated several women who have reported hiding their first periods from their mothers. Amanda, for example, did not want to acknowledge that she was now a grown woman like her devalued mother (see chapter 4). And Caroline felt that her body was a source of unhealthy curiosity, worry, and intrusion by her mother (see chapter 10). Hiding her soiled underwear was a very temporary solution to her anxieties. Since the menses is accompanied by the acquisition of breasts and curves, these mothers are suddenly confronted with large, developed, and often beautiful daughters. The blow to their feminine vanity or insecurity can be acute.

Think of the number of fairy tales in which older women (often depicted as stepmothers) attempt to thwart the sexual growth and development of young women: the stories of Snow White, Cinderella, Sleeping Beauty, and Rapunzel all have in common the theme of a young woman having to fight and defeat an old crone, bad fairy, witch, or stepmother to grow up and marry the Prince. An example from my clinical experience illustrates how some of these issues, adolescent sexuality and autonomy, can manifest.

VICTORIA'S STORY

Victoria was sent to therapy by her parents because she was disrespectful and uncommunicative. I treated Victoria during her sopho-

more and junior years of high school. Her parents had been struggling with a hyperactive younger sister, Terry, who had serious school
problems and was in therapy. At first they assumed Victoria, who
got good grades and behaved herself, did not need treatment. Two
circumstances changed their minds. Victoria's mother developed a
chronic illness that interfered with her ability to work, and her daughter became inexplicably hostile and rejecting, claiming the mother
was using her illness (which was in fact rather serious) for attention.
Victoria also felt that her "bratty" younger sister was getting the
lion's share of parental attention and was furious at both her parents
about this. Increasing sullenness and secretiveness characterized her
relationship with them. Other than running up a large telephone bill
the previous summer, she hadn't done anything delinquent or dangerous, but she wouldn't give her parents the time of day. Even Victoria's
father, to whom she had been very close, realized she needed some
help.

When I first met Victoria, I was startled. I expected a sullen, angry
teen who would not talk to me. In fact, it took some time before she
would confide in me, but it was her appearance that was startling.
She was a slender, shy-looking, beautiful young woman with long
chestnut hair and fair skin. She was dressed in clothes that I can best
describe as twenty-first-century Victorian gothic: high black laced
boots, velvet skirts and jackets, frilly white satin or lace blouses,
antique jewelry—and they all looked terrific on her. It later trans-
pired that she had designed and made most of these clothes herself
but that her parents were very distressed about the way she dressed.
In my view, compared to the bare midriffs, short shorts, tight jeans,
and T-shirts of her contemporaries, she was a class act. Nevertheless,
she was engaged in a continual struggle with her mother over clothes
that her mother felt were too sexy and inappropriate. Victoria felt her

mother dressed like a middle-aged frump and wanted to dress her that way, too. As an outside observer I could experience Victoria's way of dressing as creative and charming. But her mother, who had been raised in a strict religious household and was struggling with illness and aging, resented and envied Victoria.

Both parents worried about their daughter's relationships with boys. Victoria *preferred* the company of boys, but her parents were missing the boat. She and her male friends clung together as a kind of out-group among their peers. They considered themselves different and better than the others, more intellectual, more interesting. None of them were really ready for sex, so they protected each other by seeming sophisticated. Victoria may have looked like a femme fatale, but she was actually somewhat innocent. She still needed her parents' interest and protection but could not admit it. Her antipathy toward her mother was actually based on an unconscious fear of losing her to illness. She told me she felt her mother was exaggerating and using the illness to control her. The mother fueled this antipathy with unrealistically strict rules about traveling, staying out late, driving with other adolescents—encroaching on Victoria's autonomy in many ways.

I felt this mother, whose health and looks had been compromised by her illness, was envious of her young, beautiful daughter. In sessions with the parents I emphasized their overprotection of Victoria and the way this contributed to the hostility between them. I also pointed out to them how truly creative, intelligent, and original Victoria was, including her choice of clothing. The outcome of these interventions was some shifting on both sides. Her parents eased up on the rules, and Victoria made increasing attempts to be civil. When last seen by me, Victoria was about to take a driver's training course, doing very well in school, and thinking seriously about a good college. Victoria's situation illustrates how an objective surrogate—me in this case—could appreciate the very qualities that so troubled her mother. I felt that this mother did not want to resent her daughter, but her earlier deprivations and precarious health made her envy very difficult to overcome.

On the bright side, maternal pride in a grown daughter who is close to being a mature woman herself is one of the deepest rewards of motherhood. Some mothers are terrific with adolescents, enjoying their idealistic, experimental, and creative attitudes toward life. I found my three sons delightful as adolescents—funny, inventive, industrious. I liked their girlfriends. I liked the way they painted the old gray Volvo sedan my husband and I bequeathed them white with large green spots—ignoring my concern that every policeman in Palo Alto would recognize their car. I have known many other women who found their teenagers delightful, despite the noise, mess, and high jinks. It is the burgeoning autonomy and budding sexuality that drives other mothers mad that these mothers so much enjoy.

Adolescence is universally somewhat difficult, but when the mother herself has had a troubled adolescence or is a troubled adult, her ambivalence may not be successfully resolved. This is a stage of development that can lead to permanent familial rifts. Adolescence precedes and overlaps with the time young people depart from home, whether for college, work, or marriage. Leaving home can ease troubled family relationships or worsen them. Moving on to the next developmental step is a healthy kind of leaving, as opposed to leaving because home is unbearable or unsatisfactory. In general, young people who have been overprotected, overmanaged, and overwatched are relieved to be on their own, despite bouts of homesickness. On the other hand, those teenagers whose early dependent needs were not sufficiently fulfilled may develop a kind of pseudo-independence that is really quite fragile. The psychological services of college student health centers are filled with students struggling with anxiety and depression in the face of this pseudo-independence. Shaky independence can also lead to dropping out of school and early impulsive marriages (and pregnancies), which may in turn break down. On the other hand, marriage and motherhood may also "grow people up."

Some mothers who have trouble during their children's adolescence may be anxious and helpless, unable to intervene usefully in any of the above situations. If anything, they generate further anxiety in already anxious teens. Other mothers (like Victoria's) remain overly involved, interfering with their children's autonomy at a most crucial time.

Marriage brings a new person and the new person's family into the picture. From the point of view of ambivalent feelings, marriage can be either a threat to a possessive mother or an enrichment of life for a mother who welcomes and comes to love her child's spouse. Since a spouse becomes a "sort of" child to his or her new family, the enrichment may be in the form of financial success, social status, a child of the missing sex (a man marrying into a family of girls, a woman into a family of boys), and, perhaps most important, someone of sound psychological makeup and good sense to enrich the family. Of course, the two families of a married couple may also engage in considerable competition, envy, and jealousy, a much less pleasant outcome. Mothers now have to share their adult children with the mothers of the spouses, and if there is jealousy, it may worsen as grandchildren make their appearance.

The attainment of career success on the part of a young person is generally a plus to any family, but it is another place where parental envy can rear its ugly head. If the mother has been disappointed in her own career aspirations, it may be very painful to see a daughter or daughter-in-law, even a son or son-in-law, achieve what she has not. Obviously, this is true for fathers also. Career success may be a double-edged sword for fathers. At the very ages when they are of great interest to their children, they may be too busy to spend enough time with them. This often contributes to marital unhappiness and worsens maternal ambivalence.

To summarize, the balance of positive and negative attitudes that constitutes maternal ambivalence will have a complex course as a mother develops through stages of adulthood. Psychoanalysts such as Freud and Erikson point out that development continues throughout adulthood, making such repair possible. New experiences of the child and of oneself can ameliorate earlier difficulties. As we have seen, a stage in the child's development that is hard for the mother may give way to a different one that is easier for her to handle, leading to a more positive feeling about herself and her child. On the other hand, painful, guilty, and traumatic experiences may be too powerful for a mother to overcome, creating continuing pathological parent-child patterns. Two examples illustrate some of these potentials.

NORA'S AND WENDY'S STORIES

Nora was a patient I treated when she was in her early twenties. She was a graduate student when she first came to see me, and she left treatment to go to professional school and became a psychologist. Thirty years later she called to give me the follow-up of her story.

Nora was an only child whose father had died when she was twelve years old. She and her father had been very close; his death was a terrible loss to her. Moreover, her relationship with her mother was very troubled. Nora's was a Snow White story, a mother envious of her daughter and competing with her in many ways ("who is the fairest one of all?"). Nora's mother never got over the loss of her husband. After he died, she was more envious of her daughter than ever. Nora was young; she had her life before her; she was an attractive woman. Furthermore, this difficult mother knew that Nora had been very dear to her father and could not forgive her.

Nora came to see me because her marriage, which was only a few years old, was in trouble. She had married early, to get away from home. For this reason, as well as the mother's envy, which led to criticism, spoiling, and "preferring" her son-in-law to her daughter, the marriage was probably doomed from the start. It ended while Nora was in therapy.

Nora described her mother as "wicked" and indeed many of the stories she told me of their interactions portrayed the mother as hypercritical and destructive. An example stands out in my mind. Nora was an accomplished violinist and had invited her mother to a concert by the college orchestra in which she was playing. Her mother's comment afterward was, "I could see you so clearly from where I sat because you were the *only* one bowing in the wrong direction!"

At that point there seemed little hope that this mother and daughter would ever work things out. What Nora told me in her follow-up call was that she had developed a successful career and was remarried, to a man with whom she was happy and comfortable. She now had a teenage daughter of her own. She told me she had gone to some trouble to heal the rift with her mother "for the sake of the family," and, indeed, her mother, given a second chance at mothering, came to love her granddaughter. She did an infinitely better job dealing with the grandchild than she had with her own daughter, and this led to some forgiveness on Nora's part. For this troubled mother, the chance to do it over, better, the second time was redemption for her own angry and conflicted mothering. She was aware of this and very grateful to her daughter for this second chance.

Wendy, a young woman who baby-sat for me when my children were young, is another instance in which maternal ambivalence—that of Wendy's mother toward her daughter—was lessened by grandparenthood. Wendy's mother had no recognition of her own ambivalence toward the three children she had within four years. It was all wonderful in retrospect. But, in fact, she was overwhelmed, and she failed to protect Wendy from her sadistic older brother. Mother and daughter became so antagonistic during Wendy's adolescence that Wendy finally left home and moved in with the family of a close friend.

In Wendy's mind, the relationship with her mother was impossible. Yet once Wendy got married and had children, the situation changed. Her mother adored her grandchildren and was very helpful to Wendy and her husband in caring for them. Wendy, having two children close together, could see how difficult it had been for her mother and could admire her mother's love and patience with her grandchildren. Without specifically talking it through, relationships in this family became friendlier and much more supportive.

Interestingly, there can also be a dark side of grandmotherhood, although this is less frequent and disturbing than the dark side of motherhood. A close friend confided in me that her in-laws never visited their grandchildren and showed almost no interest in them. I was even more shocked at this than I was to find out that some women did not want children. Not want grandchildren? Impossible! But it isn't.

For some women, becoming a grandmother means the end of youth, especially if the generations are close together. A woman of forty is considered young these days but less so if she is a grandmother. Today's generations tend to have less trouble with this aspect of becoming grandparents because women are having children later and grandparents are older. In fact, if parents have had children in their mid- to late thirties or early forties, which is increasingly common these days, they may not live to relate to their grandchildren or to see them grow up, especially if their children also wait to be parents. Becoming a grandparent at eighty has its drawbacks.

In some countries and social classes, grandmothers end up taking on all or most of the care of their grandchildren. Examples of this occur in poorer countries where mothers have to work and in families where there are unwed teenage mothers who have to finish school as well as work. In such situations, the grandmother, herself not very old, has to be a mother all over again. Although she has experience on her side and the mellowing that comes with aging, she cannot enjoy one of the best parts of being a grandparent—leaving the child with the parents when you have had enough.

As wonderful as grandparents can be, we have to keep in mind that just as maternal ambivalence stems from conflicts between the child's and the mother's needs, so, too, does grandparental ambivalence stem from conflicts between the needs of the parental and grandparental generations. I have seen this in my own generation and in myself. I have four young and delightful grandchildren, whom I do not see often enough, partly because they do not live close to me. I miss them and look forward to visits back and forth as bright spots in my life. I often think, and say, that if the children lived closer, I would have them over all the time. I would bake cookies, constantly. However, if I am truthful, I am still working and enjoying my work. I would have them over more often but not all the time. Furthermore, I have never baked cookies and think it unlikely that I would start now.

One of my good friends has several grandchildren from her eldest child but also two children recently out of college and not yet fully established in their lives. The parents of her two grandchildren frequently ask her to baby-sit, especially when the children are sick or when they (the parents) need a break. Both these young parents work. My friend is a loving grandparent, but she can take just so much time away from *her* work. Several times she has contracted colds or flu from baby-sitting the grandchildren when they were ill. She has had to put her foot down—reluctantly—about the limitations on the time she has available.

A final and important factor in grandparental ambivalence is not easy to admit. Little children are adorable and delicious, but they are very tiring. When my grandchildren leave after a visit, my husband and I are exhausted (and, I am sorry to say, a bit relieved). Of course, after a few days go by we are ready to see them again, even if it does mean reading *The Little Engine That Could* for the two-hundredth time.

There is a final life-cycle issue in which ambivalence plays an important role: the care of parents as the illnesses and the disabilities of age take their toll. We now talk of the sandwich generation, where older mothers are taking care of young children as their parents become elderly and in need of more care. Aside from considerations of space and money, a daughter's (or son's) willingness to take care of aging parents has a lot to do, consciously and unconsciously, with the nature of the relationship in earlier years. Have the knots of ambivalence and resentment been sufficiently resolved for children to take on arranging for and providing care with loving-kindness? Are they willing to have their parents live with or near them, or do they willingly visit them in the care facility they are living in? Or are the elderly parents stuck away somewhere, avoided and viewed with resentment, in some extreme situations becoming victims of elder abuse?

There are so many factors at work over the long course of a mother's life that we cannot predict in general, or for a given person, what will happen. In the next chapter I discuss some of the ways in which mothers can think about their own attitudes and seek help to alter the balance of their ambivalence in the positive direction.

CHAPTER THIRTEEN

What's a Mother to Do?

Recently I went for a walk with a colleague who talked to me about her patient Rose. Rose has one child, a daughter, whom she hates. My colleague is having trouble dealing with Rose's feelings about her daughter, as well as her own feelings about Rose. "She must feel like a monster," I remarked. "That's exactly right," my colleague replied. "That's *exactly* how she feels! How did you know?" I knew because I have been thinking about maternal ambivalence for years. The kind of discomfort Rose is enduring almost always accompanies feelings of hatred toward children, especially one's own. The mother fears her feelings are monstrous, and the child may well come to feel that he or she *is* a monster.

If this patient had hated her husband, her parents, her siblings, or the therapist herself for that matter, my colleague would not have been consulting me. She was troubled by her difficulty maintaining an objective, nonjudgmental stance. After all, she told me, Rose has not hurt her daughter, nor is this likely to happen. The patient came to treatment in order to understand her feelings and to deal with them the best she can. Troubled and guilty, she wants to feel differently, but the hatred is deeply entrenched. The daughter is difficult to manage; she is spiteful; she reminds the patient of her own mother and of their unhappy relationship. For the therapist, this is a situation that resembles many others with which she has dealt—with one exception, the entrenched quality of the hatred targeted at the patient's child. It is the degree of maternal aggression and rejection that makes it hard for my colleague to empathize with her patient's dilemma. I think she is very eager for Rose's feelings toward her daughter to change because the situation seems so unnatural. But what if the result of the treatment is not that Rose comes to understand her deepest feelings and develop some affection for her daughter but that she (at most) learns to minimize damaging behaviors in their relationship, much as Eva Khatchadourian did with her son, Kevin. It is not a happy outcome to contemplate. And yet it happens.

Maternal ambivalence in its most extreme forms, the dark side of motherhood, is today's crime that dares not speak its name. It seems to be even worse as we begin the twenty-first century. As I noted in chapter 1, there has been an increasing idealization of motherhood since the Enlightenment. Today it is accompanied by vastly increased expectations of what constitutes good mothering in every area of infant and child care: eating, sleeping, play, and education, as well as emotional, social, and intellectual development. And all these expectations exist in the context of fewer extended families and a rising divorce rate, not to mention the desire of women to work, for a variety of economic and emotional reasons.

How do women do it at all? All the inbuilt instinctual behaviors that allow other mammals to feed and protect their young until they are able to manage on their own are of limited usefulness to a species in which infancy and childhood last so long and in which higher brain function allows for consciousness of what you are doing. You cannot trust your instincts if you think about them too much. And today's women, especially middle- and upper-middle-class women, who tend to be the people I see in my clinical work, certainly do a lot of thinking, a lot of reading, a lot of talking to friends, and a lot of worrying. Women from lower socioeconomic groups also do plenty of worrying about their mothering, but their choices are so much more limited by their economic situation and the social problems they face—employment, housing, health care, and education—that they don't have the luxury of choice that comes with a comfortable middle-class existence.

At the present time educated women, having made great inroads in the professional and corporate world, are discovering that day care centers and nannies, good and caring as they may be, are not the same for them or their children as their own presence. Many of these mothers are returning to the home. In *Are Men Necessary?* Maureen Dowd, talking about the demise of "alpha" women in the workplace, fears that they will become "alpha moms, armed with alpha SUV's, which they drive in an alpha, over-caffeinated manner down the freeway while clutching a venti skim latte. They're equipped with alpha muscles from daily workouts and alpha tempers from getting in teachers' faces to propel their precious alpha kids" (104). Dowd goes on to describe a Comcast TV channel developed by a former vice president of a large financial firm that is targeted at mothers who want to do their best for their children. Dowd describes this as "Alpha Mom TV." "They'll be told what to do and what not to do and how to do it better." These mothers will discover how to boost their newborns' coordination and strength. They will learn massage that will help their babies eat and sleep better. They will hear "research-based explanations of how children separate and attach" (105). Nothing need be left to common sense and imagination, and everything will be done just right.

Dowd wonders if the children raised in this way will become "scary alpha children who refuse to do as they're told." As an example, she cites a 2005 *New York Times* story that talks about the proliferation of picky eaters among toddlers. Apparently, they would rather eat French fries than green vegetables. Why is that news? Toddlers have always been picky eaters, but parents have not always been *so* obsessed with correct eating. In Dowd's view, women who have been disappointed in the work world, finding they still were secondary to men, have taken on mothering with the same aggressive spirit. I think it is more complicated than that.

Not all mothers who are so eager to follow the rules and do it right were once highly paid executives. Parenthood has always had its anxieties and rules, because, oddly enough, it doesn't come as naturally as we think it will. Some mothers seem to be naturals. For others, motherhood is more of a struggle. And, as I mentioned earlier, higher brain functioning produces its own problems. Consciousness, memory, and rational thinking lead to awareness of the consequences of one's actions and of the inevitability of the life cycle. Consciousness means knowing about the problematic feelings that may arise in mothers and their children as they interact. And it means being aware of the possibility of physical and mental illness and death. What other species knows it will die, that its children might die, and that there are things they can and cannot do to prevent the latter tragedy from happening? What other species understands the relationship between what you put in and what you get out? How can mothers just do what comes naturally (as animals do) when they are burdened by the awareness of consequences? Women's awareness of the inevitability of mixed feelings toward their offspring makes it even more urgent that they "do it right."

Advances in the understanding of human development are occurring at a rapid rate. Psychoanalytic research in child development, parent-child relationships, and attachment theory, as well as progress in the neurosciences, has vastly increased our understanding of how human beings function, both individually and socially. Some recent changes in recommendations for good parental behavior stem from this more sophisticated understanding. But, given parental anxieties about child-rearing, these higher standards bring other problems in their wake. For example, friends of mine, psychologically sophisticated people, were lectured by their daughter, a new mother, about the importance of "attachment parenting" in the development of infant and child security. They were given to understand that if they did not let their grandson sleep with them (when they were baby-sitting) it would interfere with his sense of security, possibly forever.[1] What did children do before attachment parenting came on the scene? They slept in their cribs. Surely they didn't all grow up insecure, nor do all children who are "correctly" reared grow up secure.

The biological, social, and psychological strains of pregnancy, childbirth, and mothering are enormous and, I believe, more under-rated than we are willing to admit. It doesn't always go as naturally or as easily as we wish. So of course mothers cling to every possibility of doing it right. But trying to do it right is, in itself, less of a problem than feeling that one must *love* doing it right. Conflict between the needs of the mother and the needs of the infant and child is the major source of maternal ambivalence. And maternal ambivalence is a major source of anxiety and guilt to mothers. And this anxiety and guilt leads to efforts at reparation that further interfere with the satisfying of reasonable maternal needs, needs that are already eroded by the more pressing neediness of infants and children. It would seem to be a vicious cycle, and it certainly leads to a lot of undue suffering.

I believe that women who want to have children also want to be good mothers, and I believe that most of them try as hard as they can. But every mother is also the person she is, with the temperament she was born with and the early experiences she had with her own family and society. And every child is born with some inbuilt temperament and genetic endowment, although with enormous brain plasticity and capacity for development. It is this capacity for development that can make child therapy a more hopeful venture than that of adults, where character and neurological structure are more fixed. But this does not mean that problems with mothering cannot be helped. If this book is anything, it is a strong plea for measures that can ameliorate *maternal* suffering, as well as that of children.

I believe that the place we, as a society, have to start is with the recognition of the enormous pressures mothers face and the normality of the wide range of feelings they experience toward their offspring. We have to start with the recognition that there are many different ways to mother, that each mother-child unit is unique. We have to recognize that humans, social and flexible beings that they are, follow fashion in all areas of their lives; but when the passion for fashion invades child-rearing practices, to the exclusion of common sense, it can be a recipe for disaster.

One of the saddest aspects of the decrease of extended families is the loss of the influence of experience and common sense, something that the older generation has acquired, even as it loses its strength and vitality. Is this a plea for the involvement of grandparents? It certainly is. Grandparents, aunts, uncles, and others, relatively uncluttered with the powerful emotionality of the mother-child unit, can often see solutions and alternatives.

In chapter 2 I mentioned a study I did in medical school about ways in which first-time mothers learned about infant care. I found that lower-class women tended to find out about babies from friends and family members. Middle- and upper-class women learned from friends and family, too, but also by reading. Is one way better than another? I'm not sure. Through imitation alone, lower-class women may perpetuate poor child-rearing practices—using sugar as a bribe, TV as a baby-sitter, or excessive corporal discipline. But upper-class women have their foibles, too, which are just as likely to be imitated. They may apply perfectionistic standards to otherwise reasonable practices—never giving a bottle if breast-feeding, insisting on proper nutrition at *all* times and in defiance of strong childhood preferences, pushing educational achievement as if all children were alike—and thereby end up driving themselves crazy in their devotion to "doing it right."

The cover of the May 16, 2006, *New Yorker* magazine says it all. It shows a young woman pushing what appears to be a large, plush "throne on wheels." The throne is loaded with packages, and the woman is wearing an enormous backpack, equally loaded. On closer examination we can see that these packages are baby toys and pieces of baby equipment. In the middle of the throne, a tiny head peers out. This picture needed no explanation in 2006. This is how a "good" mother takes her baby for a walk in the park.

It is not the *New Yorker* alone that publicizes the foibles of modern parenthood. Rebellion against the demands placed on parenthood, motherhood in particular, has been around for a while but is beginning to pick up momentum. On April 13, 2009, Oprah Winfrey began a week of shows on the topic "The Trouble with Motherhood" in which women with a variety of issues aired their stories. "We hear from mothers all the time who say they feel alone. They feel overwhelmed; they feel sometimes inadequate. And you say you're afraid to admit the truth for fear of being judged," Oprah says. "So today we're creating a judgment-free zone, a sisterhood of motherhood where anything goes." When Oprah goes after an issue, its time has come!

Fortunately, most fathers are not so concerned with doing it right. We hope they are concerned with doing it *well*, but this does not always involve such perfectionistic standards; therefore, they are often able to be more relaxed about their parenting, except, naturally, where their children's sports performances are concerned.

The psychoanalyst James Herzog, who has written extensively about fathers, posits a crucial set of functions that the father performs in the family, which he calls the "paternal principle."[2] The father, he believes, affirms the reality of age differences between generations and the reality of gender differences and diversity in the family. The mother, who falls in love with her baby in the grip of "primary maternal preoccupation,"[3] may forget that she is also a woman and a wife. She may wish her husband to become a second mother—what Herzog calls the "Mr. Rogers preference." There is little room in this preference for adult sexuality, and it is up to the father to make a bid for the needs of the adult couple, separate from those of the infant and child. To quote Herzog:

> In the face of this important dynamic, the father is called on to remain grounded in his adult sexuality and beckon his wife to join him in that realm even as she may experience dramatic shifts in her own libidinal life. . . . [T]his groundedness of the father and his capacity to manage the mother's need for both a second mother and a father/spouse, even while she may think that she needs only the former and is not currently interested in the latter, is, I suggest, a hallmark of good-enough masculinity and paternity. (56)

Many a marriage founders as mothers put their children's needs ahead of their own and that of their spouses, and it only becomes worse as more children join the family. Fathers keep alive the positive images of the sexual components in the marriage and the more assertive aspects of caregiving at a time when the major pressure from mothers is for nurturance, support, and protection of the baby. It is the father, after all, who tosses the baby up in the air, to the baby's delight and the mother's horror.

Although I am not writing about paternal ambivalence (a subject that merits another book), it is important to recognize how much the father's mixed feelings about his children impinge on his wife. Many men have their first (perhaps their only) affair in the aftermath of a child's birth, when their wives fall in love with their children and relatively out of love with their husbands. In such a case the father is not standing up well for the "paternal principle," but his wife's blind love for her child and anxiety about its welfare may make her unable to listen or respond to her husband's needs.

Fortunately, as children get older, the father becomes more important to them, and the husband's wounds of exclusion have a chance to heal. He feels he has broken into the exclusive mother-child bond and has found his own rewards in fathering. However, disagreements between parents about child rearing occur all through childhood and are certain to intensify ambivalence in both parents toward the child as well as each other. Adolescence is an especially loaded time as generally predictable children turn into large, impulsive, disobedient, and hormone-ridden strangers.

In the absence of extended families, more common in the middle and upper classes, friends tend to fill the gap. Mothers' groups and play groups form part of the missing support system previously provided by the mother's sisters, her maiden aunts, grandparents, and, in the days of large families, the older siblings of her younger children. On the one hand, today's peer resources are invaluable for support and the experience of universality: other mothers struggle with the same issues. On the other hand, peer resources present the serious problem of reinforcing worry and self-criticism, as all the members are of the same generation and struggling with the same impossible standards. An acquaintance confided to me that only once did her very helpful mothers' group take up the issue of "the dark side of motherhood." "And," she told me, "we all felt so guilty, we never could go back to it." Furthermore, there is no one in these groups to provide an intergenerational perspective and to raise questions from another viewpoint. There is no one to say, "We never had all these after-school activities and all this parental supervision and involvement, and we learned to read and write and think and imagine, and, furthermore, we grew up to be pretty decent people."

A most important element in both the production of ambivalence and its relief is the mother's wish/need to work or to otherwise engage in pleasurable and creative activities apart from her children. The number of available activities is large, and each mother has her own set of needs, wishes, and priorities. Even if we look askance at some of these activities—excessive shopping, compulsive reading, exercising to the point of anorectic skinniness, even extramarital affairs—the mother still faces the problem of how to balance her needs with the needs of her children. And to assume that a woman does *not* love her children if her needs outside of the home are frivolous, or even dangerous, is both a mistake and a form of subtle class-ridden snobbery.

Whatever outside activity the mother longs for, she faces two major issues: finding good child care and managing her conscience, which produces its own particular brand of torture when it comes to any manifestations of maternal ambivalence. Of course, the more the mother has to work for economic reasons (i.e., in order to be able to take care of her children in the first place), the less likely she is to be guilty and ashamed. She may be anxious, regretful, and even depressed about having to leave her children, but her conscience is less likely to punish her, especially since the alternatives—homelessness and starvation—are so much worse.

Child care is too large and complex a subject to be dealt with in summary; it is a book of its own and has been several times written. However, from the vantage point of my interest in maternal ambivalence, I would like to make a few observations. Good child care, if it can be found, may produce its own problems. Mothers want the best help they can get, but what if the nanny, day-care worker, or babysitter gets to spend more time with the child than the mother does, and what if that person is also more patient and more loving? What's a mother to do about her envy, if that's what she experiences? (Some mothers experience relief.) Fire someone the child loves, and then embark on another difficult search for the right person? The search will be hers alone because, for a society that claims to privilege its children as much as we do and also expects so much of mothers, we do precious little to encourage the profession of child-care worker, or the profession of teaching for that matter, by providing the good pay and societal respect that would lead people to seek such work.

We don't get good marks for our treatment of mothers in this country. The failure of our government to provide support for general health care extends to the lack of support for women on maternity leave. Maternity leave, as well as child care, is considered a private matter. For the government to be asked to provide these services is dubbed socialism—what you would expect from such "leftist" countries as Holland, France, Denmark, Sweden, and other enlightened societies.

Good maternity leave, legal abortions, and a wide spectrum of available and competent child care services are ways in which government services can ease the conditions that worsen maternal ambivalence. A less obvious but also important need is for changes and improvements in the public school systems in this country. Although the following two phenomena may not be related, it seems to me that as public schools have deteriorated in quality, parents have invaded them with an overinvolvement in their children's schooling that takes up time and energy and is stressful for teachers and children, as well as parents. There was a time when schools were for children and teachers alone. There were PTAs, and parents were expected to get their children to go to school and to inspect and sign their report cards, occasionally to volunteer to go on school trips.

Now parents are involved in every aspect of schooling. Children do not go to school or return home by themselves. Parents take them. Parents help them with the excessive homework they are given from kindergarten on. The whole atmosphere is one of pushing children to succeed, of testing, of expectations that are often unrealistic. Boys and girls alike are taught to read in kindergarten, even though it is clear that many little boys are not ready until the first or second grade. Yet the quality of teaching has clearly declined. It is not a respected profession. My mother was a schoolteacher in the New York City public school system when I was growing up in the forties and fifties. She and her many schoolteacher friends were highly intelligent and well educated—women who today might have become lawyers and doctors. This is not to say that teachers today do not work hard. They do, but they are underpaid, and this sometimes keeps the best and brightest from undertaking this profession. Furthermore, the excessive competitive pressures on children and parents lead to endless after-school activities that take up parental time and leave children very little free time. All this tension-creating activity worsens maternal ambivalence.

To return for a moment to child care, there is also a hidden problem in the mother/child-care person dyad that is insufficiently recognized. In the unconscious fantasies of many mothers the child-care person is also *their* mother, come to rescue them from overwhelming responsibilities and feelings. And, in the unconscious fantasies of many child-care workers, their employers are *their* parents, as well as the parents of the children for whom they are caring. So, often the mother has to take care of the nanny in order for the nanny to take care of the children. If it works as a trade-off, there doesn't have to be a problem. Sometimes a mother does better taking care of a somewhat infantile adult than she does taking care of a totally infantile infant. I think it is the failure to realize this tension in the mother/child-care person dyad that can lead to unworkable situations.

These complex wishes for nurturance are both unconscious and shame producing. After all, we are all supposed to be grown up, to no longer need parents. In my work as an analyst I find that uncovering unconscious wishes or fantasies that evoke shame is one of the most sensitive issues in treatment. Patients work very hard to keep such thoughts unconscious.

So what *is* a mother to do? This brings us to the whole issue of treatment. Let's assume we now understand that maternal aggression, the negative side of ambivalence, is inevitable and ubiquitous. And that we agree that it leads to much suffering, in the form of anxiety, depression, shame, and guilt, in both mothers and their children. And, furthermore, that it is the conflict between the mother's needs and the child's needs that leads to ambivalence. The final assumption that *I* am making is that this painful issue can be ameliorated in a variety of ways, if women can come to accept that their feelings do not make them unnatural pariahs, unfit to be mothers, unfit to be part of the human race.

Perhaps the best way to explore this is to review some of the mothering issues that spark ambivalence and talk about treatment alternatives that may be useful. To begin with, once I became aware of conflict about *having* children, I began to see it all over. It makes me wonder what I may have missed in the past. It was not that I was unaware that some mothers were more uncomfortable than others about motherhood, but I think I was not fully aware of how hard a subject it was for these women to talk about.

Amanda was the first patient I treated who told me *outright* she was frightened and ambivalent about having children. She opened the door for me on this issue. She made me aware that some women are better off without children. Although this may seem self-evident to many readers, it wasn't to me. My awareness of the intense psychological, biological, and cultural forces compelling reproduction, driven in part by evolutionary necessity, led me to ignore the powerful and self-preservative forces that lead some women to choose *not* to have children. For example, Anne, whom I discussed in chapter II, was driven to madness and suicide by her unconscious reliving of her disturbed early relationship with her mother, now aroused by her own maternity. It is, of course, impossible to say whether she would have survived if she had not had a child, but her ambivalence (demonstrated by her previous psychogenic infertility) was deeply entrenched. Furthermore, it seems to me that this child *might* well have been better off not being born than he will be having had a mother whose suicide left him abandoned so early in life. That is, perhaps Anne's ambivalence about having a child did have a self-preservative element.

In my experience, to have or not to have children is best addressed by intensive psychotherapy or psychoanalysis. In using these two terms, I am describing particular kinds of treatment. It is based on the premise that much human unhappiness and difficulty in close relationships stem from three sources: early childhood experience, traumas that may occur throughout the life cycle, and the paradoxical capacity of the human mind to *not know*—to keep unpleasant or frightening thoughts and fantasies out of consciousness, even as human behavior is deeply motivated and shaped by these same unconscious thoughts and fantasies.

Therapy based on a psychoanalytic understanding of behavior does not rely on advice or modifications of behavior, useful as these techniques may be in some circumstances. Rather, it seeks to uncover and understand what is unknown to the patient, to help the patient "know" herself, as well as to relieve painful inhibitions and feelings and to facilitate more rational life choices.

Psychoanalytic psychotherapy and psychoanalysis are both based on these assumptions. The difference between the two forms of treatment is that psychoanalysis involves a greater frequency of appointments (four or five a week) than psychotherapy (one to three appointments per week) and the use of the couch. This use facilitates a state of reverie that leads to the ability to associate and allows for the emergence of unconscious material.

Support groups and talking with friends, spouses, family, and other professionals—for example, pediatricians, obstetricians, nursing advisers—all have their place. They are very important resources but are unlikely to get to the level of unconscious fantasy that we saw previously in Amanda, Sandra, and Priscilla. All three of these women feared the destructive potential of children as well as their own aggression, and this kind of material is rarely exposed in more casual settings. Chodorow, in her article, "'Too Late,'" points out two important factors in women who seek therapy in connection with conflicts about having children. They are deeply unaware of their aggressive wishes and fantasies about prospective offspring, and they deny the passage of time. I have come across these same factors: Amanda sought therapy at thirty-five, Sandra at forty-two, and Priscilla at forty-eight. They all waited until it was "too late." None of these women had been infertile in the years when conception was possible. Their treatment actually became an attempt to understand *why* they had unconsciously made childbearing impossible, so that they could be more at peace with themselves concerning this issue.

Shorter therapies, such as crisis intervention, which may go on for a month or two, are indicated when women need to make short-term decisions, such as whether or not to have an abortion, or when they are unduly worried about pregnancy or childbirth or some aspect of infant care, such as breast-feeding. Leslie, a patient I discussed in chapter 7, came to see me because she feared she would have a postpartum depression after she delivered her baby. She responded very positively to a brief therapy that carried her through her delivery and the first three months of her child's life. Of course, brief therapy may become a longer-term treatment if the situation is not ameliorated.

If a postpartum depression or psychosis does occur, medical and psychological intervention may make all the difference. Adequate psycho-pharmacological treatment is a must to stabilize a very distressing symptomatic picture, and psychological treatment is extremely important for understanding the elements of fear and ambivalence that accompany the breakdown, as well as the antecedents that may have touched it off. Shame about having this condition may lead to reluctance to expose it. This is extremely unfortunate, because the odds of such intervention being helpful are quite high, and it makes a big difference to both mother and baby if the situation is gotten under control quickly. Having one postpartum depression does not mean that the mother shouldn't have another child. But, as in the case of Andrea Yates, increasing depressions following childbirth are a good reason to seriously reconsider having more children.

Motherhood is an enormous developmental task, and for each woman some parts are more difficult than others. The first baby is the hardest, the one most worried about. Newborn infants are totally helpless, and their new mothers are exhausted from what is, usually, the most difficult labor they will have. Every cry, hiccup, and shudder may arouse anxiety. In this phase of life, family members, friends, nurses, and pediatricians can be enormously reassuring. The most serious parenting disorder during this time is the occurrence of postpartum depression. For the most part, however, new mothers fall deeply in love with their babies and weather the first month or two of exhaustion and confusion about the baby's signals of distress, ending up feeling that they and they alone *really* understand their babies.

As I pointed out in chapter 1, women can handle their ambivalence by taking the blame on themselves *or* by blaming their children. Guilty mothers are more willing to seek help of all kinds, from the La Leche league and visiting nurses to couples and family therapy to intensive psychological treatment. Angry, blaming mothers are too ashamed of their feelings and too threatened by the prospect that the blame will be turned back on them to seek treatment easily. When they do, they are often reluctant to admit the full extent of their negative maternal feelings. Generally, these women are more troubled and less amenable to supportive measures than are guilty mothers.

I want to emphasize, once again, that the more passing the problem between mother and child, the less drastic the treatment needs to be. It is really when the mother's ambivalence reflects a deep-seated

242 / What's a Mother to Do?

issue of her own, one that preceded children but worsens under the strains of motherhood, that stronger measures are needed.

Sometimes problems between mothers and daughters occur when the daughter becomes a mother. In chapter 10, on vampyric mothering, I spoke about Caroline, who felt that her own mother envied her new motherhood and tried to spoil it by stimulating anxiety about the baby's welfare. In mother-daughter relationships characterized by envy, anything the daughter gets may be deeply resented by the mother and lead to attempts at spoiling. It is counterintuitive to think of the older generation envying the younger, but it is often the case. The loss of youth, beauty, and reproductive capacity is more than some older women can tolerate.

For some mothers, a daughter's motherhood is a final declaration of independence; if independence has been hard to tolerate in toddlerhood and adolescence, it may be intolerable at this juncture. But, happily, for *most* mothers, a daughter's motherhood is a source of great pleasure, as it confers on them the almost universally enjoyed status of grandmotherhood. Now mother and daughter are both grown women who have shared the experiences of pregnancy and childbirth and will go on to enjoy the shared experience of mothering. Grandmotherhood can be a redemptive experience for a previously troubled mother-daughter pair. It is so much simpler to be a grandmother; helpfulness and wisdom come so easily. A grandmother may be able to heal rifts and resentments between her daughter and herself. In fact, daughters often take a second look at their mothers when they see them as grandparents. A final addendum to the case of Rachel is that her mother, Hannah, turned out to be a terrific grandmother, and in later years Rachel herself took to grandmothering with an ease and lack of anxiety that had been missing during her troubled years of motherhood. And the experience of grandmotherhood allowed Rachel to further reconcile with Ethan, her eldest son. He could now recapture, through observing her care of his children, some of what had been good in her parenting of him. He could learn from her and in seeing how much she loved his children, more deeply understand that she had loved him also, that the positive side of her ambivalence had prevailed. And this is all we can ask of any mother.

NOTES

PREFACE

1. For an in-depth analysis of the relationship between literature and psychoanalytic theory, see Meredith Skura's 1981 book, *The Literary Use of the Psychoanalytic Process.*

CHAPTER ONE

1. Orenstein, quoted in Hayt, "Admitting to Mixed Feelings about Motherhood."

2. Illustrative of the idealization of childhood in the Victorian era are the number of classics written for children during this time, e.g., *Alice's Adventures in Wonderland, Little Lord Fauntleroy.* The late Victorian era became known as the golden age of children's literature.

3. Child labor laws were passed at the end of the nineteenth century and the beginning of the twentieth in the United States.

4. Putting babies to sleep on their backs to avoid SIDS is current practice. Thirty years ago they were put on their tummies to sleep to avoid aspi-

rating (getting vomit in their lungs) should they spit up. Aspiration can lead to infant death.

5. Hrdy, *Mother Nature.*

6. Winnicott, "The Capacity to Be Alone," 420.

7. Winnicott, "The Theory of the Parent-Infant Relationship," 594; emphasis mine.

8. Lamott, *Operating Instructions,* 59.

CHAPTER TWO

1. Rich, *Of Woman Born,* 81.

2. For further discussion of envy and hostility, see chapter 12.

3. The biological explanation for the increase in female sexual response is the increase of vascularization in the labia during pregnancy. Psychological factors have more to do with women's increased confidence in their female sexual and reproductive capabilities following childbirth.

4. "Transference relationship" refers to the nature of the feelings and relationship that develop between therapist and patient. The patient unconsciously equates and experiences the therapist as she experienced important others early in life. It is the difference between these early memories and fantasies and the reality of the present live relationship that is therapeutic.

5. Modell, "A Narcissistic Defense against Affects."

CHAPTER THREE

1. Mother Goose, "The Old Woman Who Lived in a Shoe."

CHAPTER FOUR

1. A brilliant cinematic rendering of the effects of maternal loss on a young child is *Ponette,* a 1996 film by the French director Jacques Coillon in which a four-year-old child loses her mother in a car accident and turns to her doll,

Ponette, for comfort. The child's anger, depression, and guilt are painfully and accurately rendered.

2. Quotation from Shelley, *Frankenstein*, xiii.

3. Shelley, *The Journals of Mary Shelley*; quoted in Mellor, *Mary Shelley*, 32.

4. Mellor, *Mary Shelley*, 41.

5. Hill-Miller, *My Hideous Progeny*.

6. Percy Shelley sometimes used the pen name Victor, the first name Mary Shelley bestowed on Dr. Frankenstein.

7. In *Mary Shelley's Frankenstein*, Kenneth Branagh's cinematic version of the novel, Frankenstein's mother dies in childbirth. Branagh's plot changes reveal *his* interpretation of Shelley's authorial motive, one with which I agree.

8. Raphael-Leff, *Pregnancy: The Inside Story*.

9. This letter is quoted in Hill-Miller, *My Hideous Progeny*, 56.

10. Psychoanalytic theory, especially early in its development, stressed the importance of "penis envy" in the psychology of women. It was only later, when the importance of the mother-child relationship was more universally recognized, that "womb envy" was considered a factor in male psychology. Interestingly, it has never gained the kind of recognition and use that penis envy once did. I believe this has to do with the power and mystery that surround female reproduction. The concept is too threatening and feminizing.

CHAPTER FIVE

1. Obsessional rituals such as hand washing and other symptoms of obsessive-compulsive syndrome have been understood in psychoanalytic theories as efforts to defend against aggressive impulses, fantasies, and wishes that may take the form of unconscious longings to damage and soil.

2. Sybil's surgeries were especially unfortunate in their timing. At six to eight months most babies experience stranger anxiety, a sign that they recognize their mothers and fathers as their source of nurturance and safety and are distressed when they disappear. The kind of anxiety that would have afflicted her at eighteen months has to do with the development of

ambivalence and her recognition that she is a separate person from her mother whom she both wants to be close to and separate from. The anxiety at the age of five has to do with issues of bodily integrity and harm. Sexual curiosity and anxiety characterizes this phase of development, the Oedipal phase.

CHAPTER SIX

1. Nine months to a year was an average time for a depression to abate in the days before modern antidepressant medication was developed. Rachel's relationship with her therapist was crucial to her recovery, but medication would have greatly shortened her period of acute suffering.

CHAPTER SEVEN

1. Note the resemblance in this description of Ben to Frankenstein's monster: ugly, sloping forehead, heavy hunched look. There are other resemblances, in particular, Ben's enormous strength and his envy, if it can be called that, of the other children, normal and loved.

2. *Sublimation* is a psychoanalytic term for the transformation of drives, such as the sexual drive and the aggressive drive, into acceptable forms and activities. The ability to sublimate is part of growth and the development of ego strength.

3. This study is described in Daniel Stern's 1985 book, *The Interpersonal World of the Infant.* In addition to recognizing the smell of mother's milk, newborns also respond to the mother's voice from the very beginning. They have heard it in utero.

4. Bowlby, *Maternal Care and Mental Health,* 67.

5. Dissociation is a defense against anxiety in which thoughts and memories are cut off from the feelings that normally would accompany them. Christine cannot let herself know what she feels about Rhoda until the attempted murder of Leroy shocks her into memory and full consciousness.

CHAPTER EIGHT

1. Huet, *Monstrous Imagination.*
2. Arthur Miller's 1953 play, *The Crucible,* takes on the Salem witch trials. One of the characters, Rebecca Nurse, a kindly older woman and midwife, is accused of causing stillbirths and miscarriages. She is found guilty and executed by hanging.
3. This is a form of dwarfism in which the head and torso are normal in size, but the limbs are very short. The actors who played the Munchkins in the movie *The Wizard of Oz* were achondroplastic dwarfs.
4. For more examples of healing relationships in novels, see Almond and Almond, *The Therapeutic Narrative.*

CHAPTER TEN

1. In other words, Caroline's object-relatedness was far enough advanced that she did not merge with her daughter or force her but rather used her as a source of narcissistic feeding, as long as Josie was willing.
2. McNally, *In Search of Dracula,* 140.

CHAPTER ELEVEN

1. Meyer and Oberman, *Mothers Who Kill Their Children,* 2.
2. Meyer and Oberman, *Mothers Who Kill Their Children,* 13–15.
3. Slavitt and Bovie, *Euripedes,* 1: *Medea.*
4. Chassay, "Death in the Afternoon."

CHAPTER TWELVE

1. Mahler, Pine, and Bergman elaborate four stages in the development of separation and individuation between infancy and the age of three. In their view, infants begin with a symbiotic relationship with the mother before

separation and individual identity develop. Awareness of separation marks the end of the first phase and leads to separation anxiety at around six to nine months. The beginning of the child's forays into the environment (the "love affair with the world"—phase two) is marked by great enthusiasm and a sense of omnipotence. As the child gradually becomes conscious of its own separate status and individual identity, there is an upsurge of anxiety that it is no longer part of mother and could lose her. This is called the rapprochement subphase, lasting from about eighteen months to three years. It is marked by both the need to do things by oneself and the equally strong need to check that mother is still there. This can be a rocky time for many mothers. The fourth phase, object constancy, is well established by three years.

CHAPTER THIRTEEN

1. Sears and Sears, *The Attachment Parenting Book.*
2. Herzog, "What Fathers Do and How They Do It," 56.
3. Winnicott, "The Capacity to Be Alone," 420.

BIBLIOGRAPHY

Almond, Barbara. 1963. Social class differences in sources of information on infant care. Thesis in fulfillment of M.D. degree. Yale University School of Medicine, New Haven.

———. 1990. A healing relationship in Margaret Drabble's novel *The Needle's Eye*. *Annual of Psychoanalysis* 19: 91–106.

———. 1998. The monster within: Mary Shelley's *Frankenstein* and a patient's fears of childbirth and mothering. *International Journal of Psychoanalysis* 75: 775–86.

———. 2007. Monstrous infants and vampyric mothers in Bram Stoker's *Dracula*. *International Journal of Psychoanalysis* 88: 219–35.

Almond, Barbara, and Richard Almond. 1996. *The Therapeutic Narrative: Fictional Relationships and the Process of Psychological Change*. Westport, CT: Praeger.

Almond, Richard. 1989. Psychological change in Jane Austen's *Pride and Prejudice*. *Psychoanalytic Study of the Child* 44: 307–24.

Austen, Jane. 1982 [1813]. *Pride and Prejudice*. New York: Washington Square Press.

Bettelheim, Bruno. 1976. *The Uses of Enchantment*. New York: Alfred A. Knopf.

Bowlby, John. 1952. *Maternal Care and Mental Health*. Geneva: World Health Organization.

Chassay, Susanne. 2006. Death in the afternoon. *International Journal of Psychoanalysis* 87: 203–17.

Chodorow, Nancy J. 1978. *The Reproduction of Mothering*. Berkeley: University of California Press.

———. 2005. "Too late": Ambivalence about motherhood, choice and time. *Journal of the American Psychoanalytic Association* 51: 1181–98.

Chodorow, Nancy J., and Susan Contratto. 1982. The fantasy of the perfect mother. In *Feminism and Psychoanalytic Theory*, 79–96. New Haven, CT: Yale University Press.

DeMarneffe, Daphne. 2006. *Maternal Desire*. Boston: Back Bay Books.

Dowd, Maureen. 2005. *Are Men Necessary? When Sexes Collide*. New York: Putnam.

Drabble, Margaret. 1965. *The Millstone*. Harmondsworth: Penguin.

Erikson, Erik. 1959. *Identity and the Life Cycle: Selected Papers*. Psychological Issues, Monograph 1. New York: International Universities Press.

Friedan, Betty. 1963. *The Feminine Mystique*. New York: Norton.

Grass, Günter. 1959. *The Tin Drum*. Greenwich, CT: Fawcett.

Hayt, Elizabeth. 2002. Admitting to mixed feelings about motherhood. *Sunday New York Times,* May 12.

Hegi, Ursula. 1994. *Stones from the River*. New York: Scribner Paperback Fiction.

Herzog, James M. 2005. What fathers do and how they do it. In *What Do Mothers Want?* 65–78. Hillsdale, NJ: Analytic Press.

Hill-Miller, Katherine C. 1995. *My Hideous Progeny: Mary Shelley, William Godwin, and the Father-Daughter Relationship*. Newark: University of Delaware Press.

Hrdy, Sarah Blaffer. 1999. *Mother Nature: A History of Mothers, Infants, and Natural Selection*. New York: Pantheon Books.

Huet, Marie-Helene. 1993. *Monstrous Imagination*. Cambridge, MA: Harvard University Press.

Klabunde, Anja. 2001. *Magda Goebbels*. London: Sphere/Little, Brown.

Lamott, Anne. 1994. *Operating Instructions: A Journal of my Son's First Year*. New York: Ballantine Books.

Lessing, Doris. 1988. *The Fifth Child.* New York: Alfred A. Knopf.

Levin, Ira. 1967. *Rosemary's Baby.* New York: Random House.

Lu, Stacy. 2006. Cosmopolitan moms. *New York Times,* November 9.

Luzinger-Bohleber, Marianne. 2001. The Medea fantasy: An unconscious determinant of psychogenic sterility. *International Journal of Psychoanalysis* 82: 323–45.

Mahler, Margaret, Fred Pine, and Anni Bergman. 1975. *The Psychological Birth of the Human Infant.* New York: Basic Books.

March, William. 1954. *The Bad Seed.* Hopewell, NJ: Ecco Press.

McNally, Florescu. 1994. *In Search of Dracula: The History of Dracula and Vampires.* New York: Houghton Mifflin.

Mellor, Anne K. 1988. *Mary Shelley: Her Life, Her Fiction, Her Monsters.* New York: Methuen.

Meyer, Cheryl, and Michelle Oberman. 2001. *Mothers Who Kill Their Children.* New York: New York University Press.

Modell, Arnold. 1975. A narcissistic defense against affects: The illusion of self-sufficiency. *International Journal of Psychoanalysis* 56: 275–85.

Morrison, Toni. 1987. *Beloved.* New York: Plume.

Orenstein, Peggy. 2000. *Flux: Women on Sex, Work, Love, Kids and Life in a Half-Changed World.* New York: Anchor Books.

Parker, Roszika. 1995. *Mother Love / Mother Hate: The Power of Maternal Ambivalence.* New York: Basic Books.

Quindlen, Anna. 2001. Playing God on no sleep. *Newsweek,* July 2, 2001, 164.

Raphael-Leff, Joan. 1993. *Pregnancy: The Inside Story.* Northvale, NJ: Jason Aronson.

Rich, Adrienne. 1976. *Of Woman Born: Motherhood as Experience and Institution.* New York: Norton.

Rosin, Hanna. 2009. The case against breast feeding. *Atlantic,* April 2009, 64–70.

Sears, William, and Martha Sears. 2001. *The Attachment Parenting Book.* Boston: Little, Brown.

Shelley, Mary. 1830 [1818]. *Frankenstein.* Indianapolis: Bobbs-Merrill.

———. 1987. *The Journals of Mary Shelley: 1814–1844.* Edited by P. R. Feldman and D. Scott-Kileved. Oxford: Clarendon Press.

———. 1980. *The Letters of Mary Wollstonecraft Shelley*. Edited by B. T. Bennett. Baltimore: Johns Hopkins University Press.

Shields, Brooke. 2005. *Down Came the Rain: My Journey through Postpartum Depression*. New York: Hyperion.

Shriver, Lionel. 2003. *We Need to Talk about Kevin*. New York: Perennial.

Simpson, Mona. 1986. *Anywhere but Here*. New York: First Vintage Contemporaries.

Skura, Meredith. 1981. *The Literary Use of the Psychoanalytic Process*. New Haven: Yale University Press.

Slavitt, David, and Palmer Bovie. 1997. *Euripedes, 1: Medea*. Philadelphia: University of Pennsylvania Press.

Stern, Daniel. 1985. *The Interpersonal World of the Infant*. New York: Basic Books.

Stoker, Bram. 1983 [1897]. *Dracula*. New York: Modern Library.

Tarkington, Booth. 1957. *The Magnificent Ambersons*. In *The Gentleman from Indianapolis*, edited by John Beecroft. Garden City, NY: Doubleday.

Trollope, Joanna. 1998. *Other People's Children*. New York: Berkley Books.

Tyler, Anne. 1985. *The Accidental Tourist*. New York: Alfred A. Knopf.

Winnicott, Donald W. 1975 [1947]. Hate in the counter-transference. In *Through Pediatrics to Psychoanalysis*, 194–203. New York: Basic Books.

———. 1958. The capacity to be alone. In *The Maturational Processes and the Facilitating Environment*, 416–20. Madison, CT: International Universities Press.

———. 1960. The theory of the parent-infant relationship. *International Journal of Psychoanalysis* 41: 585–95.

Yalom, Marilyn. 1987. *Maternity, Mortality, and the Literature of Madness*. University Park: Pennsylvania State University Press.

Yates, Richard. 1989 [1961]. *Revolutionary Road*. New York: Vintage Contemporaries.

INDEX

abandonment: and Anne (pseud.),
xxiii, 205–6, 238; in *Beloved* (Morrison), 198–99; and child murder,
198–99, 202, 204–6; from child's
point of view, 155, 157–61; in *Frankenstein* (Shelley), 20, 65, 198; and
Mary Shelley, 59–62, 65, and monstrous offspring, 20, 59–62, 65, 70;
in *Stones from the River* (Hegi), 130;
in *Tin Drum, The* (Grass), 157–61;
in *We Need to Talk about Kevin*
(Shriver), 129, 133

abortions, xii, 207–9, 236, 240; illegal,
207–8; in *Millstone, The* (Drabble),
32; and reproductive fears, 77–78,
84, 86–87; in *Revolutionary Road*
(Yates), 208–9; self-abortion, 32,
208–9

absence, maternal, 62–65, 70, 93–94,
134. *See also* abandonment

abuse, 10, 56; as child murder, 209;
and vampyric mothering, xxiii,
166, 180, 184

adolescence, 9, 11, 17, 24, 210, 212–19,
233, 242; and deformities in children, 148, 150; in *Fifth Child, The*
(Lessing), 116; and Mary Shelley,
59; and Rachel (pseud.), 94, 102;
in *We Need to Talk about Kevin*
(Shriver), 125

adoption, 24–25, 32–33, 146

aggression, 4, 8–11, 237, 239–40; and
alpha moms, 228; and Amanda
(pseud.), 65, 67; and Andrea Yates,
139; in *Bad Seed, The* (March), 134,
137–38, 188; in *Beloved* (Morrison),
198; and child murder, 187–88, 198,
204, 209; from child's point of
view, 158–60; and deformities in
children, 149; in *Dracula* (Stoker),
173; and externalization of ambivalence, 105–6, 108–9, 114, 117, 134,
137–40, 248n2; in *Fifth Child, The*
(Lessing), 114, 117, 248n2; in *Frankenstein* (Shelley), 65; inevitability
of, 23; and Mary Shelley, 61; and

Text:	10/15 Janson
Display:	Janson
Indexer:	Sharon Sweeney
Compositor:	BookMatters, Berkeley
Printer and binder:	Maple-Vail Book Manufacturing Group